IN THE EYE OF THE STORM

Other Books by Max Lucado:

On the Anvil
No Wonder They Call Him the Savior
God Came Near
Six Hours One Friday
The Applause of Heaven

IN THE EYE OF THE STORM

MAX LUCADO

GRASON

Minneapolis, MN

IN THE EYE OF THE STORM
A DAY IN THE LIFE OF JESUS

Unless noted otherwise, scripture quotations are from The Holy Bible, New International Version. Copyright © 1973, 1978, 1984 International Bible Society. Used by permission of Zondervan Bible Publishers. Those marked KJV are from the King James Version of the Bible. Those marked TLB are from *The Living Bible*, copyright 1971 by Tyndale House Publishers, Wheaton, Ill. Used by permission. Those marked NEB are from the New English Bible, Copyright © the Delegates of the Oxford University Press and the Syndics of the Cambridge University Press, 1961, 1970. Reprinted by permission.

Library of Congress Cataloging-in-Publication Data:

Lucado, Max.
    In the eye of the storm : a day in the life of Jesus / Max Lucado.
        p. cm.
    Includes bibliographical references.
    ISBN 0-89066-228-2
    1. Christian life—1960– 2. Consolation. 3. Jesus Christ—Person and offices. I. Title.
    BV4501.2.L82   1991
    248.4—dc20   91–21854
                                                         CIP

This special edition is published with the permission of Word, Inc., Irving, TX.

Printed in the United States of America

To Robert and Elsie Forcum

two ambassadors with a love for the church
and a burden for the world

CONTENTS

Acknowledgments

Here's a salute to some special friends who made this book possible.

First to the folks at Word Publishing:

Kip Jordon, Byron Williamson, Ernie Owen, Joey Paul, and Roland Lundy—It's a privilege to be on the team.

Dave Moberg, Tom Williams, Susan Russell, Ed Curtis, and Michal Rutledge—Creativity unlimited!

Nancy Norris and Leslie Hughes—We know who really keeps the office working.

Stephen and Amanda Sorenson—You can cross my "t's" and dot my "i's" anytime. Thanks for the great editorial work.

And to my church family at Oak Hills:

Mary Stain—My supersecretary who corrects my mistakes, takes my calls, keeps me prompt, and saves my neck on a daily basis. Thank you so much.

Elsie Clay, Marcelle Le Gallo, and Kathleen McCleery—Our secretarial staff who help Mary so she can help me. Thanks again.

Glen Carter, Jim Toombs, John Tuller, Pat Hile, Jeff Pickens, and Rod Chisholm—Six co-workers who make my work a joy.

Karen Hill, Rod Chisholm, and Allen Dutton, Jr.— Thanks for proofreading the manuscript.

The members of Oak Hills Church—You make every Sunday a homecoming.

And to the Lucado family:

Jenna, Andrea, and Sara—three little girls who've taken my heart hostage.

And most of all, to my wife Denalyn—a decade with you has convinced me: there is a heaven, and you don't have to die to go there.

BEFORE
YOU
BEGIN . . .

CHIPPIE THE PARAKEET NEVER saw it coming. One second he was peacefully perched in his cage. The next he was sucked in, washed up, and blown over.

The problems began when Chippie's owner decided to clean Chippie's cage with a vacuum cleaner. She removed the attachment from the end of the hose and stuck it in the cage. The phone rang, and she turned to pick it up. She'd barely said "hello" when "sssopp!" Chippie got sucked in.

The bird owner gasped, put down the phone, turned off the vacuum, and opened the bag. There was Chippie—still alive, but stunned.

Since the bird was covered with dust and soot, she grabbed him and raced to the bathroom, turned on the faucet, and held Chippie under the running water. Then, realizing that Chippie was soaked and shivering, she did what any compassionate bird owner would do . . . she reached for the hair dryer and blasted the pet with hot air.

Poor Chippie never knew what hit him.

A few days after the trauma, the reporter who'd initially written about the event contacted Chippie's owner to see how the bird was recovering. "Well," she replied, "Chippie doesn't sing much anymore—he just sits and stares."

It's hard not to see why. Sucked in, washed up, and blown over . . . that's enough to steal the song from the stoutest heart.

Can you relate to Chippie? Most of us can. One minute you're seated in familiar territory with a song on your lips, then . . . The pink slip comes. The rejection letter arrives. The doctor calls. The divorce papers are delivered. The check bounces. A policeman knocks on your door.

Sssopp! You're sucked into a black cavern of doubts, doused with the cold water of reality, and stung with the hot air of empty promises.

The life that had been so calm is now so stormy. You're hailstormed by demands. Assailed by doubts. Pummeled by questions. And somewhere in the trauma, you lose your joy. Somewhere in the storm, you lose your song.

Ever found yourself in a storm of life? If so, if Chippie's story is your story, then I'm glad you picked up this book. I wrote it with you in mind. I wrote it because there is a day in the life of Christ that you need to know about.

Aside from the Crucifixion, it is the most stressful day of his life. A roaring sequence of bad news, demanding crowds, and doubting friends. Twenty-four hours in which Jesus faces the same gale-force fears that you and I face. Waves of pressure slam. Winds of anxiety blow. Clouds of darkness billow.

Yet through it all Jesus remains calm. He endures the day without losing his song. I'd like to help you see how he did it.

First we'll consider the *stress of demands*. Jesus handled twelve hours of chaos. What did he do to keep his cool? What did he know that gave him strength? If your days are bookended with deadlines and "chuck-it-all" frustrations—then you'll like this section.

The second section is entitled *Storms of Doubt*. Have you ever found yourself in a storm and wondered why Jesus doesn't pull you out? The disciples did. While Jesus went up the mountain, they went out on the sea. The storm came, their boat bounced, and they were left with a long night of fear and a long list of questions. "Jesus knows we're in a storm. Why doesn't he come?"

Sound familiar?

The final section of the book deals with a third source of anxiety—the *sting of failure*. In the twilight hours of that night we discover a sweet story of grace, Peter's attempt to walk on water. What began as a step of faith ended up as a belly flop of fear. If you've ever wondered what God does when we fail, then read this section and allow the hand that saved Peter to touch you.

Storms come. They come quickly. They pounce ferociously. If you are in one, then you know what I mean. If you're not in one today, you know as well as I—one may be in tomorrow's forecast.

My prayer is that this book will leave you better prepared. My prayer is that you will find some word, some story, some verse, or some thought that will convince you that he is very near. I pray that as you read you will be reminded that the same voice that stilled the rage on the Sea of Galilee can still the storm in your world.

Read on, friend, and be assured—he is closer than you've ever dreamed.

STRESS
OF
DEMANDS

1

FROM
CALM
TO
CHAOS

*M*AYBE YOU CAN RELATE TO the morning I just had.
It's Sunday. Sundays are always busy days for me.
Sundays are always early days for me. Today promised to
be no exception.

With a full slate of activities planned, I got up early
and drove to church. There was not much traffic at 6:00
A.M. I had the roads to myself. The orange of dawn had yet
to break the nighttime spell on the summer's black sky.
The twilight sparkled. Cool air wafted.

I parked outside my church office and took a minute
to enjoy the quietude. I set down my books, picked up my
coffee, and leaned against the car.

It was just the star-studded sky and me. Across the
city, lights flickered. Shadowed trees slept. The night was
calm: no noise, no hurry, no demands. That would all
change within a couple of hours. Let a few thousand alarm
clocks buzz and a few thousand garage doors open, and the
serenity would be invaded as suburbia awakened. But at
the moment, suburbia slept.

Life is like that sometimes. There are jaunts in life's
journey that are as glassy as a midnight lake on a windless night. No noise. No rushing. No crises. There are
measures in our music where the conductor silences the
kettledrum, and only the flute is allowed to sing.

And sing she does. Under the spell of her song, deadlines aren't as deadly. Death is distant. Dear ones are still dear and sometimes near. The eclipsing clouds of fear and debts and angry phone calls have passed. And, for a while, your world is moonlit.

Mine was. I sat on the hood of my car, sipped my coffee, and toasted the stars. They twinkled their response.

It was calm. But calm has a way of becoming chaos.

With a briefcase in one hand and a coffee cup in the other, I walked and whistled across the parking lot to the office door. To enter my office, I had to get past the sleeping dog of the twentieth century: the alarm system. I set down my briefcase and unlocked the door. I picked up my briefcase and walked in.

The code box on the wall was flashing a red light.

I'm not too electronically inclined, but I do know what a red light on an alarm system means: "Punch in the code, buddy, or get ready for the music."

I punched in the code. Nothing happened. I punched in the code again. The little red light kept blinking. I punched it in again. Time was running out. The little light snickered at me. I could hear the message being sent up and down the wires to all the neon-eyed alarm gremlins. "Man your sirens, everybody. Ol' do-do brain is entering his bank-card number again!"

I kept pushing, the clock kept ticking, the light kept flashing, and the gremlins were getting excited. "Get ready! Ten seconds and counting. Ten, nine, eight . . ."

"Oh, no," I groaned, "it's about to hit."

The siren pounced on me like a mountain lion. I thought we were under nuclear attack. Floodlights flash flooded the hallway, and red strobes turned. I kept pushing buttons, and the alarm kept blaring. You'd have thought it was a breakout at Alcatraz.

My pulse raced, my forehead moistened, and my situation was desperate. I raced down the hall to my office, pulled open the lap drawer of my desk, and found the phone number of the alarm company.

I could barely hear what the man said when he answered. When I understood what he said, I could scarcely believe he had said it.

"What do you mean, 'What's the matter?'" I exclaimed. "Can't you hear?"

"Yes, I punched in the code," I screamed. "It didn't do any good!"

The next twenty minutes were loud, demanding, confusing, and aggravating. I was speaking to technicians I couldn't see about equipment I didn't understand trying to understand words I couldn't hear.

That's when the policeman came. He tapped on the window. I opened it. "I can't get the thing to shut off!" I yelled.

"You the preacher here?" he asked.

"Yes," I yelled.

He just shook his head and walked away, probably muttering something about what they don't teach in theology courses.

Finally, for no apparent reason, the siren ceased. The lights shut off. What had been an air-raid shelter became an office again. I walked back to my desk, sat down, and sighed. *What a way to begin the day.* The morning lesson I had prepared was lying on my credenza. I picked it up and read the first line: "When calm becomes chaos."

"Appropriate," I muttered.

Ever happened to you? When was the last time your life went from calm to chaos in half a minute? ("How many examples would you like?" you ask.) When was the last time you found yourself pushing buttons that didn't respond, struggling with instructions you couldn't hear, or operating a system you didn't understand?

You enter the wrong computer code and lose eighteen months worth of ledgers in a matter of seconds. Calm volcanoes into chaos.

A message on your answering machine tells you that the report you are scheduled to give next week is due tomorrow. Good-bye sleep. Hello all-nighter. Good-bye calm. Hello chaos.

The mechanic who promised that the car would be ready today in time for the trip says, "I know I promised, but it's much worse than we thought. Your side axle disjointed, causing the U-joint to descramble the electronic ignition that is hand-assembled in Lower Tasmania and . . ."

"Grrrr."

If you've ever had your spouse call you at the office and say, "Just got a letter from the IRS. They are going to audit . . ."

If your boss has ever begun a conversation with these words: "You're a good worker, but with all this talk about a recession we have to cut back . . ."

If your teenager has ever walked in and asked, "Does our car insurance cover the other guy's car?"

Then you know that life can go from calm to chaos in a matter of moments. No warnings. No announcements. No preparation.

Little red lights blink, and you start pushing buttons. Sometimes you silence the alarm; sometimes it rips the air like a demon. The result can be peace or panic. The result can be calm or chaos.

It all depends on one factor: Do you know the code?

For me, this morning became chaos. Had I been prepared . . . had I known the code . . . had I known what to do when the warning flashed . . . calm would have triumphed.

The next few pages will usher you into a day in Jesus' life when the calm could have become chaos. It has all the elements of anxiety: bad news and a death threat, followed by swarming demands, interruptions, inept disciples, and a blazing temptation to follow the crowd. In twenty-four pressure-packed hours, Jesus was carried from the summit of celebration to the valley of frustration.

It was the second most stressful day of his life. As soon as one alarm was disarmed, another began blinking. The rulers threatened. The crowds pressed. The followers doubted. The people demanded. When you see what he endured that day, you will wonder how he kept his cool.

Somehow, though, he did. Although the people pressed and the problems monsooned, Jesus didn't blow up or bail out. In fact, he did just the opposite. He served people, thanked God, and made cool-headed decisions.

I want to help you see how he did it. I'd like to share with you a few "internal codes" that you desperately need. Equip yourself with these internal codes, punch them in when the red lights of your world start to flash, and you will be amazed at how quickly the alarms will be disarmed.

A few words of explanation:

If you are looking for external adjustments, you won't find them here. I won't say anything about dressing for success or power language or popularity schemes. You can buy many books that will help you externally, but this isn't one of them.

What you will discover in this book are attitudes . . . godly attitudes . . . a way of viewing people and problems as modeled by the Master.

If you want external alteration, look elsewhere. If you want internal development, read on. If you want to see how

God handled—and handles—hassles, then I've got some thoughts to share with you.

Let's do something. Let's take the principles modeled by Jesus into our day-to-day whirlwind of demands and decisions. Let's take a few minutes and observe God under pressure. Let's watch his face. Listen to his words. Observe his choices. And see what we can learn. Let's watch Christ in a pressure-cooker environment and try to answer this question:

What did Jesus know that allowed him to do what he did?

2

GOD
UNDER
PRESSURE

A DAY IN THE LIFE of Christ.
Call it a tapestry of turmoil, a noisy pictorial in which the golden threads of triumph entwine with the black, frazzled strings of tragedy.

Call it a symphony of emotions, a sunrise-to-sunset orchestration of extremes. One score is brassy with exuberance; the next moans with sorrow. On one page, the orchestra swells in adoration. On the next, Jesus solos the ballad of loneliness.

Whatever you call it, call it real. Call it a day in which Jesus experiences more stress than he will any other day of his life—aside from his crucifixion. Before the morning becomes evening, he has reason to weep . . . run . . . shout . . . curse . . . praise . . . doubt.

From calm to chaos. From peace to perplexity. Within moments his world is turned upside down.

In the tapestry, though, there is one thread that sparkles. In the symphony, there is one song that soars. In the story, there is one lesson that comforts. You've heard it before, but you may have forgotten it. Look closely. Listen intently. Be reminded:

Jesus knows how you feel.

If you've ever had a day in which you've been blitzkrieged by demands, if you've ever ridden the roller coaster of sorrow and celebration, if you've ever wondered if God in heaven can relate to you on earth, then read and reread about this pressure-packed day in the life of Christ.

Take heart. Jesus knows how you feel.

———————————————

He begins the morning by hearing about the death of John the Baptist: his cousin, his forerunner, his coworker, his friend.[1] The man who came closer to understanding Jesus than any other is dead.

Imagine losing the one person who knows you better than anyone else, and you will feel what Jesus is feeling. Reflect on the horror of being told that your dearest friend has just been murdered, and you will relate to Jesus' sorrow. Consider your reaction if you were told that your best friend had just been decapitated by a people-pleasing, incestuous monarch, and you'll see how the day begins for Christ. His world is beginning to turn upside down.

The emissaries brought more than news of sorrow, however; they brought a warning: "The same Herod who took John's head is interested in yours." Listen to how Luke presents the monarch's madness: "Herod said, 'I beheaded John. Who, then, is this I hear such things about?' *And he tried to see him*"[2] (emphasis mine). Something tells me that Herod wanted more than a social visit.

So, with John's life taken and his own life threatened, Jesus chooses to get away for a while. "When Jesus heard what had happened, he withdrew by boat privately to a solitary place."[3]

But before he can get away, his disciples arrive. The Gospel of Mark states that the "apostles gathered around Jesus and reported to him all they had done and taught."[4]

They return exuberant. Jesus had commissioned them to proclaim the gospel and authenticate it with miracles. "They went out and preached that people should repent. They drove out many demons and anointed many sick people with oil and healed them."[5]

Can you imagine the excitement? Can you envision the scene? A reunion of twelve friends. A reuniting of disciples with their teacher. A homecoming bubbling with testimonies:

- Peter describing a lame man he healed.
- John telling of a crowd he taught.
- Andrew recounting the deliverance of an epileptic.
- James relating to Jesus how the crowds followed him wherever he went.
- Matthew reporting the healing of a blind woman.

Remember, these disciples were ordinary men. They weren't orators, scholars, kings, or saints. They were fishermen and a tax collector, common laborers who, by God's power, had taken a nation by storm. The emotion? Exuberance. In a matter of moments, Jesus' heart goes from the pace of a funeral dirge to the triumphant march of a ticker-tape parade.

And look who follows the disciples to locate Jesus. About five thousand men plus women and children![6] Rivers of people cascade out of the hills and villages. Some scholars estimate the crowd to be as high as twenty-five thousand.[7] They swarm around Jesus, each with one desire: to meet the man who had empowered the disciples.

What had been a calm morning now buzzes with activity. "So many people were coming and going that they did not even have a chance to eat."[8]

I've had people demand my attention. I know what it's like to have a half-dozen kids wanting different things at the same time. I know the feeling of receiving one call with two other people waiting impatiently on other lines. I even know what it's like to be encircled by a dozen or so people, each making a separate request.

But twenty-five thousand? That's larger than many cities! No wonder the disciples couldn't eat. I'm surprised they could breathe!

The morning has been a jungle trail of the unexpected. First Jesus grieves over the death of a dear friend and relative. Then his life is threatened. Next he celebrates the triumphant return of his followers. Then he is nearly suffocated by a brouhaha of humanity. Bereavement . . . jeopardy . . . jubilation. . . bedlam.

Are you beginning to see why I call this the second most stressful day in the life of Christ? And it's far from over.

Jesus decides to take the disciples to a quiet place where they can rest and reflect. He shouts a command over the noise of the crowd. "Come with me by yourselves to a quiet place and get some rest."[9] The thirteen fight their way to the beach and climb into a boat.

And, for a few precious moments, the world is quiet again. The din of the crowd grows distant and the only sound is the slap of the water against the hull. Jesus' heart is weighted by sorrow and buoyed by joy. He watches his followers swapping stories of victory. Then he raises his glance and sees on the horizon Tiberias, the city constructed by John the Baptist's murderer, Herod. Joy suddenly alloyed with indignation causes his fists to clench and his eyes to moisten.

Who would question his desire to get away from the people? He just needs a few hours alone. Just a respite. Just a retreat. Time to pray. Time to ponder. Time to weep. A time without crowds or demands. A campfire wreathed with friends. An evening with those he loves. *The people can wait until tomorrow.*

The people, however, have other ideas. "The crowds learned about it and followed him."[10] It's a six-mile walk around the northeastern corner of the Sea of Galilee, so the crowd takes a hike. When Jesus got to Bethsaida, his desired retreat had become a roaring arena.

"Surprise!"

Add to the list of sorrow, peril, excitement, and bedlam the word *interruption.* Jesus' plans are interrupted. What he has in mind for his day and what the people have in mind for his day are two different agendas. What Jesus seeks and what Jesus gets are not the same.

Sound familiar?

Remember when you sought a night's rest and got a colicky baby? Remember when you sought to catch up at the office and got even further behind? Remember when you sought to use your Saturday for leisure, but ended up fixing your neighbor's sink?

Take comfort, friend. It happened to Jesus, too.

In fact, this would be a good time to pause and digest the central message of this chapter.

Jesus knows how you feel.

Ponder this and use it the next time your world goes from calm to chaos.

His pulse has raced. His eyes have grown weary. His heart has grown heavy. He has had to climb out of bed with a sore throat. He has been kept awake late and has gotten up early. He knows how you feel.

You may have trouble believing that. You probably believe that Jesus knows what it means to endure heavy-duty tragedies. You are no doubt convinced that Jesus is acquainted with sorrow and has wrestled with fear. Most people accept that. But can God relate to the hassles and headaches of my life? Of your life?

For some reason this is harder to believe.

Perhaps that's why portions of this day are recorded in all the Gospel accounts. No other event, other than the Crucifixion, is told by all four Gospel writers. Not Jesus' baptism. Not his temptation. Not even his birth. But all four writers chronicle this day. It's as if Matthew, Mark, Luke, and John knew that you would wonder if God understands. And they proclaim their response in four-part harmony:

Jesus knows how you feel.

A friend of mine was recently trying to teach his six-year-old son how to shoot a basket. The boy would take the basketball and push it as hard as he could toward the goal, but it always fell short. The father would then take the ball and toss it toward the basket, saying something like, "Just do it like this, son. It's easy."

Then the boy would try, and miss, again. My friend would then take the ball and make another basket, encouraging his son to push the ball a bit harder.

After several minutes and many misses, the boy responded to his father's encouragement by saying, "Yeah, but it's easy for you up there. You don't know how hard it is from down here."

You and I can never say that about God. Of the many messages Jesus taught us that day about stress, the first one is this: "God knows how you feel."

Read how J. B. Phillips translates Hebrews 4:15:

For we have no superhuman High Priest to whom our weaknesses are unintelligible—he himself has shared fully in all our experience of temptation, except that he never sinned.

The writer of Hebrews is adamant almost to the point of redundancy. It's as if he anticipates our objections. It's as if he knows that we will say to God what my friend's son said to him: "God, it's easy for you up there. You don't know how hard it is from down here." So he boldly proclaims Jesus' ability to understand. Look at the wording again.

He himself. Not an angel. Not an ambassador. Not an emissary, but Jesus himself.

Shared fully. Not partially. Not nearly. Not to a large degree. Entirely! Jesus shared fully.

In all our experience. Every hurt. Each ache. All the stresses and all the strains. No exceptions. No substitutes. Why? So he could sympathize with our weaknesses.

A politician dons a hardhat and enters the factory like he is one of the employees. A social worker goes to the inner city and spends the night on the streets with the homeless. A general walks into the mess hall and sits down with the soldiers like he is one of the enlisted men.

All three want to communicate the same message: "I identify with you. I can understand. I can relate." There is one problem, though. The factory employees know that the politician's hardhat will come off when the television crew is gone. The derelicts know that the social worker will be in a warm bed tomorrow night. And the soldiers are well aware that for every meal the general eats in the mess hall, he'll eat dozens in the officers' quarters.

Try as they might, these well-meaning professionals don't really understand. Their participation is partial. Jesus' participation, however, was complete. The writer of Hebrews states with double clarity that Jesus "shared *fully* in *all* our experience" (emphasis mine).

A bookstore owner in the Northwest once told me about an angry lady who stomped into his store carrying my book, *God Came Near*. She slammed the book on the counter, said a few less-than-kind things about the book, and then screamed loudly enough for everyone on the block to hear, "My God didn't have pimples!"

I know the paragraph that put the spark in her tinderbox. It reads like this:

> Jesus may have had pimples. He may have been tone-deaf. Perhaps a girl down the street had a crush on him or vice-versa. It could be that his knees were bony. One thing's for sure: He was, while completely divine, completely human.[11]

I can understand why the woman became upset. I can relate to her discomfort. We quickly fix a crack in the stained glass. We rub away any smudges on the altar. There is something *safe* about a God who never had callouses. There is something *awesome* about a God who never felt pain. There is something *majestic* about a God who never scraped his elbow.

But there is also something *cold* about a God who cannot relate to what you and I feel.

If I had a moment with that lady, I would ask her, "Jesus may not have had pimples, but don't you hope that he could have?"

Every page of the Gospels hammers home this crucial principle: God knows how you feel. From the funeral to the factory to the frustration of a demanding schedule. Jesus understands. When you tell God that you've reached your limit, he knows what you mean. When you shake your head at impossible deadlines, he shakes his, too. When your plans are interrupted by people who have other plans, he nods in empathy. He has been there. He knows how you feel.[12]

Before we resume our chronicling of this stressful day in Jesus' life, let me take you to another day—one far more recent, in a place closer to home.

———————————

February 15, 1921. New York City. The operating room of the Kane Summit Hospital. A doctor is performing an appendectomy.

In many ways the events leading to the surgery are uneventful. The patient has complained of severe abdominal pain. The diagnosis is clear: an inflamed appendix. Dr. Evan O'Neill Kane is performing the surgery. In his distinguished thirty-seven-year medical career, he has performed nearly four thousand appendectomies, so this surgery will be uneventful in all ways except two.

The first novelty of this operation? The use of local anesthesia in major surgery. Dr. Kane is a crusader against the hazards of general anesthesia. He contends that a local application is far safer. Many of his colleagues agree with him in principle, but in order for them to agree in practice, they will have to see the theory applied.

Dr. Kane searches for a volunteer, a patient who is willing to undergo surgery while under local anesthesia. A volunteer is not easily found. Many are squeamish at the thought of being awake during their own surgery. Others are fearful that the anesthesia might wear off too soon.

Eventually, however, Dr. Kane finds a candidate. On Tuesday morning, February 15, the historic operation occurs.

The patient is prepped and wheeled into the operating room. A local anesthetic is applied. As he has done thousands of times, Dr. Kane dissects the superficial tissues and locates the appendix. He skillfully excises it and concludes the surgery. During the procedure, the patient complains of only minor discomfort.

The volunteer is taken into post-op, then placed in a hospital ward. He recovers quickly and is dismissed two days later.

Dr. Kane had proven his theory. Thanks to the willingness of a brave volunteer, Kane demonstrated that local anesthesia was a viable, and even preferable, alternative.

But I said there were two facts that made the surgery unique. I've told you the first: the use of local anesthesia. The second is the patient. The courageous candidate for surgery by Dr. Kane was Dr. Kane.

To prove his point, Dr. Kane operated on himself![13]

A wise move. The doctor became a patient in order to convince the patients to trust the doctor.

I've shared this story with several health professionals. They each gave me the same response: furrowed brow, suspicious grin, and the dubious words, "That's hard to believe."

Perhaps it is. But the story of the doctor who became his own patient is mild compared to the story of the God who became human. But Jesus did. So that you and I would believe that the Healer knows our hurts, he voluntarily became one of us. He placed himself in our position. He suffered our pains and felt our fears.

Rejection? He felt it. Temptation? He knew it. Loneliness? He experienced it. Death? He tasted it.

And stress? He could write a best-selling book about it.

Why did he do it? One reason. So that when you hurt, you will go to him—your Father and your Physician—and let him heal.

3

A
MOTHER'S
LOVE—
A
FRIEND'S
EMPATHY

T HERESA BRIONES IS A TENDER, loving mother. She also has a stout left hook that she used to punch a lady in a coin laundry. Why'd she do it?

Some kids were making fun of Theresa's daughter, Alicia.

Alicia is bald. Her knees are arthritic. Her nose is pinched. Her hips are creaky. Her hearing is bad. She has the stamina of a seventy-year-old. And she is only ten.

"Mom," the kids taunted, "come and look at the monster!"

Alicia weighs only twenty-two pounds and is shorter than most preschoolers. She suffers from progeria—a genetic aging disease that strikes one child in eight million. The life expectancy of progeria victims is twenty years. There are only fifteen known cases of this disease in the world.

"She is not an alien. She is not a monster," Theresa defended. "She is just like you and me."

Mentally, Alicia is a bubbly, fun-loving third grader. She has a long list of friends. She watches television in a toddler-sized rocking chair. She plays with Barbie dolls and teases her younger brother.

Theresa has grown accustomed to the glances and questions. She is patient with the constant curiosity. Genuine inquiries she accepts. Insensitive slanders she does not.

The mother of the finger-pointing children came to investigate. "I see 'it,'" she told the kids.

"My child is not an 'it,'" Theresa stated. Then she decked the woman.

Who could blame her? Such is the nature of parental love. Mothers and fathers have a God-given ability to love their children regardless of imperfections. Not because the parents are blind. Just the opposite. They see vividly.

Theresa sees Alicia's inability as clearly as anyone. But she also sees Alicia's value.

So does God.

God sees us with the eyes of a Father. He sees our defects, errors, and blemishes. But he also sees our value.

Two chapters ago, I closed with this question: What did Jesus know that enabled him to do what he did?

Here's part of the answer. He knew the value of people. He knew that each human being is a treasure. And because he did, people were not a source of stress, but a source of joy.

When Jesus lands on the shore of Bethsaida, he leaves the Sea of Galilee and steps into a sea of humanity. Keep in mind, he has crossed the sea to get *away* from the crowds. He needs to grieve. He longs to relax with his followers. He needs anything but another crowd of thousands to teach and heal.

But his love for people overcomes his need for rest.

When Jesus landed and saw a large crowd, he had compassion on them and healed their sick.[1]

He had compassion on them, because they were like sheep without a shepherd.[2]

He welcomed them and spoke to them about the kingdom of God, and healed those who needed healing.[3]

It is doubtful that anyone in the crowd thinks to ask Jesus how he is doing. There is no indication that anyone is concerned with how Jesus is feeling. No one has come to give; all have come to take.

———————————

In our house we call 5:00 P.M. the piranha hour. That's the time of day when everyone wants a piece of Mom. Sara, the baby, is hungry. Andrea wants Mom to read her a book. Jenna wants help with her homework. And I—the ever-loving, ever-sensitive husband—want Denalyn to drop everything and talk to me about my day.

When is your piranha hour? When do people in your world demand much and offer little?

Every boss has had a day in which the requests outnumber the results. There's not a businessperson alive who hasn't groaned as an armada of assignments docks at his or her desk. For the teacher, the piranha hour often begins when the first student enters and ends when the last student leaves.

Piranha hours: parents have them, bosses endure them, secretaries dread them, teachers are besieged by them, and Jesus taught us how to live through them successfully.

When hands extended and voices demanded, Jesus responded with love. He did so because the code within him disarmed the alarm. The code is worth noting: "People are precious."

―――――――――――――――――――

I can hear somebody raising an objection at this point. "Yes, but it was easier for Jesus. He was God. He could do more than I can. After all, he was divine."

True, Jesus was equally God and man. But don't be too quick to dismiss what he did. Consider his loving response from another angle.

Consider that, along with his holy strength, he also had a holy awareness. There were no secrets on the mountain that day; Jesus knew the hearts of each person. He knew why they were there and what they would do.[4]

Matthew writes that Jesus "healed their sick."[5] Not *some* of their sick. Not the *righteous* among the sick. Not the *deserving* among the sick. But *"the sick."*

Surely, among the many thousands, there were a few people unworthy of good health.

The same divinity that gave Jesus the power to heal also gave him the power to perceive. I wonder if Jesus was tempted to say to the rapist, "Heal you? After what you've done?" Or to the child molester, "Why should I restore your health?" Or to the bigot, "Get out of here, buddy, and take your arrogance with you."

And he could see not only their past, he could see their future.

Undoubtedly, there were those in the multitude who would use their newfound health to hurt others. Jesus released tongues that would someday curse. He gave sight to eyes that would lust. He healed hands that would kill.

Many of those he healed would never say "thank you," but he healed them anyway. Most would be more concerned with being healthy than being holy, but he healed them anyway. Some of those who asked for bread today would cry for his blood a few months later, but he healed them anyway.

Jesus chose to do what you and I seldom, if ever, choose to do. He chose to give gifts to people, knowing full well that those gifts could be used for evil.

Don't be too quick to attribute Jesus' compassion to his divinity. Remember both sides. For each time Jesus healed, he had to overlook the future and the past.

Something, by the way, that he still does.

Have you noticed that God doesn't ask you to prove that you will put your salary to good use? Have you noticed that God doesn't turn off your oxygen supply when you misuse his gifts? Aren't you glad that God doesn't give you only that which you remember to thank him for? (Has it been a while since you thanked God for your spleen? Me, too. But I still have one.)

God's goodness is spurred by his nature, not by our worthiness.

Someone asked an associate of mine, "What biblical precedent do we have to help the poor who have no desire to become Christians?"

My friend responded with one word: "God."

God does it daily, for millions of people.

What did Jesus know that allowed him to do what he did? What internal code kept his calm from erupting into chaos? He knew the value of people.

Interestingly, the stress seen that day is not on Jesus' face, but on the faces of the disciples. "Send the crowds away,"[6] they demand. Fair request. "After all," they are saying, "you've taught them. You've healed them. You've accommodated them. And now they're getting hungry. If we don't send them away, they'll want you to feed them, too!"

I wish I could have seen the expression on the disciples' faces when they heard the Master's response. "They do not need to go away. You give them something to eat."[7]

I used to think that this was a rhetorical request. I used to think that Jesus knew the disciples couldn't feed the crowd, but that he asked them anyway. I used to think that it was a "test" to teach them to rely on God for what they couldn't do.

I don't see it like that anymore.

I still think it was a test—not a test to show them what they couldn't do, but a test to demonstrate what they could do. After all, they had just gone on tour achieving the impossible. Jesus is asking them to do it again. "You give them something to eat."[8]

I wish I could tell you that the disciples did it. I wish I could say that they knew God wouldn't ask them to do something he wouldn't empower them to do, so they fed the crowd. I wish I could tell you that the disciples miraculously fed the five thousand men plus women and children.

But I can't . . . because they didn't.

Rather than look to God, they looked in their wallets. "That would take eight months of a man's wages! Are we to go and spend that much on bread and give it to them to eat?"[9]

"Y-y-y-you've got to be kidding."

"He can't be serious."

"It's one of Jesus' jokes."

"Do you know how many people are out there?"

Eyes watermelon-wide. Jaws dangling open. One ear hearing the din of the crowd, the other the command of God.

Don't miss the contrasting views. When Jesus saw the people, he saw an opportunity to love and affirm value. When the disciples saw the people, they saw thousands of problems.

Also, don't miss the irony. In the midst of a bakery—in the presence of the Eternal Baker—they tell the "Bread of Life" that there is no bread.

How silly we must appear to God.

Here's where Jesus should have given up. This is the point in the pressure-packed day where Jesus should have exploded. The sorrow, the life threats, the exuberance, the crowds, the interruptions, the demands, and now this. His own disciples can't do what he asks them. In front of five thousand men, they let him down.

"Beam me up, Father," should have been Jesus' next words. But they weren't. Instead he inquires, "How many loaves do you have?"

The disciples bring him a little boy's lunch. A lunch pail becomes a banquet, and all are fed. No word of reprimand is given. No furrowed brow of anger is seen. No "I-told-you-so" speech is delivered. The same compassion Jesus extends to the crowd is extended to his friends.

Look at this day one more time. Review what our Lord faced.

Intense sorrow—the death of a dear friend and relative.

Immediate threat—his name is on the wanted poster.

Immeasurable joy—a homecoming with his followers.

Immense crowds—a Niagara of people followed him everywhere.

Insensitive interruptions—he sought rest and got people.

Incredible demands—crowds of thousands clamored for his touch.

Inept assistance—the one and only time he asked for help, he got a dozen "you're-pulling-my-leg" expressions.

But the calm within Christ never erupted. The alarm never sounded. What did Jesus know that enabled him to do what he did? He knew the incredible value of people. As a result:

- He didn't stamp his feet and demand his own way.
- He didn't tell the disciples to find another beach where there were no people.
- He didn't ask the crowds why they hadn't brought their own food.
- He didn't send the apostles back into the field for more training.
- Most important, he stayed calm in the midst of chaos. He even paused, in the midst of it all, to pray a prayer of thanks.[10]

A boy went into a pet shop, looking for a puppy. The store owner showed him a litter in a box. The boy looked at the puppies. He picked each one up, examined it, and put it back into the box.

After several minutes, he walked back to the owner and said, "I picked one out. How much will it cost?"

The man gave him the price, and the boy promised to be back in a few days with the money. "Don't take too long," the owner cautioned. "Puppies like these sell quickly."

The boy turned and smiled knowingly, "I'm not worried," he said. "Mine will still be here."

The boy went to work—weeding, washing windows, cleaning yards. He worked hard and saved his money. When he had enough for the puppy, he returned to the store.

He walked up to the counter and laid down a pocketful of wadded bills. The store owner sorted and counted the cash. After verifying the amount, he smiled at the boy and said, "All right, son, you can go get your puppy."

The boy reached into the back of the box, pulled out a skinny dog with a limp leg, and started to leave.

The owner stopped him.

"Don't take that puppy," he objected. "He's crippled. He can't play. He'll never run with you. He can't fetch. Get one of the healthy pups."

"No thank you, sir," the boy replied. "This is exactly the kind of dog I've been looking for."

As the boy turned to leave, the store owner started to speak but remained silent. Suddenly he understood. For extending from the bottom of the boy's trousers was a brace—a brace for his crippled leg.

Why did the boy want the dog? Because he knew how it felt. And he knew it was very special.

What did Jesus know that enabled him to do what he did? He knew how the people felt, and he knew that they were special.

I hope you never forget that.

Jesus knows how you feel. You're under the gun at work? Jesus knows how you feel. You've got more to do than is humanly possible? So did he. You've got children who make a "piranha hour" out of your dinner hour? Jesus knows what that's like. People take more from you than they give? Jesus understands. Your teenagers won't listen? Your students won't try? Your employees give you blank stares when you assign tasks? Believe me, friend, Jesus knows how you feel.

You are precious to him. So precious that he became like you so that you would come to him.

When you struggle, he listens. When you yearn, he responds. When you question, he hears. He has been there. You've heard that before, but you need to hear it again.

He loves you with the love of a Theresa Briones.

He understands you with the compassion of the crippled boy.

Like Theresa, he battles with hell itself to protect you.

And, like the boy, he paid a great price to take you home.

4

WHEN
FISHERMEN
DON'T
FISH

They were like sheep without a shepherd. So he began teaching them many things.[1]

When Jesus landed and saw a large crowd, he had
compassion on them and healed their sick.[2]

*I*T'S A GOOD THING THOSE VERSES weren't written about me.
It's a good thing thousands of people weren't depending
on Max for their teaching and nourishment. Especially on
a day when I'd just heard of the death of a dear friend. Especially on a day when I wanted to be alone with my friends.
Especially after I'd gotten into a boat to escape the crowds.
Had that been me in Jesus' sandals on that Bethsaida
beach, the verses would read something like:

They were like sheep without a shepherd. So Max told
them to quit grazing on his pasture and to head back
to their pens.

When Max landed and saw a large crowd, he mumbled
something about how hard it was to get a day off and
radioed for the helicopter. Then he and the disciples
escaped to a private retreat.

It's a good thing I wasn't responsible for those people.
I would have been in no mood to teach them, no mood to
help them. I would have had no desire even to be with them.

But, as I think about it, Jesus had no desire to be with them either. After all, he did leave them, didn't he? He had every intention of getting away and being alone. So what happened? Why didn't he tell them to get lost? What made him change his mind and spend the day with the people he was trying to avoid?

Answer? Take a look at five words in Matthew 14:14: "He had compassion on them."

The Greek word used for compassion in this passage is *splanchnizomai*, which won't mean much to you unless you are in the health professions and studied "splanchnology" in school. If so, you remember that "splanchnology" is a study of the visceral parts. Or, in contemporary jargon, a study of the gut.

When Matthew writes that Jesus had compassion on the people, he is not saying that Jesus felt casual pity for them. No, the term is far more graphic. Matthew is saying that Jesus felt their hurt in his gut:

- He felt the limp of the crippled.
- He felt the hurt of the diseased.
- He felt the loneliness of the leper.
- He felt the embarrassment of the sinful.

And once he felt their hurts, he couldn't help but heal their hurts. He was moved in the stomach by their needs. He was so touched by their needs that he forgot his own needs. He was so moved by the people's hurts that he put his hurts on the back burner.

Maybe that's why God brings hurting people into your world, too. All solitude and no service equals selfishness. Some solitude and some service, however, equals perspective.

Here's a story to illustrate my point.

When I was in high school, our family used to fish every year during spring break. One year my brother and my mom couldn't go, so my dad let me invite a friend. I asked Mark. He was a good pal and a great sport. He got permission from his parents, and we began planning our trip.

Days before leaving, we could already anticipate the vacation. We could feel the sun warming our bodies as we floated in the boat. We could feel the yank of the rod and hear the spin of the reel as we wrestled the white bass into the boat. And we could smell the fish frying in an open skillet over an open fire.

We could hardly wait. Days passed like cold molasses. Finally spring break arrived. We loaded our camper and set out for the lake.

We arrived late at night, unfolded the camper, and went to bed—dreaming of tomorrow's day in the sun. But during the night, an unseasonably strong norther blew in. It got cold fast! The wind was so strong that we could barely open the camper door the next morning. The sky was gray. The lake was a mountain range of white-topped waves. There was no way we could fish in that weather.

"No problem," we said. "We'll spend the day in the camper. After all, we have Monopoly. We have *Reader's Digest*. We all know a few jokes. It's not what we came to do, but we'll make the best of it and fish tomorrow."

So, huddled in the camper with a Coleman stove and a Monopoly board, we three fishermen passed the day—indoors. The hours passed slowly, but they did pass. Night finally came, and we crawled into the sleeping bags dreaming of angling.

Were we in for a surprise. The next morning it wasn't the wind that made the door hard to open, it was the ice!

We tried to be cheerful. "No problem," we mumbled. "We can play Monopoly . . . again. We can reread the stories in *Reader's Digest*. And surely we know another joke or two." But as courageous as we tried to be, it was obvious that some of the gray had left the sky and entered our camper.

I began to notice a few things I hadn't seen before. I noticed that Mark had a few personality flaws. He was a bit too cocky about his opinions. He was easily irritated and constantly edgy. He couldn't take any constructive criticism. Even though his socks did stink, he didn't think it was my business to tell him.

"Just looking out for the best interest of my dad's camper," I defended, expecting Dad to come to my aid.

But Dad just sat over in the corner, reading. *Humph*, I thought, *where is he when I need him?* And then, I began to see Dad in a different light. When I mentioned to him that the eggs were soggy and the toast was burnt, he invited me to try my hand at the portable stove. *Touchy, touchy*, I said to myself. *Nothing like being cooped up in a camper with someone to help you see his real nature.*

It was a long day. It was a long, cold night.

When we awoke the next morning to the sound of sleet slapping the canvas, we didn't even pretend to be cheerful. We were flat-out grumpy. Mark became more of a jerk with each passing moment; I wondered what spell of ignorance I must have been in when I invited him. Dad couldn't do anything right; I wondered how someone so irritable could have such an even-tempered son. We sat in misery the whole day, our fishing equipment still unpacked.

The next day was even colder. "We're going home" were my father's first words. No one objected.

I learned a hard lesson that week. Not about fishing, but about people.

When those who are called to fish don't fish, they fight.

When energy intended to be used outside is used inside, the result is explosive. Instead of casting nets, we cast stones. Instead of extending helping hands, we point accusing fingers. Instead of being fishers of the lost, we become critics of the saved. Rather than helping the hurting, we hurt the helpers.

The result? Church Scrooges. "Bah humbug" spirituality. Beady eyes searching for warts on others while ignoring the warts on the nose below. Crooked fingers that bypass strengths and point out weaknesses.

Split churches. Poor testimonies. Broken hearts. Legalistic wars.

And, sadly, poor go unfed, confused go uncounseled, and lost go unreached.

When those who are called to fish don't fish, they fight.

But note the other side of this fish tale: When those who are called to fish, fish—they flourish!

Nothing handles a case of the gripes like an afternoon service project. Nothing restores perspective better than a visit to a hospital ward. Nothing unites soldiers better than a common task.

Leave soldiers inside the barracks with no time on the front line and see what happens to their attitude. The soldiers will invent things to complain about. Bunks will be too hard. Food will be too cold. Leadership will be too tough. The company will be too stale. Yet place those same soldiers in the trench and let them duck a few bullets, and what was a boring barracks will seem like a haven. The beds will feel great. The food will be almost ideal. The leadership will be courageous. The company will be exciting.

When those who are called to fish, fish—they flourish!

Jesus knew that.

When he arrived at Bethsaida, he was sorrowful, tired, and anxious to be alone with the disciples. No one would have blamed him had he dismissed the crowds a second time. No one would have criticized him had he waved away the people. But he didn't. Later he would. Later he would demand their departure and seek solitude.

But not before he "healed their sick"[3] and taught them "many things."[4] Self was forgotten . . . others were served . . . and stress was relieved.

Make a note of that. The next time the challenges "outside" tempt you to shut the door and stay inside, stay long enough to get warm. Then get out. When those who are called to fish don't fish, they fight.

5

THE
JOY
IN
THE
JOURNEY

S HE SAT IN 14E, and I sat in 14D.

She was rural, and I was urban. She was backward, and I was sophisticated. She was homey, and I was "professional." But she could see, and I was blind.

"They sure do put these seats close up against each other, don't they," she said as I sat down.

Her face was ten inches from mine. She had basset-hound cheeks; her eyebrows peaked over her nose; and her jowls sagged. She smiled so widely you could see the cavity on her upper side. Her neck seemed to lean out of her shoulders at a forty-five-degree angle, leaving her head in front of her shoulders rather than above them. She wore a Dutch-bob haircut and a blue, velour pants suit.

I don't know if she was old or just looked old. But I do know one thing: She'd never flown.

"I don't do this too much, do you?"

When I told her I did, her eyes widened. "Oooh, that must be fu-un." (She could add a syllable to any word.)

I groaned to myself. I already had a bad attitude. My week had been hectic. The plane was late and overbooked. I had a toothache and had left the tooth medicine at the hotel. I wanted to sleep, but I had work to do. And now I was sitting next to Gomer Pyle's mother.

"Oooh, boy, look at that one!"

She pointed at the plane ahead of us on the runway.

"Is this one that big?"

"Yes." I hoped my brief response would show her that I wasn't up for chitchat. It didn't.

"I'm going to see my boy in Dallas. Do you ever go to Dallas? I hope he's OK. He had a stomach flu last week. He's got a new dog. I can't wait to see it. It's a Labrador. Do you know what that is? They are big and lovable and . . ."

She was uncanny. Not only could she add a syllable to every word, she could answer her own questions.

As we were taking off, however, she got quiet. For several moments she said nothing. Then she suddenly let out a sound that would have called the pigs for dinner.

"Oooooeeee, those trees down there look like peat moss!"

People seated around us turned and stared like I was E. F. Hutton.

"What river is that?"

I told her I didn't know, so she flagged down a stewardess.

When the drinks came around, I asked for a Coke; she asked for the list.

"Tell me again?" So the stewardess told her again. "Oh, it's so hard to choose," she giggled. But she finally chose.

When they brought her the drink, she exclaimed that she didn't know apple juice came in cans. And when they brought her a sandwich, she opened the box and proclaimed loud enough for the pilot to hear, "Why, they even put mayonnaise in here."

When I pulled out my laptop computer, she was enthralled. "Now isn't that clever."

And that went on . . . the whole flight. She didn't miss a thing. If she wasn't staring out the window, she was amazed by a magazine. If she wasn't talking, she was "ooohing." She played with her fan. She turned her light on and off. She toyed with her seat belt. She savored her lunch. When we went through turbulence, I looked over at her to be sure she was all right, and she was grinning. You'd have thought she was riding the Ferris wheel at the county fair!

It occurred to me, about mid-journey, that she was the only person enjoying the trip.

The rest of us, the "sophisticated," were too mature to have fun. The man in front of me was discussing business trips to Japan, dropping more names than the U.S. Bureau of the Census. The fellow behind me was ordering beers—two at a time. The lady to my right was up to her eyebrows in paperwork. And I was staring at a computer screen—eyes tired, mouth hurting, stressed-out, trying to find a message for stress-filled people and never noticing that the message was sitting beside me.

And I might never have noticed had she not leaned over and said to me at the end of the flight. "Son, I may be out of place in saying this, but you've worked the entire trip. You need to relax, boy. You need to put that machine up and enjoy the journey."

Gulp.

I smiled weakly and mumbled some excuse about needing to get the work done before tomorrow. But she wasn't listening. She was squeezing her hands together in excitement as we landed.

"Wasn't that a fu-un trip?" she asked as we were leaving the plane.

I didn't say anything. I just nodded and smiled. Off she walked, bouncing down the concourse as curious as a six-year-old. I watched her as long as I could, then turned to go to my next flight with a lesson learned.

I resolved to keep my eyes open.

It does little good, I decided, to make the trip and miss the journey.

6

REMARKABLE

SOMETHING HAPPENED A FEW weeks ago that could be filed in the folder labeled "Remarkable."

I was playing basketball at the church one Saturday morning. (A good number of guys show up each week to play.) Some are flat-bellies—guys in their twenties who can touch their toes when they stretch and touch the rim when they jump. The rest of us are fat-bellies—guys who are within eyesight of, if not over the top of, the hill. Touching our toes is no longer an option. Looking down and *seeing* our toes is the current challenge. We never touch the rim when we jump and seldom touch it when we shoot.

But the flat-bellies don't mind if the fat-bellies play. (They don't have a choice. We have the keys to the building.)

Anyway, a few Saturdays back we were in the middle of a game when I went up for a rebound. I must have been pretty slow because, just as I was going up for the ball, someone else was already coming down with it. And the only thing I got from the jump was a finger in the eye.

When I opened my eye, everything was blurry. I knew my contact lens was not where it used to be. I thought I felt it in the corner of my eye, so I waved out of the game and ran to the rest room. But after I looked in the mirror, I realized that it must have fallen out on the floor somewhere.

I ran back onto the court. The guys were at the opposite end, leaving the goal under which I had lost my contact lens vacant.

I hurried out, got down on my knees, and began to search. No luck. When the fellows started bringing the ball downcourt, they saw what I was doing and came to help. All ten of us were down on our knees, panting like puppies and sweating like Pony Express horses.

But no one could find the silly lens.

We were just about to give up when one fellow exclaimed, "There it is." I looked up. He was pointing at a player's shoulder. The same guy whose finger had explored my cornea.

There, on his shoulder, was my lens. It had fallen on him . . . stuck to his skin . . . stayed on his back all the way down the court while he jumped and bounced . . . and then ridden all the way back.

Remarkable.

Even more remarkable when you consider that the contact lens made this round trip on the back of a flat-belly. One of the guys who can touch the rim and his toes. Had it landed on the shoulder of one of the "top-of-the-hill guys," no one would have been impressed. Some of us have the mobility of grazing buffalo. But when you think of the ride the tiny piece of plastic took, when you think of the odds of it being found, you have only one place to put this event: in the folder labeled "Remarkable."

The more I thought about this event, the more remarkable it became.

The more remarkable it became, the more I learned about remarkable things.

I learned that remarkable things usually occur in unremarkable situations, i.e., Saturday morning basketball games.

I also noticed that there are more remarkable things going on than those I usually see. In fact, as I began to look around, I found more and more things that I'd labeled "To be expected" that deserve to be labeled "Well what do you know."

Examples?

My money is in a bank with at least several thousand other folks' money. Who knows how many transactions are made every day? Who knows how much money goes into that place and is taken out? But somehow, if I want some money or just want to know how much money I have, the bank teller can give me what I want.

Remarkable.

Each morning I climb into a truck that weighs half a ton and take it out on an interstate where I—and a thousand other drivers—turn our vehicles into sixty-mile-per-hour missiles. Although I've had a few scares and mishaps, I still whistle while I drive at a speed that would have caused my great-grandfather to pass out.

Remarkable.

Every day I have the honor of sitting down with a book that contains the words of the One who created me. Every day I have the opportunity to let him give me a thought or two on how to live.

If I don't do what he says, he doesn't burn the book or cancel my subscription. If I disagree with what he says, lightning doesn't split my swivel chair or an angel doesn't mark my name off the holy list. If I don't understand what he says, he doesn't call me a dummy.

In fact, he calls me "Son," and on a different page explains what I don't understand.

Remarkable.

At the end of the day when I walk through the house, I step into the bedrooms of three little girls. Their covers are usually kicked off, so I cover them up. Their hair usually hides their faces, so I brush it back. And one by one, I bend over and kiss the foreheads of the angels God has loaned me. Then I stand in the doorway and wonder why in the world he would entrust a stumbling, fumbling fellow like me with the task of loving and leading such treasures.

Remarkable.

Then I go and crawl into bed with a woman far wiser than I . . . a woman who deserves a man much better looking than I . . . but a woman who would argue that fact and tell me from the bottom of her heart that I'm the best thing to come down her pike.

After I think about the wife I have, and when I think that I get to be with her for a lifetime, I shake my head and thank the God of grace for grace and think, *Remarkable*.

In the morning, I'll do it all again. I'll drive down the same road. Go to the same office. Call on the same bank. Kiss the same girls. And crawl into bed with the same woman. But I'm learning not to take these everyday miracles for granted.

Just think, it all came out of a basketball game. Ever since I found that contact, I've seen things a lot clearer.

I'm discovering many things: traffic jams eventually clear up, sunsets are for free, Little League is a work of art, and most planes take off and arrive on time. I'm learning that most folks are good folks who are just as timid as I am about starting a conversation.

I'm meeting people who love their country and their God and their church and would die for any of the three.

I'm learning that if I look . . . if I open my eyes and observe . . . there are many reasons to take off my hat, look at the Source of it all, and just say thanks.

7

THANKS FOR THE BREAD

*D*EAR FRIEND,

I'm writing to say thanks. I wish I could thank you personally, but I don't know where you are. I wish I could call you, but I don't know your name. If I knew your appearance, I'd look for you, but your face is fuzzy in my memory. But I'll never forget what you did.

There you were, leaning against your pickup in the West Texas oil field. An engineer of some sort. A supervisor on the job. Your khakis and clean shirt set you apart from us roustabouts. In the oil field pecking order, we were at the bottom. You were the boss. We were the workers. You read the blueprints. We dug the ditches. You inspected the pipe. We laid it. You ate with the bosses in the shed. We ate with each other in the shade.

Except that day.

I remember wondering why you did it.

We weren't much to look at. What wasn't sweaty was oily. Faces burnt from the sun; skin black from the grease. Didn't bother me, though. I was there only for the summer. A high-school boy earning good money laying pipe. For me, it was a summer job. For the others, it was a way of life. Most were illegal immigrants from Mexico. Others were drifters, bouncing across the prairie as rootless as tumbleweeds.

We weren't much to listen to, either. Our language was sandpaper coarse. After lunch, we'd light the cigarettes and begin the jokes. Someone always had a deck of cards with lacy-clad girls on the back. For thirty minutes in the heat of the day, the oil patch became Las Vegas—replete with foul language, dirty stories, blackjack, and barstools that doubled as lunch pails.

In the middle of such a game, you approached us. I thought you had a job for us that couldn't wait another few minutes. Like the others, I groaned when I saw you coming.

You were nervous. You shifted your weight from one leg to the other as you began to speak.

"Uh, fellows," you started.

We turned and looked up at you.

"I, uh, I just wanted, uh, to invite . . ."

You were way out of your comfort zone. I had no idea what you might be about to say, but I knew that it had nothing to do with work.

"I just wanted to tell you that, uh, our church is having a service tonight and, uh . . ."

"What?" I couldn't believe it. "He's talking church? Out here? With us?"

"I wanted to invite any of you to come along."

Silence. Screaming silence. The same silence you'd hear if a nun asked a madam if she could use the brothel for a mass. The same silence you'd hear if an IRS representative invited the Mafia to a seminar on tax integrity.

Several guys stared at the dirt. A few shot glances at the others. Snickers rose just inches from the surface.

"Well, that's it. Uh, if any of you want to go . . . uh, let me know."

After you turned and left, we turned and laughed. We called you "reverend," "preacher," and "the pope." We poked fun at each other, daring one another to go. You became the butt of the day's jokes.

I'm sure you knew that. I'm sure you went back to your truck knowing the only good you'd done was to make a good fool out of yourself. If that's what you thought, then you were wrong.

That's the reason for this letter.

I thought of you this week. I thought of you when I read about someone else who took a risk at lunch. I thought of you when I read the story of the little boy who gave his lunch to Jesus.[1]

His lunch wasn't much. In fact, it wasn't anything compared to what was needed for more than five thousand people.

He probably wrestled with the silliness of it all. What was one lunch for so many? He probably asked himself if it was even worth the effort.

How far could one lunch go?

I think that's why he didn't give the lunch to the crowd. Instead he gave it to Jesus. Something told him that if he would plant the seed, God would grant the crop.

So he did.

He summoned his courage, got up off the grass, and walked into the circle of grownups. He was as out of place in that cluster as you were in ours. He must have been nervous. No one likes to appear silly.

Someone probably snickered at him, too.

If they didn't snicker, they shook their heads. "The little fellow doesn't know any better."

If they didn't shake their heads, they rolled their eyes. "Here we have a hunger crisis, and this little boy thinks that a sack lunch will solve it."

But it wasn't the men's heads or eyes that the boy saw; he saw only Jesus.

You must have seen Jesus, too, when you made your decision. Most people would have considered us to be unlikely deacon material. Most would have saved their seeds for softer soil. And they'd have been almost right. But Jesus said to give . . . so you gave.

As I think about it, you and the little boy have a lot in common:

- You both used your lunch to help others.
- You both chose faith over logic.
- You both brought a smile to your Father's face.

There's one difference, though. The boy got to see what Jesus did with his gift, and you didn't. That's why I'm writing. I want you to know that at least one of the seeds fell into a fertile crevice.

Some five years later, a college sophomore was struggling with a decision. He had drifted from the faith given to him by his parents. He wanted to come back. He wanted to come home. But the price was high. His friends might laugh. His habits would have to change. His reputation would have to be overcome.

Could he do it? Did he have the courage?

That's when I thought of you. As I sat in my dorm room late one night, looking for the guts to do what I knew was right, I thought of you.

I thought of how your love for God had been greater than your love for your reputation.

I thought of how your obedience had been greater than your common sense.

I remembered how you had cared more about making disciples than about making a good first impression. And when I thought of you, your memory became my motivation.

So I came home.

I've told your story dozens of times to thousands of people. Each time the reaction is the same: The audience becomes a sea of smiles, and heads bob in understanding. Some smile because they think of the "clean-shirted engineers" in their lives. They remember the neighbor who brought the cake, the aunt who wrote the letter, the teacher who listened . . .

Others smile because they have done what you did. And they, too, wonder if their "lunchtime loyalty" was worth the effort.

You wondered that. What you did that day wasn't much. And I'm sure you walked away that day thinking that your efforts had been wasted.

They weren't.

So I'm writing to say thanks. Thanks for the example. Thanks for the courage. Thanks for giving your lunch to God. He did something with it; it became the Bread of Life for me.

Gratefully,
Max

P.S. If by some remarkable coincidence you read this and remember that day, please give me a call. I owe you lunch.

8

MUSINGS
IN
MINNEAPOLIS

*I*T'S A LONG WAY FROM BOSTON, Massachusetts to Edmonton, Canada. No matter how you cut it or route it, it's a long way.

My journey today began around 1:30 P.M. I spoke where I was supposed to speak and changed into my Reeboks just in time to fight traffic all the way to Logan Airport.

The plane was overbooked; some folks were mad. The plane was also designed by a five-foot, four-inch engineer who hates tall people. (I ate my knees for lunch.) The plane arrived late into Minneapolis, where I was to change planes.

Now, I know I'm not supposed to complain. I've heard myself preach sermons on gratitude. And I know that a million people in the world would love to have the airline peanuts I threw away today. But still, I got off the plane with a cramp in my leg, an empty stomach, a bad attitude, and three more hours of travel to go.

On the way to my next plane, I saw a McDonald's. Looked good. Did I have time? Then I saw something better: a phone.

I walked over, set down my bags, and called home. Denalyn answered. I love it when she answers. She's always glad when I call. When she gets to heaven, Saint Peter will give her the receptionist job at the gate.

We spent twenty minutes talking about major Pentagon-level topics like the weather in New England and the weather in San Antonio. We talked about the fact that Jenna had a friend coming over to spend the night and that Sara might have a fever. I told her about the Canadian, French-speaking English teacher I sat next to on the plane, and she told me about the new elementary school.

We made no decisions. We solved no problems. We re-solved no major conflicts. We just talked. And I felt better.

Jenna got on the phone and asked me when I was coming home, and it felt good to be wanted.

Andrea got on the phone and told me she loved me, and it felt good to be loved.

Jenna put the phone next to baby Sara's ear, and I talked baby talk in the middle of the airport. (Some people turned to stare.) But I didn't care because Sara cooed, and it felt good to be cooed at.

Denalyn got back on the phone and said, "I'm glad you called." And I hung up happy.

Now I'm back on the plane and my attitude is back on track. The plane is delayed because the runway is backed up, which means I'll get into Edmonton an hour later than I planned. I don't know who is going to pick me up, and I can't remember to whom I'm supposed to speak tomorrow. But that's OK.

I can handle being a pilgrim as long as I know that I can call home whenever I want.

Jesus could . . . and he did.

Maybe that's the rationale behind verse 19 of Matthew 14: "Taking the five loaves and the two fish and looking up to heaven, he gave thanks and broke the loaves." I'd always chalked this prayer up to, at best, a good example—at worst, a good habit.

Until now.

Now it occurs to me that Jesus needed to call home in the middle of the hassles as much as I did. He was surrounded by people who wanted food and disciples who wanted a break. His heart was heavy from the death of John the Baptist.

He needed a minute with someone who would understand.

Maybe he, like me, got a bit weary of the hassles of getting a job done in a distant land and needed to call home.

So he did. He chatted with the One he loved. He heard the sound of the home he missed. And he was reminded that when all hell breaks loose, all heaven draws near.

Maybe you should call home, too. God will be glad when you do—but not half as glad as you will be.

9

FENDING
OFF
THE
VOICES

Y OU WANT SUCCESS? Here's your model. You want achievement? Here's your prototype. You want bright lights, pageants, and media attention? Consider the front-page, center article of the nation's largest daily newspaper.

It is a caricature of "Miss America." The "vital" data of the fifty-one participants has been compiled to present the perfect woman. She has brown hair. She has brown eyes. She knows how to sing and has a perfect figure: 35–24–35. She is Miss America. She is the ideal.

The message trumpets off the page: "This is the standard for American women." The implication is clear: Do what it takes to be like her. Firm your thighs. Deepen your cleavage. Pamper your hair. Improve your walk.

No reference is made to her convictions . . . to her honesty . . . to her faith . . . or to her God. But you are told her hip size.

In a small photo, four inches to the left, is another woman. Her face is thin. Her skin is wrinkled, almost leathery. No makeup . . . no blush . . . no lipstick. There is a faint smile on her lips and a glint in her eyes.

She looks pale. Perhaps it's my imagination or perhaps it's true. The caption reads, "Mother Teresa: In serious condition."[1]

Mother Teresa. You know her story. When she won the Nobel Peace Prize in 1985, she gave the two hundred

thousand dollars to the poor of Calcutta. When a businessman bought her a new car, she sold it and gave the money
to the underprivileged. She owns nothing. She owes nothing.

Two women: Miss America and Mother Teresa. One
walks the boardwalk; the other works the alley. Two voices.
One promises crowns, flowers, and crowds. The other
promises service, surrender, and joy.

Now, I have nothing against beauty pageants (although
I have my reservations about them). But I do have something against the lying voices that noise our world.

You've heard them. They tell you to swap your integrity
for a new sale. To barter your convictions for an easy deal. To
exchange your devotion for a quick thrill.

They whisper. They woo. They taunt. They tantalize.
They flirt. They flatter. "Go ahead, it's OK." "Just wait until tomorrow." "Don't worry, no one will know." "How could
anything that feels so right be so wrong?"

The voices of the crowd.

Our lives are Wall Streets of chaos, stock markets loud
with demands. Grown men and women barking in a frenzied
effort to get all they can before time runs out. "Buy. Sell.
Trade. Swap. But whatever you do, do it fast—and loud."

A carnival of gray-flannel suits where no one smiles
and everyone dashes.

An endless chorus of booming voices: some offering,
some taking, and all screaming.

What do we do with the voices?

As I work on this manuscript, I'm seated at a desk in a
hotel room. I'm away from home. Away from people who
know me. Away from family members who love me.

Voices that encourage and affirm are distant.

But voices that tantalize and entice are near. Although
the room is quiet, if I listen, their voices are crystal clear.

A placard on my nightstand invites me to a lounge in the lobby, where I can "make new friends in a relaxing atmosphere." An advertisement on top of the television promises me that with the request of a late-night adult movie my "fantasies will come true." In the phone book, several columns of escort services offer "love away from home." An attractive, gold-lettered volume in the drawer of the nightstand beckons: *The Book of Mormon—Another Testament of Jesus Christ.* On television a talk-show host discusses the day's topic: "How to succeed at sex in the office."

Voices. Some for pleasure. Some for power.

Some promise acceptance. Some promise tenderness. But all promise something.

Even the voices that Jesus heard promised something.

"After the people saw the miraculous sign that Jesus did, they began to say, 'Surely this is the Prophet who is to come into the world.'"[2]

To the casual observer, these are the voices of victory. To the untrained ear, these are the sounds of triumph. What could be better? Five thousand men plus women and children proclaiming Christ to be the prophet. Thousands of voices swelling into a roar of revival, an ovation of adulation.

The people have everything they need for a revolution.

They have an enemy: Herod. They have a martyr: John the Baptist. They have leadership: the disciples. They have ample supplies: Jesus the bread maker. And they have a king: Jesus of Nazareth.

Why wait? The time has come. Israel will be restored. God's people have heard God's voice.

"King Jesus!" someone proclaims. And the crowd chimes in.

And don't think for a minute that Christ didn't hear their chant.

A chorus promising power intoxicates. No cross needed. No sacrifice required. An army of disciples at his fingertips. Power to change the world without having to die doing it.

Revenge would be sweet. *The one who took the head of John the Baptist is only a few miles away. I wonder if he has ever felt a cold blade on his neck.*

Yes, Jesus heard the voices. He heard the lurings. But he also heard someone else.

And when Jesus heard him, he sought him.

"Jesus, knowing that they intended to come and make him king by force, withdrew again to a mountain by himself."[3]

Jesus preferred to be alone with the true God rather than in a crowd with the wrong people.

Logic didn't tell him to dismiss the crowds. Conventional wisdom didn't tell him to turn his back on a willing army. No, it wasn't a voice from without that Jesus heard. It was a voice from within.

The mark of a sheep is its ability to hear the Shepherd's voice.

"The sheep listen to his voice. He calls his own sheep by name and leads them out."[4]

The mark of a disciple is his or her ability to hear the Master's voice.

"Here I am! I stand at the door and knock. If anyone hears my voice and opens the door, I will come in and eat with him, and he with me."[5]

The world rams at your door; Jesus taps at your door. The voices scream for your allegiance; Jesus softly and tenderly requests it. The world promises flashy pleasure;

Jesus promises a quiet dinner . . . with God. "I will come in and eat."

Which voice do you hear?

Let me state something important. There is never a time during which Jesus is not speaking. Never. There is never a place in which Jesus is not present. Never. There is never a room so dark . . . a lounge so sensual . . . an office so sophisticated . . . that the ever-present, ever-pursuing, relentlessly tender Friend is not there, tapping gently on the doors of our hearts—waiting to be invited in.

Few hear his voice. Fewer still open the door.

But never interpret our numbness as his absence. For amidst the fleeting promises of pleasure is the timeless promise of his presence.

"Surely I am with you always, to the very end of the age."[6]

"'Never will I leave you; never will I forsake you.'"[7]

There is no chorus so loud that the voice of God cannot be heard . . . if we will but listen.

That's true in this hotel room.

It took me a few minutes to find it, but I did. It wasn't as visible as the lounge placard or the movie advertisement. But it was there. It wasn't as fancy as the Mormon Bible or as attention-grabbing as the escort ads. But I'd give up those lies every time for the peace I've found in this treasure.

A Bible. A simple, hard-covered, Gideon-placed, King James Version Bible. It took me a few minutes to find it, but I did. And when I did, I opened it to one of my favorite voice passages:

A time is coming when all who are in their graves will hear his voice and come out—those who have done good will rise to live, and those who have done evil will rise to be condemned.[8]

Interesting. A day is coming when everyone will hear his voice. A day is coming when all the other voices will be silenced; his voice—and his voice only—will be heard.

Some will hear his voice for the very first time. It's not that he never spoke, it's just that they never listened. For these, God's voice will be the voice of a stranger. They will hear it once—and never hear it again. They will spend eternity fending off the voices they followed on earth.

But others will be called from their graves by a familiar voice. For they are sheep who know their shepherd. They are servants who opened the door when Jesus knocked.

Now the door will open again. Only this time, it won't be Jesus who walks into our house; it will be we, who walk into his.

10

THE
PHOTO
AND
THE
FILE

*E*ACH JUNE I PUT MY CALENDAR together for the coming year. June is the month of D-Day. I don't mean D-Day as in Normandy invasion. I mean D-Day as in decisions to be made.

This morning I began the process of decision. I opened the "Decision File" and began reading the speaking invitations. A church planter in Wyoming wonders if I could spend time with his church. A church camp in Washington invites me to speak to its campers. A missionary in India has read my books and asks, "If I can come up with the money, can you spend a week with us?"

Something happens as a person fields the invitations of others. He or she begins to feel important.

As I looked at the letters, it dawned on me how vital I was to the progress of humanity.

I wondered how the earth stayed on its axis before I was born. I nodded my head in understanding at the letter that read, "You are the one for this meeting." I put my hand under my shirt and rubbed the S on the red jersey—"Super Max."

I was feeling puffy and proud when I read the last letter. But as I put down the file, I noticed another request. One that didn't make it into the folder. One that was lying on my desk.

It had no date, no signature, no deadline. It wasn't a letter or a phone message. It was a photograph—a photograph so recent that it had no frame. It was a portrait of a mom and a dad encircled by three little girls. Our family portrait.

The positioning of the photo and the file struck me. There was something symbolic about the way I'd unintentionally placed the letters next to the family picture. The singular photo lying in the shadow of the stack of requests seemed to whisper a question that only I could answer:

"Max, who will win?"

There is only so much sand in the hourglass. Who gets it?

You know what I'm talking about, don't you? Since you don't stockpile your requests until June, your situation may not be as graphic as mine. But it's every bit as real.

"The PTA needs a new treasurer. With your background and experience and talent and wisdom and love for kids and degree in accounting, YOU are the perfect one for the job!"

"There's going to be some shuffling in the ranks. With the retirement of the branch manager, *somebody* will move up. The company is looking for a bright, young salesman— someone like you—who is willing to demonstrate his dedication to the organization by taking on some extra projects . . . and working some late hours."

"I apologize that I have to ask you again, but you are such a good Sunday-school teacher. If you could only take one more quarter . . ."

"I just lost my hygienist. Will you come back to work for me? I know you don't want to go back to work until your children start school. But it's only four hours a day and there's a day-care center just a few blocks from my office now. Wouldn't the extra money be nice?"

"Would I be willing to serve as chapter president? Well, to be honest, I was going to sit out this term because our youngest goes to college next fall. Yes, I realize this is a critical year for the organization. . . . Oh, no, I wouldn't want the club to falter. . . . Yes, we have made great progress over the last few months. It's just that . . ."

It's tug-of-war, and you are the rope.

On one side are the requests for your time and energy. They call. They compliment. They are valid and good. Great opportunities to do good things. If they were evil, it'd be easy to say no. But they aren't, so it's easy to rationalize.

On the other side are the loved ones in your world. They don't write you letters. They don't ask you to consult your calendar. They don't offer to pay your expenses. They don't use terms like "appointment," "engagement," or "do lunch." They don't want you for what you can do for them; they want you for who you are.

Clovis Chappell, a minister from a century back, used to tell the story of two paddleboats. They left Memphis about the same time, traveling down the Mississippi River to New Orleans. As they traveled side by side, sailors from one vessel made a few remarks about the snail's pace of the other.

Words were exchanged. Challenges were made. And the race began. Competition became vicious as the two boats roared through the Deep South.

One boat began falling behind. Not enough fuel. There had been plenty of coal for the trip, but not enough for a race. As the boat dropped back, an enterprising young sailor took some of the ship's cargo and tossed it into the ovens. When the sailors saw that the supplies burned as well as the coal, they fueled their boat with the material they had been assigned to transport. They ended up winning the race, but burned their cargo.

God has entrusted cargo to us, too: children, spouses, friends. Our job is to do our part in seeing that this cargo reaches its destination.

Yet when the program takes priority over people, people often suffer.

How much cargo do we sacrifice in order to achieve the number one slot? How many people never reach the destination because of the aggressiveness of a competitive captain?

A world of insight is hidden in four words in Matthew 14:22: "He dismissed the crowd." This wasn't just *any* crowd that Jesus dismissed.

These weren't casually curious.

These weren't coincidental bystanders.

This was a multitude with a mission. They had heard the disciples. They had left their homes. They had followed Jesus around the sea. They had heard him teach and had seen him heal. They had eaten the bread. And they were ready to make him king.

Surely Jesus will commandeer the crowd and focus their frenzy. Surely he will seize the chance to convert the thousands. Surely he will spend the night baptizing the willing followers. No one would turn down an opportunity to minister to thousands of people, right?

Jesus did.

"He dismissed the crowd." Why? Read verse 23: "After he had dismissed them, he went up on a mountainside by himself to pray."

He said no to the important in order to say yes to the vital.

He said no to a good opportunity in order to say yes to a better opportunity. It wasn't a selfish decision. It was a deliberate choice to honor priorities. If Jesus thought it necessary to say no to the demands of the crowds in order to pray, don't you think you and I should, too?

"Blessed are the meek,"[1] Jesus said. The word *meek* does not mean weak. It means focused. It is a word used to describe a domesticated stallion. Power under control. Strength with a direction.

Blessed are those who are harnessed. Blessed are those who recognize their God-given responsibilities. Blessed are those who acknowledge that there is only one God and have quit applying for his position. Blessed are those who know what on earth they are on earth to do and set themselves about the business of doing it. Blessed are those who are able to "discern what is best."[2]

As I looked at the photo and the file, I decided to try something. I decided to make a list of what I would lose by saying no to my family one night. It wasn't hard to do; I just made a list of what I would have missed by not being home with my family last night.

I could have been out of town this week. I had an invitation to be in the Midwest at a church. I turned it down. What if I hadn't? If I had gone, I would have had the attention of a thousand people for an hour. I would have had the opportunity to speak about Jesus to some people who don't know him. Is a Tuesday evening at home with three children and a spouse more important than preaching to an audience?

Read my list of what I would have missed. Then you decide.

I would have missed a trip to the swimming pool in which I saw Jenna climb onto her inner tube for the first time.

I would have missed fifteen minutes of bouncing up and down in the shallow end of the pool, with Andrea clinging to my neck singing the theme from "Sleeping Beauty."

I would have missed seeing Denalyn get sentimental as she unpacked a box of baby clothes.

I wouldn't have gone on a walk with the girls during which Jenna found ten "special" rocks.

I wouldn't have been there to hold Andrea when her finger got slammed in the door.

I wouldn't have been there to answer Jenna's question: "Daddy, what is a handicapped person?"

I would have missed seeing Andrea giggle as she took Jenna's straw when Jenna's back was turned.

I wouldn't have heard Jenna tell the story of Jesus on the cross during our family devotional (when she assured us, "But he didn't stay dead!").

I wouldn't have seen Andrea make a muscle with her arm and sing, "Our God is so BIIIIIIG!"

What do you think? I know my vote. There are a hundred speakers who could have addressed that crowd, but my girls just have one daddy.

After I made my list, just for the fun of it I picked up the phone and called the church that had asked me to come and speak this week. The minister wasn't in, but his secretary was. "Isn't this the week of your seminar?" I asked.

"Oh, yes! It has been a wonderful success!"

They didn't even miss me.

Now I've got a better idea what to do with my stack of requests.

STORMS
OF
DOUBT

11

SEEING GOD THROUGH SHATTERED GLASS

*T*HERE IS A WINDOW IN YOUR heart through which you can see God. Once upon a time that window was clear. Your view of God was crisp. You could see God as vividly as you could see a gentle valley or hillside. The glass was clean, the pane unbroken.

You knew God. You knew how he worked. You knew what he wanted you to do. No surprises. Nothing unexpected. You knew that God had a will, and you continually discovered what it was.

Then, suddenly, the window cracked. A pebble broke the window. A pebble of pain.

Perhaps the stone struck when you were a child and a parent left home—forever. Maybe the rock hit in adolescence when your heart was broken. Maybe you made it into adulthood before the window was cracked. But then the pebble came.

Was it a phone call? "We have your daughter at the station. You'd better come down."

Was it a letter on the kitchen table? "I've left. Don't try to reach me. Don't try to call me. It's over. I just don't love you anymore."

Was it a diagnosis from the doctor? "I'm afraid our news is not very good."

Was it a telegram? "We regret to inform you that your son is missing in action."

Whatever the pebble's form, the result was the same— a shattered window. The pebble missiled into the pane and shattered it. The crash echoed down the halls of your heart. Cracks shot out from the point of impact, creating a spider web of fragmented pieces.

And suddenly God was not so easy to see. The view that had been so crisp had changed. You turned to see God, and his figure was distorted. It was hard to see him through the pain. It was hard to see him through the fragments of hurt.

You were puzzled. God wouldn't allow something like this to happen, would he? Tragedy and travesty weren't on the agenda of the One you had seen, were they? Had you been fooled? Had you been blind?

The moment the pebble struck, the glass became a reference point for you. From then on, there was life before the pain and life after the pain. Before your pain, the view was clear; God seemed so near. After your pain, well, he was harder to see. He seemed a bit distant . . . harder to perceive. Your pain distorted the view—not eclipsed it, but distorted it.

Maybe these words don't describe your situation. There are some people who never have to redefine or refocus their view of God. Most of us do.

Most of us know what it means to feel disappointed by God.

Most of us have a way of completing this sentence: "If God is God, then . . ." Call it an agenda, a divine job description. Each of us has an unspoken, yet definitive, expectation of what God should do. "If God is God, then . . ."

• There will be no financial collapse in my family.

• My children will never be buried before me.

- People will treat me fairly.
- This church will never divide.
- My prayer will be answered.

These are not articulated criteria. They are not written down or notarized. But they are real. They define the expectations we have of God. And when pain comes into our world—when the careening pebble splinters the window of our hearts—these expectations go unmet and doubts may begin to surface.

We look for God, but can't find him. Fragmented glass hinders our vision. He is enlarged through this piece and reduced through that one. Lines jigsaw their way across his face. Large sections of shattered glass opaque the view.

And now you aren't quite sure what you see.

―――――――――――――――――

The disciples weren't sure what they saw, either.

Jesus failed to meet their expectations. The day Jesus fed the five thousand men he didn't do what they wanted him to do.

The Twelve returned from their mission followed by an army. They finished their training. They recruited the soldiers. They were ready for battle. They expected Jesus to let the crowds crown him as king and attack the city of Herod. They expected battle plans . . . strategies . . . a new era for Israel.

What did they get?

Just the opposite.

Instead of weapons, they got oars. Rather than being sent to fight, they were sent to float. The crowds were sent away. Jesus walked away. And they were left on the water with a storm brewing in the sky.

What kind of Messiah would do this?

Note carefully the sequence of the stormy evening as Matthew records it:

> Immediately Jesus made the disciples get into the boat and go on ahead of him to the other side, while he dismissed the crowd. After he had dismissed them, he went up on a mountainside by himself to pray. *When evening came* [emphasis mine], he was there alone, but the boat was already a considerable distance from land, buffeted by the waves because the wind was against it.[1]

Matthew is specific about the order of events. Jesus sent the disciples to the boat. Then he dismissed the crowd and ascended a mountainside. It was evening, probably around 6:00 P.M. The storm struck immediately. The sun had scarcely set before typhoon-like winds began to roar.

Note that Jesus sent the disciples out into the storm *alone*. Even as he was ascending the mountainside, he could feel and hear the gale's force. Jesus was not ignorant of the storm. He was aware that a torrent was coming that would carpet-bomb the sea's surface. But he didn't turn around. The disciples were left to face the storm . . . alone.

The greatest storm that night was not in the sky; it was in the disciples' hearts. The greatest fear was not from seeing the storm-driven waves; it came from seeing the back of their leader as he left them to face the night with only questions as companions.

It was this fury that the disciples were facing that night. Imagine the incredible strain of bouncing from wave to wave in a tiny fishing vessel. One hour would weary you. Two hours would exhaust you.

Surely Jesus will help us, they thought. They'd seen him still storms like this before. On this same sea, they had awakened him during a storm, and he had commanded the skies to be silent. They'd seen him quiet the wind and soothe the waves. *Surely he will come off the mountain.*

But he doesn't. Their arms begin to ache from rowing. Still no sign of Jesus. Three hours. Four hours. The winds rage. The boat bounces. Still no Jesus. Midnight comes. Their eyes search for God—in vain.

By now the disciples have been on the sea for as long as six hours.

All this time they have fought the storm and sought the Master. And, so far, the storm is winning. And the Master is nowhere to be found.

"Where is he?" cried one.

"Has he forgotten us?" yelled another.

"He feeds thousands of strangers and yet leaves us to die?" muttered a third.

The Gospel of Mark adds compelling insight into the disciples' attitude. "They had not understood about the loaves; their hearts were hardened."[2]

What does Mark mean? Simply this. The disciples were mad. They began the evening in a huff. Their hearts were hardened toward Jesus because he fed the multitude. Their preference, remember, had been to "send the crowds away."[3] And Jesus had told them to feed the people. But they wouldn't try. They said it couldn't be done. They told Jesus to let the people take care of themselves.

Also keep in mind that the disciples had just spent some time on center stage. They'd tasted stardom. They were celebrities. They had rallied crowds. They had recruited an army. They were, no doubt, pretty proud of themselves. With chests a bit puffy and heads a bit swollen, they'd told Jesus, "Just send them away."

Jesus didn't. Instead, he chose to bypass the reluctant disciples and use the faith of an anonymous boy. What the disciples said couldn't be done was done—in spite of them, not through them.

They pouted. They sulked. Rather than being amazed at the miracle, they became mad at the Master. After all, they had felt foolish passing out the very bread they said could not be made. Add to that Jesus' command to go to the boat when they wanted to go to battle, and it's easier to understand why these guys are burning!

"Now what is Jesus up to, leaving us out on the sea on a night like this?"

It's 1:00 A.M., no Jesus.

It's 2:00 A.M., no Jesus.

Peter, Andrew, James, and John have seen storms like this. They are fishermen; the sea is their life. They know the havoc the gale-force winds can wreak. They've seen the splintered hulls float to shore. They've attended the funerals. They know, better than anyone, that this night could be their last. "Why doesn't he come?" they sputter.

Finally, he does. "During the fourth watch of the night [3:00 to 6:00 A.M.] Jesus went out to them, walking on the lake."[4]

Jesus came. He finally came. But between verse 24—being buffeted by waves—and verse 25—when Jesus appeared—a thousand questions are asked.

Questions you have probably asked, too. Perhaps you know the angst of being suspended between verses 24 and 25. Maybe you're riding a storm, searching the coastline for a light, a glimmer of hope. You know that Jesus knows what you are going through. You know that he's aware of your storm. But as hard as you look to find him, you can't see him. Maybe your heart, like the disciples' hearts, has been hardened by unmet expectations. Your pleadings for help are salted with angry questions.

The first section of this book spoke of stress; the second is about storms. Stress attacks your nerves. Storms attack your faith. Stress interrupts. Storms destroy. Stress comes like a siren. Storms come like a missile. Stress clouds the day. Storms usher in the night.

The question of stress is, *"How can I cope?"* The question of storms is, *"Where* is God and *why* would he do this?"

The second section of this book is for you if the pebble of pain has struck the window of your heart, if you've known the horror of looking for God's face and seeing only his back as he ascends a mountainside.

In the following pages, you will discover hopeful chronicles to help you deal with your doubts. Let me introduce you to a few friends who learned to see through shattered glass.

- An entrepreneur, stripped of treasures, who found one treasure that no one could take.

- A father who learned of trust during a six-hour drive with three children.

- A mother superior in New Mexico who discovered that prayer—her last resort—was her best resort.

- A woodsman who taught a village the virtue of patience.

- God's son—dog-tired and heartsore—who found strength through heaven's friends.

Some stories are fiction, some are fact. Some are legendary, others are biblical. Some are humorous, others are serious. But all have a message for those who know the anxiety of searching for God in a storm.

The message? When you can't see him, trust him. The figure you see is not a ghost. The voice you hear is not the wind.

Jesus is closer than you've ever dreamed.

12

TWO FATHERS, TWO FEASTS

I DROVE THE FAMILY TO Grandma's last night for Thanksgiving. Three hours into the six-hour trip, I realized that I was in a theology lab.

A day with a car full of kids will teach you a lot about God. Transporting a family from one city to another is closely akin to God transporting us from our home to his. And some of life's stormiest hours occur when the passenger and the Driver disagree on the destination.

A journey is a journey, whether the destination be the Thanksgiving table or the heavenly one. Both demand patience, a good sense of direction, and a driver who knows that the feast at the end of the trip is worth the hassles in the midst of the trip.

The fact that my pilgrims were all under the age of seven only enriched my learning experience.

As minutes rolled into hours and our car rolled through the hills, I began to realize that what I was saying to my kids had a familiar ring. I had heard it before—from God. All of a sudden, the car became a classroom. I realized that I was doing for a few hours what God has done for centuries: encouraging travelers who'd rather rest than ride.

I shared the idea with Denalyn. We began to discover similarities between the two journeys. Here are a few we noted.

In order to reach the destination, we have to say no to some requests.

Can you imagine the outcome if a parent honored each request of each child during a trip? We'd inch our bloated bellies from one ice-cream store to the next. Our priority would be popcorn and our itinerary would read like a fast-food menu. "Go to the Cherry Malt and make a right. Head north until you find the Chili Cheeseburger. Stay north for 1,300 calories and bear left at the Giant Pizza. When you see the two-for-one Chili Dog Special, take the Pepto-Bismol Turnpike east for five convenience stores. At the sixth toilet . . ."

Can you imagine the chaos if a parent indulged every indulgence?

Can you imagine the chaos if God indulged each of ours?

No is a necessary word to take on a trip. Destination has to reign over Dairy Deluxe Ice Cream Sundae.

"For God has not *destined* us [emphasis mine] to the terrors of judgement, but to the full attainment of salvation through our Lord Jesus Christ."[1]

Note God's destiny for your life. Salvation.

God's overarching desire is that you reach that destiny. His itinerary includes stops that encourage your journey. He frowns on stops that deter you. When his sovereign plan and your earthly plan collide, a decision must be made. Who's in charge of this journey?

If God must choose between your earthly satisfaction and your heavenly salvation, which do you hope he chooses?

Me, too.

When I'm in the driver's seat as the father of my children, I remember that I'm in charge. But when I'm in the passenger's seat as a child of my Father, I forget that he's in charge. I forget that God is more concerned with my destiny than my belly (although my belly hasn't done too badly). And I complain when he says no.

The requests my children made last night on the road to Grandma's weren't evil. They weren't unfair. They weren't rebellious. In fact, we had a couple of cones and Cokes. But most of the requests were unnecessary.

My four-year-old daughter would argue that fact. From her viewpoint, another soft drink is indispensable to her happiness. I know otherwise, so I say no.

A forty-year-old adult would argue that fact. From his standpoint, a new boss is indispensable to his happiness. God knows otherwise and says no.

A thirty-year-old woman would argue that fact. From her standpoint, *that* man with *that* job and *that* name is exactly who she needs to be happy. Her Father, who is more concerned that she arrive at his City than at the altar, says, "Wait a few miles. There's a better option down the road."

"Wait!" she protests. "How long do I have to wait?"

Which takes us to a second similarity between the two journeys.

Children have no concept of minutes or miles.

"We'll be there in three hours," I said.

"How long is three hours?" Jenna asked. (How do you explain time to a child who can't tell time?)

"Well, it's about as long as three Sesame Streets," I ventured.

The children groaned in unison. "Three Sesame Streets?! That's forever!"

And to them, it is.

And to us, it seems that way, too.

He who "lives forever"[2] has placed himself at the head of a band of pilgrims who mutter, "How long, O Lord? How long?"[3]

"How long must I endure this sickness?"

"How long must I endure this spouse?"

"How long must I endure this paycheck?"

Do you really want God to answer? He could, you know. He could answer in terms of the here and now with time increments we know. "Two more years on the illness." "The rest of your life in the marriage." "Ten more years for the bills."

But he seldom does that. He usually opts to measure the *here and now* against the *there and then*. And when you compare *this* life to *that* life, this life ain't long.

Our days on earth are like a shadow.[4]

Each man's life is but a breath.[5]

You are a mist that appears for a little while and then vanishes.[6]

As for man, his days are like grass, he flourishes like a flower of the field; the wind blows over it and it is gone, and its place remembers it no more.[7]

"It's a short journey," I offer to the children. "We're almost there."

I know. I've been there before. I've driven this road. I've covered this territory. For me, it's no challenge. Ah, but for the children, it's eternal.

So I try another approach. "Just think how good it will be," I depict. "Turkey, dressing, pie . . . I promise you, when you get there, the trip will have been worth it."

But they still groan.

Which takes us to the third similarity.

———————————————

Children can't envision the reward.

For me, six hours on the road is a small price to pay for my mom's strawberry cake. I don't mind the drive because I know the reward. I have three decades of Thanksgivings under my belt, literally. As I drive, I can taste the turkey. Hear the dinner-table laughter. Smell the smoke from the fireplace.

I can endure the journey because I know the destiny.

My daughters have forgotten the destiny. After all, they are young. Children easily forget. Besides, the road is strange, and the dark night has come. They can't see where we're going. It's my job, as their father, to guide them.

I try to help them see what they can't see.

I tell them how we'll feed the ducks at the lake. How we'll play on the swings. How they can spend the night with their cousins. We speak of sleeping on the floor in sleeping bags and staying up late since there is no school.

And it seems to work. Their grumbling decreases as their vision clears—as their destiny unfolds.

Perhaps that's how the apostle Paul stayed motivated. He had a clear vision of the reward.

Therefore we do not lose heart. Though outwardly we are wasting away, yet inwardly we are being renewed day by day. For our light and momentary troubles are achieving for us an eternal glory that far outweighs them all. So we fix our eyes not on what is seen, but on what is unseen.[8]

It's not easy to get three girls under the age of seven to see a city they can't see. But it's necessary.

It's not easy for us to see a City we've never seen, either, especially when the road is bumpy . . . the hour is late . . . and companions are wanting to cancel the trip and take up residence in a motel. It's not easy to fix our eyes on what is unseen. But it's necessary.

One line in the 2 Corinthians passage you just read makes me smile: "our light and momentary troubles."

I wouldn't have called them that if I were Paul. Read what he called *light and momentary,* and I think you'll agree:

- Imprisoned.
- Beaten with a whip five times.
- Faced death.
- Beaten with rods three times.
- Stoned once.
- Shipwrecked three times.
- Stranded in the open sea.
- Left homeless.
- In constant danger.
- Hungry and thirsty.[9]

Long and trying ordeals, perhaps. *Arduous and deadly afflictions,* OK. But *light and momentary troubles?* How could Paul describe endless trials with that phrase?

He tells us. He could see "an eternal glory that far outweighs them all."

⸻

Can I speak candidly for a few lines?

For some of you, the journey has been long. Very long and stormy. In no way do I wish to minimize the difficulties that you have had to face along the way. Some of you have shouldered burdens that few of us could ever carry. You have bid farewell to life-long partners. You have been robbed of life-long dreams. You have been given bodies that can't sustain your spirit. You have spouses who can't tolerate your faith. You have bills that outnumber the paychecks and challenges that outweigh the strength.

And you are tired.

It's hard for you to see the City in the midst of the storms. The desire to pull over to the side of the road and get out entices you. You want to go on, but some days the road seems so long.

Let me encourage you with one final parallel between your life's journey and the one our family took last night.

⸻

It's worth it.

As I write, the Thanksgiving meal is over. My legs are propped up on the hearth. My tablet is on my lap.

I have every intention of dozing off as soon as I finish this chapter.

The turkey has been attacked. The giblet gravy has been gobbled. The table is clear. The kids are napping. And the family is content.

As we sat around the table today, no one spoke of the long trip to get here. No one mentioned the requests I didn't honor. No one grumbled about my foot being on the accelerator when their hearts were focused on the banana splits. No one complained about the late hour of arrival.

Yesterday's challenges were lost in today's joy.

That's what Paul meant. God never said that the journey would be easy, but he did say that the arrival would be worthwhile.

Remember this: God may not do what you want, but he will do what is right . . . and best. He's the Father of forward motion. Trust him. He will get you home. And the trials of the trip will be lost in the joys of the feast.

Now, if you'll excuse me, I'll close my eyes. I'm a bit tired from the journey, and it feels good to rest.

13

DOUBTSTORMS

*T*HERE ARE SNOWSTORMS. There are hailstorms. There are rainstorms. And there are doubtstorms.

Every so often a doubtstorm rolls into my life, bringing with it a flurry of questions and gale-force winds of fear. And, soon after it comes, a light shines through it.

Sometimes the storm comes after the evening news. Some nights I wonder why I watch it. Some nights it's just too much. From the steps of the Supreme Court to the steppes of South Africa, the news is usually gloomy . . . thirty minutes of bite-sized tragedies. A handsome man in a nice suit with a warm voice gives bad news. They call him the anchorman. Good title. One needs an anchor in today's tempestuous waters.

Sometimes I wonder, *How can our world get so chaotic?*

Sometimes the storm comes when I'm at work. Story after story of homes that won't heal and hearts that won't melt. Always more hunger than food. More needs than money. More questions than answers. On Sundays I stand before a church with a three-point outline in my hand, thirty minutes on the clock, and a prayer on my lips. I do my best to say something that will convince a stranger that an unseen God still hears.

And I sometimes wonder why so many hearts have to hurt.

Do you ever get doubtstorms? Some of you don't, I know. I've talked to you. Some of you have a "Davidish" optimism that defies any Goliath. I used to think that you were na-ive at best and phony at worst.

I don't think that anymore.

I think you are gifted. You are gifted with faith. You can see the rainbow before the clouds part. If you have this gift, then skip this chapter. I won't say anything you need to hear.

But others of you wonder . . .

You wonder what others know that you don't. You wonder if you are blind or if they are. You wonder why some proclaim "Eureka" before the gold is found. You wonder why some shout "Land ho" before the fog has cleared. You wonder how some people believe so confidently while you believe so reluctantly.

As a result, you are a bit uncomfortable on the padded pew of blind belief. Your Bible hero is Thomas. Your middle name is Caution. Your queries are the bane of every Sunday school teacher.

"If God is so good, why do I sometimes feel so bad?"

"If his message is so clear, why do I get so confused?"

"If the Father is in control, why do good people have gut-wrenching problems?"

You wonder if it is a blessing or a curse to have a mind that never rests. But you would rather be a cynic than a hypocrite, so you continue to pray with one eye open and wonder:

- about starving children

- about the power of prayer

- about the depths of grace

- about Christians in cancer wards

- about who you are to ask such questions anyway.

Tough questions. Throw-in-the-towel questions. Questions the disciples must have asked in the storm.

All they could see were black skies as they bounced in the battered boat. Swirling clouds. Wind-driven white caps. Pessimism that buried the coastline. Gloom that swamped the bow. What could have been a pleasant trip became a white-knuckled ride through a sea of fear.

Their question—What hope do we have of surviving a stormy night?

My question—Where is God when his world is stormy?

Doubtstorms: turbulent days when the enemy is too big, the task too great, the future too bleak, and the answers too few.

Every so often a storm will come, and I'll look up into the blackening sky and say, "God, a little light, please?"

The light came for the disciples. A figure came to them walking on the water. It wasn't what they expected. Perhaps they were looking for angels to descend or heaven to open. Maybe they were listening for a divine proclamation to still the storm. We don't know what they were looking for. But one thing is for sure, they weren't looking for Jesus to come walking on the water.

"'It's a ghost,' they said and cried out in fear" (Matt. 14:26).

And since Jesus came in a way they didn't expect, they almost missed seeing the answer to their prayers.

And unless we look and listen closely, we risk making the same mistake. God's lights in our dark nights are as numerous as the stars, if only we'll look for them.

Can I share a few lights with you that have illuminated my world recently?

A friend and I sat in front of my house in his car and talked about his dilemma. His chief client pulled out on him, leaving him big bills and few solutions. What the client did wasn't right, but he did it anyway. The client's company was big and my friend's was small, and there wasn't a lot he could do. My friend was left with a den of hungry lions wanting six figures' worth of satisfaction.

"I called my uncle and told him what had happened. I told him I was thinking of filing for bankruptcy."

"What did he say?" I asked.

"He didn't say anything," my friend responded. "After he was silent for a long time, I said it for him. 'We don't do it like that, do we?'"

"'No, we don't,' he told me. So I'll pay the bills. If I have to sell my house, I'll pay my bills."

I was encouraged. Somebody still believed that if he did what was right, God would do what was best. There was still some we-don't-do-it-like-that faith in the world. The sky began to clear.

Light number two came from a cancer ward.

"We will celebrate forty-four years tomorrow," Jack said, feeding his wife.

She was bald. Her eyes were sunken, and her speech was slurred. She looked straight ahead, only opening her mouth when he brought the fork near. He wiped her cheek. He wiped his brow.

"She has been sick for five years," he told me. "She can't walk. She can't take care of herself. She can't even feed herself, but I love her. And," he spoke louder so she could hear, "we are going to beat this thing, aren't we, Honey?"

He fed her a few bites and spoke again, "We don't have insurance. When I could afford it, I thought I wouldn't need it. Now I owe this hospital more than $50,000." He was quiet for a few moments as he gave her a drink. Then he continued. "But they don't pester me. They know I can't pay, but they admitted us with no questions asked. The doctors treat us like we are their best-paying patients. Who would've imagined such kindness?"

I had to agree with him. Who would've imagined such kindness? In a thorny world of high-tech, expensive, often criticized health care, it was reassuring to find professionals who would serve two who had nothing to give in return.

Jack thanked me for coming, and I thanked God that once again a sinew of light reminded me of the sun behind the clouds.

Then, a few days later, another light.

Larry Brown is the coach of the San Antonio Spurs, the local professional basketball team. I don't know him personally (although rumor has it that he wants me to sign a multi-year contract and play point guard for the team . . . nice fantasy).

Coach Brown recently spent an afternoon at a local men's store, signing autographs. He was scheduled to spend two hours, but ended up spending three. Pencil-and-pad-toting kids besieged the place, asking him questions and shaking his hand.

When he was finally able to slip out, he climbed into his car, only to notice a touching sight. A late-arriving youngster pedaled up, jumped off his bike, and ran to the window to see if the coach was still in the store. When he saw he wasn't, he turned slowly and sadly, walked over to his bike, and began to ride off.

Coach Brown turned off the ignition, climbed out of the car, and walked over to the boy. They chatted a few minutes, went next door to a drugstore, sat down at a table, and had a soft drink.

No reporters were near. No cameras were on. As far as these two knew, no one knew. I'm sure Larry Brown had other things to do that afternoon. No doubt he had other appointments to keep. But it's doubtful that anything he might have done that afternoon was more important than what he did.

In a world of big-bucked, high-glossed professional sports, it did me good to hear of one coach who is still a coach at heart. Hearing what he did was enough to blow away any lingering clouds of doubt and to leave me warmed by God's light . . . his gentle light.

Gentle lights. God's solutions for doubtstorms. Gold-flecked glows that amber hope into blackness. Not thunderbolts. Not explosions of light. Just gentle lights. A businessman choosing honesty. A hospital choosing compassion. A celebrity choosing kindness.

Visible evidence of the invisible hand.

Soft reminders that optimism is not just for fools.

Funny. None of the events were "religious." None of the encounters occurred in a ceremony or a church service. None will make the six o'clock news.

But such is the case with gentle lights.

When the disciples saw Jesus in the middle of their stormy night, they called him a ghost. A phantom. A hallucination. To them, the glow was anything but God.

When we see gentle lights on the horizon, we often have the same reaction. We dismiss occasional kindness as apparitions, accidents, or anomalies. Anything but God.

"When Jesus comes," the disciples in the boat may have thought, "he'll split the sky. The sea will be calm. The clouds will disperse."

"When God comes," we doubters think, "all pain will flee. Life will be tranquil. No questions will remain."

And because we look for the bonfire, we miss the candle. Because we listen for the shout, we miss the whisper.

But it is in burnished candles that God comes, and through whispered promises he speaks: "When you doubt, look around; I am closer than you think."

14

THE
MIRACLE
OF
THE
CARPENTER

*I*T'S NO ACCIDENT THAT NEW MEXICO is called the "Land of Enchantment." Sprawling deserts spotted with sage. Purple mountains wreathed with clouds. Adobe homes hidden on hillsides. Majestic pines. Endless artifacts. A cloverleaf of cultures from the conquistador to the Comanche to the cowboy. New Mexico enchants.

And in this land of enchantment, there is a chapel of wonder.

A block south of the La Fonda Hotel in Santa Fe, on the corner of Water Street and Old Santa Fe Trail, you will find Loretto Chapel. As you step through its iron gate, you enter more than a chapel courtyard. You enter another era. Pause for a moment under the sprawling branches of the ancient trees. Imagine what it was like when the Mexican carpenters completed the chapel in 1878.

Can you see the settlers stomping through the muddy streets? Can you hear the donkeys braying? The wagon wheels groaning? And can you see the early morning sun spotlighting this gothic chapel—so simple, so splendid—as it sits against the backdrop of the desert hills?

Loretto Chapel took five years to complete. Modeled after the Sainte-Chapelle in Paris, its delicate sanctuary contains an altar, a rose window, and a choir loft.

The choir loft is the reason for wonder.

Were you to stand in the newly built chapel in 1878, you might see the Sisters of Loretto looking forlornly at the balcony. Everything else was complete: the doors had been hung, the pews had been placed, the floor had been laid. Everything was finished. Even the choir loft. Except for one thing. No stairs.

The chapel was too small to accommodate a conventional stairway. The best builders and designers in the region shook their heads when consulted. "Impossible," they murmured. There simply wasn't enough room. A ladder would serve the purpose, but mar the ambiance.

The Sisters of Loretto, whose determination had led them from Kentucky to Santa Fe, now faced a challenge greater than their journey: a stairway that couldn't be built.

What they had dreamed of and what they could do were separated by fifteen impossible feet.

So what did they do? The only thing they could do. They ascended the mountain. Not the high mountains near Santa Fe. No, they climbed even higher. They climbed the same mountain that Jesus climbed 1,800 years earlier in Bethsaida. They climbed the mountain of prayer.

━━━━━━━━━━━━━━━━━

"He went up on a mountainside by Himself to pray."[1]

Jesus faced an impossible task. More than five thousand people were ready to fight a battle he had not come to fight. How could he show them that he didn't come to be a king, but to be a sacrifice? How could he take their eyes off an earthly kingdom so that they would see the spiritual one? How could they see the eternal when they only had eyes for the temporal?

What Jesus dreamed of doing and what he seemed able to do were separated by an impossible gulf. So Jesus prayed.

We don't know what he prayed about. But I have my guesses:

- He prayed that eyes blinded by power could see God's truth.

- He prayed that disciples dizzied by success could endure failure.

- He prayed that leaders longing for power would follow him to a cross.

- He prayed that people desiring bread for the body would hunger for bread for the soul.

He prayed for the impossible to happen.

Or maybe I'm wrong. Maybe he didn't ask for anything. Maybe he just stood quietly in the presence of Presence and basked in the Majesty. Perhaps he placed his war-weary self before the throne and rested.

Maybe he lifted his head out of the confusion of earth long enough to hear the solution of heaven. Perhaps he was reminded that hard hearts don't faze the Father. That problem people don't perturb the Eternal One.

We don't know what he did or what he said. But we do know the result. The hill became a steppingstone; the storm became a path. And the disciples saw Jesus as they had never seen him before.

During the storm, Jesus prayed. The sky darkened. The winds howled. Yet he prayed. The people grumbled. The disciples doubted. Yet he prayed. When forced to choose between the muscles of men and the mountain of prayer, he prayed.

Jesus did not try to do it by himself. Why should you?

There are crevasses in your life that you cannot cross alone. There are hearts in your world that you cannot change without help. There are mountains that you cannot climb until you climb His mountain.

Climb it. You will be amazed.

The Sisters of Loretto were.

As the story goes, the nuns prayed for nine days. On the last day of the novena, a Mexican carpenter with a beard and a wind-burned face appeared at the convent. He explained that he had heard they needed a stairway to a chapel loft. He thought he could help.

The mother superior had nothing to lose, so she gave him permission.

He went to work with crude tools, painstaking patience, and uncanny skill. For eight months he worked.

One morning the Sisters of Loretto entered the chapel to find their prayers had been answered. A masterpiece of carpentry spiraled from the floor to the loft. Two complete three-hundred-sixty-degree turns. Thirty-three steps held together with wooden pegs and no central support. The wood is said to be a variety of hard fir, one nonexistent in New Mexico!

When the sisters turned to thank the craftsman, he was gone. He was never seen again. He never asked for money. He never asked for praise. He was a simple carpenter who did what no one else could do so singers could enter a choir loft and sing.

See the stairway for yourself, if you like. Journey into the land of Enchantment. Step into this chapel of amazement and witness the fruit of prayer.

Or, if you prefer, talk to the Master Carpenter yourself. He has already performed one impossible feat in your world. He, like the Santa Fe carpenter, built a stairway no one else could build. He, like the nameless craftsman, used material from another place. He, like the visitor to Loretto, came to span the gap between where you are and where you long to be.

Each year of his life is a step. Thirty-three paces. Each step of the stair is an answered prayer. He built it so you can climb it.

And sing.

15

THE
WOODCUTTER'S
WISDOM

WOULD YOU BUY A HOUSE IF you were only allowed to see one of its rooms? Would you purchase a car if you were permitted to see only its tires and a taillight? Would you pass judgment on a book after reading only one paragraph?

Nor would I.

Good judgment requires a broad picture. Not only is that true in purchasing houses, cars, and books, it's true in evaluating life. One failure doesn't make a person a failure; one achievement doesn't make a person a success.

"The end of the matter is better than its beginning,"[1] penned the sage.

"Be . . . patient in affliction,"[2] echoed the apostle Paul.

"Don't judge a phrase by one word," stated the woodcutter.

The woodcutter? Oh, you may not know him. Let me present him to you.

I met him in Brazil. He was introduced to me by a friend who knew that I needed patience. Denalyn and I were six months into a five-year stint in Brazil, and I was frustrated. My fascination with Rio de Janeiro had turned into exasperation with words I couldn't speak and a culture I didn't understand.

"Tenha paciência," Maria would tell me. "Just be patient." She was my Portuguese instructor. But, more than that, she was a calm voice in a noisy storm. With maternal persistence, she corrected my pronunciation and helped me learn to love her homeland.

Once, in the midst of a frustrating week of trying to get our goods out of customs (which eventually took three months), she gave me this story as a homework assignment. It helped my attitude far more than it helped my Portuguese.

It's a simple fable. Yet for those of us who try to pass judgment on life with only one day's evidence, the message is profound. I've done nothing to embellish it; I've only translated it. I pray that it will remind you, as it did me, that patience is the greater courage.

Once there was an old man who lived in a tiny village. Although poor, he was envied by all, for he owned a beautiful white horse. Even the king coveted his treasure. A horse like this had never been seen before—such was its splendor, its majesty, its strength.

People offered fabulous prices for the steed, but the old man always refused. "This horse is not a horse to me," he would tell them. "It is a person. How could you sell a person? He is a friend, not a possession. How could you sell a friend?" The man was poor and the temptation was great. But he never sold the horse.

One morning he found that the horse was not in the stable. All the village came to see him. "You old fool," they scoffed, "we told you that someone would steal your horse. We warned you that you would be robbed. You are so poor.

How could you ever hope to protect such a valuable animal? It would have been better to have sold him. You could have gotten whatever price you wanted. No amount would have been too high. Now the horse is gone, and you've been cursed with misfortune."

The old man responded, "Don't speak too quickly. Say only that the horse is not in the stable. That is all we know; the rest is judgment. If I've been cursed or not, how can you know? How can you judge?"

The people contested, "Don't make us out to be fools! We may not be philosophers, but great philosophy is not needed. The simple fact that your horse is gone is a curse."

The old man spoke again. "All I know is that the stable is empty, and the horse is gone. The rest I don't know. Whether it be a curse or a blessing, I can't say. All we can see is a fragment. Who can say what will come next?"

The people of the village laughed. They thought that the man was crazy. They had always thought he was a fool; if he wasn't, he would have sold the horse and lived off the money. But instead, he was a poor woodcutter, an old man still cutting firewood and dragging it out of the forest and selling it. He lived hand to mouth in the misery of poverty. Now he had proven that he was, indeed, a fool.

After fifteen days, the horse returned. He hadn't been stolen; he had run away into the forest. Not only had he returned, he had brought a dozen wild horses with him. Once again the village people gathered around the woodcutter and spoke. "Old man, you were right and we were wrong. What we thought was a curse was a blessing. Please forgive us."

The man responded, "Once again, you go too far. Say only that the horse is back. State only that a dozen horses returned with him, but don't judge. How do you know if this is a blessing or not? You see only a fragment. Unless you know the whole story, how can you judge? You read only one page of a book. Can you judge the whole book? You read only one word of a phrase. Can you understand the entire phrase?

"Life is so vast, yet you judge all of life with one page or one word. All you have is a fragment! Don't say that this is a blessing. No one knows. I am content with what I know. I am not perturbed by what I don't."

"Maybe the old man is right," they said to one another. So they said little. But down deep, they knew he was wrong. They knew it was a blessing. Twelve wild horses had returned with one horse. With a little bit of work, the animals could be broken and trained and sold for much money.

The old man had a son, an only son. The young man began to break the wild horses. After a few days, he fell from one of the horses and broke both legs. Once again the villagers gathered around the old man and cast their judgments.

"You were right," they said. "You proved you were right. The dozen horses were not a blessing. They were a curse. Your only son has broken his legs, and now in your old age you have no one to help you. Now you are poorer than ever."

The old man spoke again. "You people are obsessed with judging. Don't go so far. Say only that my son broke his legs. Who knows if it is a blessing or a curse? No one knows. We only have a fragment. Life comes in fragments."

It so happened that a few weeks later the country engaged in war against a neighboring country. All the young men of the village were required to join the army. Only the son of the old man was excluded, because he was injured. Once again the people gathered around the old man, crying and screaming because their sons had been taken. There was little chance that they would return. The enemy was strong, and the war would be a losing struggle. They would never see their sons again.

"You were right, old man," they wept. "God knows you were right. This proves it. Your son's accident was a blessing. His legs may be broken, but at least he is with you. Our sons are gone forever."

The old man spoke again. "It is impossible to talk with you. You always draw conclusions. No one knows. Say only this: Your sons had to go to war, and mine did not. No one knows if it is a blessing or a curse. No one is wise enough to know. Only God knows."

The old man was right. We only have a fragment. Life's mishaps and horrors are only a page out of a grand book. We must be slow about drawing conclusions. We must reserve judgment on life's storms until we know the whole story.

I don't know where the woodcutter learned his patience. Perhaps from another woodcutter in Galilee. For it was the Carpenter who said it best:

"Do not worry about tomorrow, for tomorrow will worry about itself."[3]

He should know. He is the Author of our story. And he has already written the final chapter.

16

LAWS
OF
THE
LIGHTHOUSE

*T*HE FIRST OF THE YEAR IS known for three things: black-eyed peas, bowl games, and lists. Some don't eat black-eyed peas. Others hate football. But everybody likes lists.

Lists are reassuring. They comfort us. They suggest that the crazy, zooming, blooming chaos of the universe can be mastered and tamed within the cage of a tidy column. To list is to understand, solve, and even control. For that reason we can't resist the urge, at the end of the year, to spew out lists like Washington, D.C. spews out documents.

We list the best movies . . . the best books . . . the worst dressed . . . the most used . . . the least popular . . . the most mysterious . . . the highest paid. We salute the good. We satire the bad. And we sum up the year on lists—"end-list" lists.

Although New Year's Day ranks at the top of the list of list-producing days, the rest of the year is by no means "list-less."

- Your grocery list makes a trip to the market manageable.

- Your calendar probably has a "to do" space, where you organize and number things you'd like to do but probably won't.

- Your syllabus tells you which books to buy.

- Your itinerary tells you which plane to take.
- Your telephone book tells you which numbers to dial.

The Bible certainly has its share of lists. Moses brought one down from the mountain. Noah might have used one as he loaded the ark. Jesus gave a list of principles in the Sermon on the Mount. (Paul gave his version in Romans 12.) Matthew and Luke listed the genealogies of Jesus. John listed the splendors of heaven.

There are lists of the gifts of the Spirit. Lists of good fruit and bad. Lists of salutations and greetings. Even the disciples' boat got into the action as it listed in the stormy Sea of Galilee. (If you smiled at that, then I've got a list of puns you'd enjoy.)

But the greatest day of lists is still New Year's Day. And the number one list is the list I call the Laws of the Lighthouse.

The Laws of the Lighthouse list contains immutable, immovable truths. Candidates for this inventory only qualify if they have lighthouse characteristics:

- They warn you of potential danger.
- They signal safe harbor.
- They are stronger than the storm.
- They shine brightest in the fog.

The Laws of the Lighthouse contain more than good ideas, personal preferences, and honest opinions. They are God-given, time-tested truths that define the way you should navigate your life. Observe them and enjoy secure passage. Ignore them and crash against the ragged rocks of reality.

In *U.S. Naval Institute Proceedings,* the magazine of the Naval Institute, Frank Koch illustrates the importance of obeying the Laws of the Lighthouse.[1]

> Two battleships assigned to the training squadron had been at sea on maneuvers in heavy weather for several days. I was serving on the lead battleship and was on watch on the bridge as night fell. The visibility was poor with patchy fog, so the captain remained on the bridge keeping an eye on all activities.
>
> Shortly after dark, the lookout on the wing reported, "Light, bearing on the starboard bow."
>
> "Is it steady or moving astern?" the captain called out.
>
> The lookout replied, "Steady, Captain," which meant we were on a dangerous collision course with that ship.
>
> The captain then called to the signalman, "Signal that ship: 'We are on a collision course, advise you change course twenty degrees.'"
>
> Back came the signal, "Advisable for you to change course twenty degrees."
>
> The captain said, "Send: 'I'm a captain, change course twenty degrees.'"
>
> "I'm a seaman second-class," came the reply. "You had better change course twenty degrees."
>
> By that time the captain was furious. He spat out, "Send: 'I'm a battleship. Change course twenty degrees.'"
>
> Back came the flashing light, "I'm a lighthouse."
>
> We changed course.

Smart move. The wise captain shifts the direction of his craft according to the signal of the lighthouse. A wise person does the same.

Herewith, then, are the lights I look for and the signals I heed:

- Love God more than you fear hell.
- Once a week, let a child take you on a walk.
- Make major decisions in a cemetery.
- When no one is watching, live as if someone is.
- Succeed at home first.
- Don't spend tomorrow's money today.
- Pray twice as much as you fret.
- Listen twice as much as you speak.
- Only harbor a grudge when God does.
- Never outgrow your love of sunsets.
- Treat people like angels; you will meet some and help make some.
- 'Tis wiser to err on the side of generosity than on the side of scrutiny.
- God has forgiven you; you'd be wise to do the same.
- When you can't trace God's hand, trust his heart.
- Toot your own horn and the notes will be flat.
- Don't feel guilty for God's goodness.
- The book of life is lived in chapters, so know your page number.
- Never let the important be the victim of the trivial.

- Live your liturgy.

To sum it all up:

Approach life like a voyage on a schooner. Enjoy the view. Explore the vessel. Make friends with the captain. Fish a little. And then get off when you get home.

17

HE SPEAKS THROUGH THE STORM

I HAD HEARD ABOUT YOU BEFORE, *but now I have seen you.*"[1]
It all happened in one day. One day he could choose his
tee time at the nicest golf course in the country; the next
he couldn't even be the caddie. One day he could Lear jet
across the country to see the heavyweight bout at the Las
Vegas Mirage. The next he couldn't afford a city bus across
town.

Talk about calm becoming chaos . . .

The first thing to go is his empire. The market crashes;
his assets tumble. What is liquid goes dry. What has been
up goes down. Stocks go flat, and Job goes broke. There he
sits in his leather chair and soon-to-be-auctioned-off mahogany desk when the phone rings with news of calamity
number two:

The kids were at a resort for the holidays when a storm
blew in and took them with it.

Shell-shocked and dumbfounded, Job looks out the
window into the sky that seems to be getting darker by
the minute. He starts praying, telling God that things can't
get any worse . . . and that's exactly what happens. He
feels a pain in his chest that is more than last night's
ravioli. The next thing he knows, he is bouncing in an
ambulance with wires stuck to his chest and needles stuck
in his arm.

He ends up tethered to a heart monitor in a community hospital room. Next to him lies an illegal immigrant who can't speak English.

Not, however, that Job lacks for conversation.

First there is his wife. Who could blame her for being upset at the week's calamities? Who could blame her for telling Job to curse God? But to curse God *and die?* If Job doesn't already feel abandoned, you know he does the minute his wife tells him to pull the plug and be done with it.

Then there are his friends. They have the bedside manner of a drill sergeant and the compassion of a chainsaw killer. A revised version of their theology might read like this: "Boy, you must have done something really bad! We know that God is good, so if bad things are happening to you, then you have been bad. Period."

Does Job take that lying down? Not hardly.

"You are doctors who don't know what they are doing," he says. "Oh, please be quiet! That would be your highest wisdom."[2]

Translation? "Why don't you take your philosophy back to the pigpen where you learned it."

"I'm not a bad man," Job argues. "I paid my taxes. I'm active in civic duties. I'm a major contributor to United Way and a volunteer at the hospital bazaar."

Job is, in his eyes, a good man. And a good man, he reasons, deserves a good answer.

"Your suffering is for your own good," states Elihu, a young minister fresh out of seminary who hasn't lived long enough to be cynical and hasn't hurt enough to be quiet. He paces back and forth in the hospital room, with his Bible under his arm and his finger punching the air.

"God does all these things to a man—twice, even three times—to turn back his soul from the pit, that the light of life may shine on him."[3]

Job follows his pacing like you'd follow a tennis player, head turning from side to side. What the young man says isn't bad theology, but it isn't much comfort, either. Job steadily tunes him out and slides lower and lower under the covers. His head hurts. His eyes burn. His legs ache. And he can't stomach any more hollow homilies.

Yet his question still hasn't been answered:

"God, why is this happening to me?"

So God speaks.

Out of the thunder, he speaks. Out of the sky, he speaks. For all of us who would put ditto marks under Job's question and sign our names to it, he speaks.

- For the father who holds a rose taken off his son's coffin, he speaks.

- For the wife who holds the flag taken off her husband's casket, he speaks.

- For the couple with the barren womb and the fervent prayers, he speaks.

- For any person who has tried to see God through shattered glass, he speaks.

- For those of us who have dared to say, "If God is God, then . . . ," God speaks.

He speaks out of the storm and into the storm, for that is where Job is. That is where God is best heard.

God's voice thunders in the room. Elihu sits down. Job sits up. And the two will never be the same again.

"Who is this that darkens my counsel with words without knowledge?"[4]

Job doesn't respond.

"Brace yourself like a man; I will question you, and you shall answer me."[5]

"Where were you when I laid the foundations of the earth? Tell me, if you know so much."[6]

One question would have been enough for Job, but it isn't enough for God.

"Do you know how its dimensions were determined and who did the surveying?" God asks. "What supports its foundations, and who laid its cornerstone, as the morning stars sang together and all the angels shouted for joy?"[7]

Questions rush forth. They pour like sheets of rain out of the clouds. They splatter in the chambers of Job's heart with a wildness and a beauty and a terror that leave every Job who has ever lived drenched and speechless, watching the Master redefine who is who in the universe.

> Have you ever once commanded the morning to appear, and caused the dawn to rise in the east? Have you ever told the daylight to spread to the ends of the earth, to end the night's wickedness?[8]

God's questions aren't intended to teach; they are intended to stun. They aren't intended to enlighten; they are intended to awaken. They aren't intended to stir the mind; they are intended to bend the knees.

> Has the location of the gates of Death been revealed to you? Do you realize the extent of the earth? Tell me about it if you know! Where does the light come from, and how do you get there? Or tell me about the darkness. Where does it come from? Can you find its boundaries, or go to its source? But of course you know all this! For you were born before it was all created, and you are so very experienced![9]

Finally Job's feeble hand lifts, and God stops long enough for him to respond. "I am nothing—how could I ever

find the answers? I lay my hand upon my mouth in silence.
I have said too much already."[10]

God's message has connected:

- Job is a peasant, telling the King how to run the
  kingdom.
- Job is an illiterate, telling e. e. cummings to
  capitalize his personal pronouns.
- Job is the bat boy, telling Babe Ruth to change
  his batting stance.
- Job is the clay, telling the potter not to press so
  hard.

"I owe no one anything," God declares in the crescendo
of the wind. "Everything under the heaven is mine."[11]

Job couldn't argue. God owes no one anything. No
explanations. No excuses. No help. God has no debt, no outstanding balance, no favors to return. God owes no man
anything.

Which makes the fact that he gave us everything even
more astounding.

How you interpret this holy presentation is key. You
can interpret God's hammering speech as a divine "in-your-
face" tirade if you want. You can use the list of unanswerable questions to prove that God is harsh, cruel, and distant.
You can use the Book of Job as evidence that God gives us
questions and no answers. But to do so, you need some
scissors. To do so, you need to cut out the rest of the Book
of Job.

For that is not how Job heard it. All his life, Job had been a good man. All his life, he had believed in God. All his life, he had discussed God, had notions about him, and had prayed to him.

But in the storm Job sees him!

He sees Hope. Lover. Destroyer. Giver. Taker. Dreamer. Deliverer.

Job sees the tender anger of a God whose unending love is often received with peculiar mistrust. Job stands as a blade of grass against the consuming fire of God's splendor. Job's demands melt like wax as God pulls back the curtain and heaven's light falls uneclipsed across the earth.

Job sees God.

God could turn away at this point. The gavel has been slammed, the verdict has been rendered. The Eternal Judge has spoken.

Ah, but God is not angry with Job. Firm? Yes. Direct? No doubt. Clear and convincing? Absolutely. But angry? No.

God is never irritated by the candle of an honest seeker.

If you underline any passage in the Book of Job, underline this one: "I had heard about you before, but now I have seen you."[12]

Job sees God—and that is enough.

But it isn't enough for God.

The years to come find Job once again sitting behind his mahogany desk with health restored and profits up. His lap is once again full of children and grandchildren and great-grandchildren—for four generations!

If Job ever wonders why God doesn't bring back the children he had taken away, he doesn't ask. Maybe he doesn't ask because he knows that his children could never be happier than they are in the presence of this One he has seen so briefly.

Something tells me that Job would do it all again, if that's what it took to hear God's voice and stand in the Presence. Even if God left him with his bedsores and bills, Job would do it again.

For God gave Job more than Job ever dreamed. God gave Job Himself.

18

PILGRIM
PONDERINGS

After six days Jesus took with him Peter, James and John the brother of James, and led them up a high mountain by themselves. There he was transfigured before them. His face shone like the sun, and his clothes became as white as the light. Just then there appeared before them Moses and Elijah, talking with Jesus.

Peter said to Jesus, "Lord, it is good for us to be here. If you wish, I will put up three shelters—one for you, one for Moses, and one for Elijah." While he was still speaking, a bright cloud enveloped them, and a voice from the cloud said, "This is my Son, whom I love; with him I am well pleased. Listen to him!"[1]

THE YOUNG WOMAN, EIGHT MONTHS heavy with child, waddles into her mother's house. Flops onto the sofa. Kicks off her tennis shoes. Props her puffy feet on the coffee table. And groans, "I don't think I can make it."

Wise from the years, the mother picks up a photo album and sits down beside her daughter. She opens the album to photos of her children in diapers and ankle-high walking shoes. Slowly the two turn the memory-filled pages. They smile at the kids blowing out candles and sitting in front of Christmas trees.

As the mother sees yesterday, the daughter sees tomorrow.

And, for just a moment, the daughter is changed. The *here and now* becomes the *there and then*. Her child is born. She sees the first stumbling step taken. She hears the first word, discernible only to Mommy. She places the shiny, black, patent-leather shoes on the stockinged feet and Karo-syrups a ribbon on the nearly bald but ever-so-precious head.

A transformation occurs. The pain in her back is now overshadowed by the joy approaching. The hand that had rubbed the neck now rests on her stomach. For the first time that day, she smiles.

A snowstorm in Chicago. Stranded at O'Hare. No place to sit in the lobby, so he walks to the coffee shop. No place to sit in the coffee shop, so he buys a cup to go, wanders back to the lobby, sits on his briefcase, and drapes his overcoat over his lap.

He looks at his watch. *Should I go to a hotel for the night?* he wonders. *It's nearly midnight! I should be halfway home by now. Who knows when I'll be able to leave?*

He sighs, leans back against a wall, and waits. He unbuttons his collar. Loosens his tie. Rubs his whiskered neck. His thoughts drift back over the week. Many calls made. Few orders placed. Blame it on the economy. Blame it on the system. Blame it on God. But blame doesn't put money in the bank.

There's an executive lobby across the hall with empty couches, snacks, and a television. In better times, he could afford the membership; now that money goes toward college tuition and braces for the kids.

A flight is announced. He pulls his boarding pass out of his overcoat breast pocket. The flight isn't his. He sticks the pass back into the coat that stretches across his lap. A leather calendar tumbles out. He picks it up and, for no real reason, looks inside.

There, amidst taxi receipts and credit cards, is a laminated photo of a family—his family. Teenage daughter with eyes like her mom's and the metallic smile. College-bound son wearing a necktie and blue jeans, mid-step between adolescence and adulthood. And his wife. My, has it been twenty-five years? Take away a few wrinkles and pounds, and he can see her in the white gown again.

For just a moment, he is home. The television is off. The kids are in bed. The dog is outside. The doors are locked. The fire is golden. His wife is asleep on the couch. For just a moment, the world of O'Hare, hotels, and sales calls are a world away. He is where it's all worthwhile. He is home.

Someone taps him on the shoulder, and he hears a kind voice. "Is that your flight?" He looks up into the half-empty lobby . . . sees the line forming at the gate . . . and smiles.

"Yeah," the salesman says, standing. "It's my flight home."

———————

Four people snake their way up the mountain. The trip has been long; the hour is late. A level place on the hillside is reached, and they sit down. They're tired. Their muscles hurt. The grayness of twilight settles over them like a soft cloth.

The quartet of pilgrims longs to sleep, but only three do.

The fourth sits in the shadows. Legs crossed. Face skyward. The stars wink at their Maker. Winds waft over the shoulders of their Designer, cooling his neck. He slips off his sandals and rubs his sore feet and reflects on the wildness of it all.

A God with sore legs? Holiness with hunger? Divinity with thirst? A World Maker made weary by his world?

His thoughts drift homeward. *Nazareth. How good it would be to be home again.*

The memories surface so easily. Sawdust-covered workbench. Friends stopping to talk. Dinner-table laughter. Wrestling with his brothers. The synagogue. The house. The home.

What I'd give to go home.

But Nazareth would never be home again. They tried to kill him the last time he was there. Neighbors, friends, teachers, schoolmates . . . they squeezed the stones intended for his body. Even his brothers and sisters considered him insane. They wanted to hide him, to put him away. They were ashamed to be known as his family.

No, Nazareth can never be home again.

What about Galilee? He could go back to Galilee. There the crowds listened. There the people followed. But he shook his head. *As long as I made them bread . . . As long as I said what they wanted to hear . . .* He remembered the crowds as they turned away. He heard their jeering. He felt their rejection.

No, I can never go back to Galilee.

He thinks of Jerusalem. She offers no comfort. He knows what she will do to him. A foreboding pain stabs his wrists. He winces at the slicing of his brow. He sees the world around him growing darker, darker . . . *My God!* a premonition inside him cries.

He shakes his head and breathes a staggered breath. His thoughts return to the present.

He plucks a shoot of grass, puts it into his mouth, and sits in the shadow of his fear.

He looks at his followers, as asleep as they are naive. They have no idea. They just can't understand. He speaks of suffering; they think of conquering. He speaks of sacrifice; they think of celebration. He's an artist painting for the color-blind. He's a singer singing for the deaf. They nod their heads and clap their hands. They think they see. They think they hear. But they don't.

They can't see. No one sees.

Part of him knew it would be like this. And part of him never knew it would be so bad.

Part of him wonders, *Would it be so bad to give up?* After all, there might be a better era. There will be other generations . . . other people.

He has given his best, and what does he have? A ragged band of good-hearted but hardheaded followers who are destined to fall face-flat over promises they can't keep. He puts his face into his cupped hands and closes his eyes and prays. It's all he knows to do.

Sounds familiar, doesn't it, seeker? Was it so long ago that you were on a quest for truth—Galahad in search of the grail? But the forest of questions was deep. The thicket of perplexities thick. It was easier to say nothing than to ask why. So you stopped.

Sounds familiar, doesn't it, dreamer? You wanted so badly to change the world. Sure the mountain was high, but you were brave. Then the winds came. Sharp rocks of reality cut your feet, breaking your stride . . . breaking your heart. And you found that the role of the cynic was less costly than the role of the dreamer. So you sat down.

You need to know something: Jesus sat down, too.

Oh, sure, there were moments when he stood tall. There were hours of splendor. There were dynamic days during which the lepers leapt and the dead came alive and the people worshiped. Those days came.

But his plateaus of popularity were gorged by canyons of isolation.

And on this day, the crevasse is deep. Steep walls mock an easy escape. Rocky abutments imprison his vision. His strength has reached its solstice.

He sits down and puts a tear-streaked face into cupped palms and prays. It's all he can do.

And when his Father sees him, it's all his Father can take.

From another dimension, a light comes. It enters the solitary figure and glows.

"As he was praying," Luke writes, "the appearance of his face changed, and his clothes became as bright as a flash of lightning."[2]

Jesus implodes with glory. For just a moment, he is transfigured; a roaring radiance pours from him. He becomes as he was before he came. For one brief, shining moment, the burden of his humanity is lifted. "Decarnation" occurs. He is elevated above earth's horizon and escorted into the eternal. He is home again. Familiar sounds surround him. Those who understand welcome him. And the One who sent him . . . holds him.

Dusty trails and hard hearts are, literally, a world away.

The One who felt weary is reminded: the weariness will soon pass.

Moses and Elijah, aflame with eternal robes, stand beside their King. When Jesus was preparing himself in the desert for the work of life, angels came to encourage him. Now, on the mountain, preparing himself for the work of death, Moses and Elijah draw near: Moses, the Lawgiver whose grave no man knew; Elijah, the prophet who side-stepped death in a fiery chariot.

The One who saw death is reminded: the grave is impotent.

And then, the voice thunders. God inhabits a cloud. It becomes a bonfire, puffy with brilliance. It consumes the shadows. It transforms the nightened mountain into a shining monument. And from the belly of the cloud, the Father speaks:

"This is my Son, whom I love; with him I am well pleased. Listen to him!"[3]

The One who had despaired is affirmed. "What people think doesn't matter," God shouts. "What I think does. And I'm proud."

By now Jesus is standing. By now the apostles are awake.

For Peter, James, and John, the scene is bizarre: dazzling white clouds, a voice from the sky, living images from the past. But for Jesus, it is a view of home. A view into yesterday. A glimpse into tomorrow.

He is the mother—pregnant with new life, dreading the pains of childbirth.

He is the father—on a long journey in a cold place.

He is—as they were, as we are—given a glimpse of home.

And tomorrow's dream becomes today's courage.

19

OUR STORM WAS HIS PATH

*S*UPPOSE ONE OF JESUS' DISCIPLES *kept a journal. And suppose that disciple made an entry in the journal on the morning after the storm. And suppose we discovered that journal. Here is how it would read . . . I suppose.*

═══════════════════════════

Only minutes before, chaos had erupted.

Oh, how the storm roared. Stars were hidden by a black ceiling. Clouds billowed like smoke. Bolts of lightning were the conductor's baton that cued the kettledrums of thunder to rumble.

And rumble they did. The clouds seemed to rise as a bear on hind legs and growl. The booms shook everything: the heavens, the earth, and—most of all—the sea. It was as if the Sea of Galilee were a bowl in the hands of a dancing giant. From the bowels of the lake the waves came, turning the glassy surface into a mountain range of snow-topped waves. Five, ten, even fifteen feet into the air they mounted, rising and falling like swallows chasing mosquitoes.

In the midst of the sea, our boat bounced. The waves slapped it as easily as children would a ball. Our straining at the oars scarcely budged it. We were at the storm's mercy. The waves lifted us up so high that we felt like we were in midair. Then down into the valley we plunged.

We were a twig in a whirlpool . . . a leaf in the wind. We were helpless.

That's when the light appeared. At first I thought it was a reflection of the moon, a gleam on the surface of the water. But the night held no moon. I looked again. The light was moving toward us, not over the waves but through them. I wasn't the only one who saw it.

"A ghost," someone screamed. Fear of the sea was eclipsed by a new terror. Thoughts raced as the specter drew near. *Was it a figment of our imagination? Was it a vision? Who? How? What was this mystical light that appeared so . . . ?*

A flash of lightning illuminated the sky. For a second I could see its face . . . his face. A second was all I needed.

It was the Master!

He spoke:

"Take courage! It is I. Don't be afraid."[1]

Nothing had changed. The storm still raged. The wind still shrieked. The boat still pitched. The thunder still boomed. The rain still slapped. But in the midst of the tumult, I could hear his voice. Although he was still far away, it was like he was by my side. The night was ferocious, yet he spoke as though the sea were placid and the sky silent.

And, somehow, courage came.

"Lord, if it's you, . . . tell me to come to you on the water."[2]

The voice was Peter's. He wasn't being cocky. He wasn't demanding proof. He was scared. Like me, he knew what this storm could do. He knew that the boat would soon go down. He knew that Jesus was standing up. And he knew where he wanted to be . . . where we all wanted to be.

"Come on," Jesus invited.

So Peter climbed over the side and stepped onto the sea. Before him opened a trail through a forest of waves. He stepped quickly. Water splashed. But he kept going. This path to Jesus was a ribbon of calm. It was peaceful. Serene.

Jesus radiated light at the end of the trail. Smiling.

Peter stepped toward the light like it was his only hope. He was halfway there when we all heard the thunder. It boomed, and he stopped. I saw his head turn. He looked up at the sky. He looked up at the clouds. He felt the wind. And down he went.

Boy did he yell!

A hand came through the water sheets and grabbed Peter. Lightning flashed again, and I could see the face of Jesus. I noticed that his smile was gone. Hurt covered his face. It was like he couldn't believe that we couldn't believe. Danger to us was just a detour to him. I wanted to ask him, "Aren't you afraid, Jesus? Aren't you afraid?"

But I said nothing. Before I knew it, he was in the boat with us.

The sea stilled as silk.

The winds hushed.

A canyon opened in the clouds; soft moonlight fell over the water.

It happened instantaneously. It didn't take the rest of the night. It didn't take an hour. It didn't take a minute. It happened in a blink.

From chaos to calm. From panic to peace. The sky was so suddenly silent that I could hear my heart pounding. I thought I was dreaming. Then I saw the wide eyes of the others and felt my clothing soaked against my skin. This was no dream. I looked at the water. I looked at Peter. I looked at the others. And then I looked at him.

And I did the only thing I could have done. With the stars as my candles and the stilled boat as my altar, I fell at his feet and worshiped.

There are times in a person's life when, even in the midst of them, you know you'll never be the same. Moments that forever serve as journey posts. This was one.

I had never seen Jesus as I saw him then. I had seen him as powerful. I had seen him as wise. I had witnessed his authority and marveled at his abilities. But what I witnessed last night, I know I'll never forget.

I saw God. The God who can't sit still when the storm is too strong. The God who lets me get frightened enough to need him and then comes close enough for me to see him. The God who uses my storms as his path to come to me.

I saw God. It took a storm for me to see him. But I saw him. And I'll never be the same.

20

THEY'D
DO
IT
AGAIN

*T*HEY'D DO IT AGAIN. I'm confident they would. The disciples would get into the same boat and ride through the same storm. They'd do it again in a heartbeat. Why?

Because through the storm they saw the Savior.

Read this verse: "Then those who were in the boat worshiped him, saying, 'Truly you are the Son of God.'"[1]

After the storm, they worshiped him. They had never, as a group, done that before. Never. Check it out. Open your Bible. Search for a time when the disciples corporately praised him.

You won't find it.

You won't find them worshiping when he heals the leper. Forgives the adulteress. Preaches to the masses. They were willing to follow. Willing to leave family. Willing to cast out demons. Willing to be in the army.

But only after the incident on the sea did they worship him. Why?

Simple. This time, they were the ones who were saved. This time, their necks were removed from the noose. Their bodies were plucked from the deep. One minute, they were dangling over the edge of the abyss, staring into the throat of the slack-jawed canyon. The next, they were bottom-plopped and wide-eyed on the deck of a still boat on a placid sea.

So they worshiped. They did the only thing that they could do when their death sentence was stayed at the eleventh hour: They looked to the Eternal Governor who gave the pardon and thanked him.

═══════════════

When you recognize God as Creator, you will admire him. When you recognize his wisdom, you will learn from him. When you discover his strength, you will rely on him. But only when he saves you will you worship him.

It's a "before and after" scenario. Before your rescue, you could easily keep God at a distance. Comfortably dismissed. Neatly shelved. Sure he was important, but so was your career. Your status. Your salary. He was high on your priority list, but he shared the spot with others.

Then came the storm . . . the rage . . . the fight . . . the ripped moorings . . . the starless night. Despair fell like a fog; your bearings were gone. In your heart, you knew there was no exit.

Turn to your career for help? Only if you want to hide from the storm . . . not escape it. Lean on your status for strength? A storm isn't impressed with your title. Rely on your salary for rescue? Many try . . . many fail.

Suddenly you are left with one option: God.

And when you ask . . . genuinely ask . . . he will come.

And from that moment on, he is not just a deity to admire, a teacher to observe, or a master to obey. He is the Savior. The Savior to be worshiped.

That's why I'm convinced that the disciples would do it again. They'd endure the storm another night . . . a thousand other nights . . . if that's what it took.

A season of suffering is a small price to pay for a clear view of God.

STING
OF
FAILURE

21

CASTLES
OF
SORROW

S ARAH WAS RICH. SHE HAD inherited twenty million dollars. Plus she had an additional income of one thousand dollars a day.

That's a lot of money any day, but it was immense in the late 1800s.

Sarah was well known. She was the belle of New Haven, Connecticut. No social event was complete without her presence. No one hosted a party without inviting her.

Sarah was powerful. Her name and money would open almost any door in America. Colleges wanted her donations. Politicians clamored for her support. Organizations sought her endorsement.

Sarah was rich. Well known. Powerful. And miserable.

Her only daughter had died at five weeks of age. Then her husband had passed away. She was left alone with her name, her money, her memories, . . . and her guilt.

It was her guilt that caused her to move west. A passion for penance drove her to San Jose, California. Her yesterdays imprisoned her todays, and she yearned for freedom.

She bought an eight-room farmhouse plus one hundred sixty adjoining acres. She hired sixteen carpenters and put them to work. For the next thirty-eight years, craftsmen labored every day, twenty-four hours a day, to build a mansion.

Observers were intrigued by the project. Sarah's instructions were more than eccentric . . . they were eerie.

The design had a macabre touch. Each window was to have thirteen panes, each wall thirteen panels, each closet thirteen hooks, and each chandelier thirteen globes.

The floor plan was ghoulish. Corridors snaked randomly, some leading nowhere. One door opened to a blank wall, another to a fifty-foot drop. One set of stairs led to a ceiling that had no door. Trapdoors. Secret passageways. Tunnels. This was no retirement home for Sarah's future; it was a castle for her past.

The making of this mysterious mansion only ended when Sarah died. The completed estate sprawled over six acres and had six kitchens, thirteen bathrooms, forty stairways, forty-seven fireplaces, fifty-two skylights, four hundred sixty-seven doors, ten thousand windows, one hundred sixty rooms, and a bell tower.

Why did Sarah want such a castle? Didn't she live alone? "Well, sort of," those acquainted with her story might answer. "There were the visitors . . ."

And the visitors came each night.

Legend has it that every evening at midnight, a servant would pass through the secret labyrinth that led to the bell tower. He would ring the bell . . . to summon the spirits. Sarah would then enter the "blue room," a room reserved for her and her nocturnal guests. Together they would linger until 2:00 A.M., when the bell would be rung again. Sarah would return to her quarters; the ghosts would return to their graves.

Who comprised this legion of phantoms?

Indians and soldiers killed on the U.S. frontier. They had all been killed by bullets from the most popular rifle in America—the Winchester. What had brought millions of dollars to Sarah Winchester had brought death to them.

So she spent her remaining years in a castle of regret, providing a home for the dead.

You can see this poltergeist place in San Jose, if you wish. You can tour its halls and see its remains.

But to see what unresolved guilt can do to a human being, you don't have to go to the Winchester mansion. Lives imprisoned by yesterday's guilt are in your own city. Hearts haunted by failure are in your own neighborhood. People plagued by pitfalls are just down the street . . . or just down the hall.

There is, wrote Paul, a "worldly sorrow" that "brings death."[1] A guilt that kills. A sorrow that's fatal. A venomous regret that's deadly.

How many Sarah Winchesters do you know? How far do you have to go to find a soul haunted by ghosts of the past? Maybe not very far.

Maybe Sarah's story is your story.

If so, I'm especially grateful that this book has made its way into your hands. This final section has been written with you in mind. In these final chapters, I have assembled thoughts on failure and forgiveness.

For in the twilight hours during the storm's black night, there is a story of grace.

It is the story of Peter: recognizing the Master's voice . . . seeing the Master's face . . . scrambling to safety from the storm.

It is also another story of Peter: hearing the winds. . . seeing the torrent . . . sinking into the water.

But most of all, it is the story of Jesus. It is the story of God extending his hand during stormy seas. It is the answer to the question every person asks: "What does God do when I fail?"

The answers to guilt's questions are not found in a new house.

The answer is found in the foundation of the one you have.

22

FEAR
THAT
BECOMES
FAITH

"They saw Jesus . . . walking on the water; and they were terrified."[1]

*F*AITH IS OFTEN the child of fear.

Fear propelled Peter out of the boat. He'd ridden these waves before. He knew what these storms could do. He'd heard the stories. He'd seen the wreckage. He knew the widows. He knew the storm could kill. And he wanted out.

All night he wanted out. For nine hours he'd tugged on sails, wrestled with oars, and searched every shadow on the horizon for hope. He was soaked to the soul and bone weary of the wind's banshee wail.

Look into Peter's eyes and you won't see a man of conviction. Search his face and you won't find a gutsy grimace. Later on, you will. You'll see his courage in the garden. You'll witness his devotion at Pentecost. You'll behold his faith in his epistles.

But not tonight. Look into his eyes tonight and see fear—a suffocating, heart-racing fear of a man who has no way out.

But out of this fear would be born an act of faith, for faith is often the child of fear.

"The fear of the Lord is the beginning of wisdom,"[2] wrote the wise man.

Peter could have been his sermon illustration.

If Peter had seen Jesus walking on the water during a calm, peaceful day, do you think that he would have walked out to him?

Nor do I.

Had the lake been carpet smooth and the journey pleasant, do you think that Peter would have begged Jesus to take him on a stroll across the top of the water? Doubtful.

But give a man a choice between sure death and a crazy chance, and he'll take the chance . . . every time.

Great acts of faith are seldom born out of calm calculation.

It wasn't logic that caused Moses to raise his staff on the bank of the Red Sea.[3]

It wasn't medical research that convinced Naaman to dip seven times in the river.[4]

It wasn't common sense that caused Paul to abandon the Law and embrace grace.[5]

And it wasn't a confident committee that prayed in a small room in Jerusalem for Peter's release from prison.[6] It was a fearful, desperate, band of backed-into-a-corner believers. It was a church with no options. A congregation of have-nots pleading for help.

And never were they stronger.

At the beginning of every act of faith, there is often a seed of fear.

Biographies of bold disciples begin with chapters of honest terror. Fear of death. Fear of failure. Fear of loneliness. Fear of a wasted life. Fear of failing to know God.

Faith begins when you see God on the mountain and you are in the valley and you know that you're too weak to make the climb. You see what you need . . . you see what you have . . . and what you have isn't enough to accomplish anything.

Peter had given it his best. But his best wasn't enough.

Moses had a sea in front and an enemy behind. The Israelites could swim or they could fight. But neither option was enough.

Naaman had tried the cures and consulted the soothsayers. Traveling a long distance to plunge into a muddy river made little sense when there were clean ones in his backyard. But what option did he have?

Paul had mastered the Law. He had mastered the system. But one glimpse of God convinced him that sacrifices and symbols were not enough.

The Jerusalem church knew that they had no hope of getting Peter out of prison. They had Christians who would fight, but too few. They had clout, but too little. They didn't need muscle. They needed a miracle.

So does Peter. He is aware of two facts: He is going down, and Jesus is staying up. He knows where he would rather be.

There's nothing wrong with this response. Faith that begins with fear will end up nearer the Father.

I went to West Texas some time back to speak at the funeral of a godly, family friend. He had raised five children. One son, Paul, told a story about his earliest memory of his father.

It was spring in West Texas—tornado season. Paul was only three or four years old at the time, but he remembers vividly the day that a tornado hit their small town.

His father hustled the kids indoors and had them lie on the floor while he laid a mattress over them. But his father didn't climb under the protection. Paul remembers peeking out from under the mattress and seeing him standing by an open window, watching the funnel cloud twist and churn across the prairie.

When Paul saw his father, he knew where he wanted to be. He struggled out of his mother's arms, crawled out from under the mattress, and ran to wrap his arms around his dad's leg.

"Something told me," Paul said, "that the safest place to stand in a storm was next to my father."

Something told Peter the same thing.

"Lord, if it's you," Peter says, "tell me to come to you on the water."[7]

Peter is not testing Jesus; he is pleading with Jesus. Stepping onto a stormy sea is not a move of logic; it is a move of desperation.

Peter grabs the edge of the boat. Throws out a leg . . . follows with the other. Several steps are taken. It's as if an invisible ridge of rocks runs beneath his feet. At the end of the ridge is the glowing face of a never-say-die friend.

We do the same, don't we? We come to Christ in an hour of deep need. We abandon the boat of good works. We realize, like Moses, that human strength won't save us. So we look to God in desperation. We realize, like Paul, that all the good works in the world are puny when laid before the Perfect One. We realize, like Peter, that spanning the gap between us and Jesus is a feat too great for our feet.

So we beg for help. Hear his voice. And step out in fear, hoping that our little faith will be enough.

Faith is not born at the negotiating table where we barter our gifts in exchange for God's goodness. Faith is not an award given to the most learned. It's not a prize given to the most disciplined. It's not a title bequeathed to the most religious.

Faith is a desperate dive out of the sinking boat of human effort and a prayer that God will be there to pull us out of the water. Paul wrote about this kind of faith in the letter to the Ephesians:

"For it is by grace you have been saved, through faith—and this not from yourselves, it is the gift of God—not by works, so that no one can boast."[8]

Paul is clear. The supreme force in salvation is God's grace. Not our works. Not our talents. Not our feelings. Not our strength.

Salvation is God's sudden, calming presence during the stormy seas of our lives. We hear his voice; we take the step.

We, like Paul, are aware of two things: We are great sinners and we need a great Savior.

We, like Peter, are aware of two facts: We are going down and God is standing up. So we scramble out. We leave behind the *Titanic* of self-righteousness and stand on the solid path of God's grace.

And, surprisingly, we are able to walk on water. Death is disarmed. Failures are forgivable. Life has real purpose. And God is not only within sight, he is within reach.

With precious, wobbly steps, we draw closer to him. For a season of surprising strength, we stand upon his promises. It doesn't make sense that we are able to do this. We don't claim to be worthy of such an incredible gift. When people ask how in the world we can keep our balance during such stormy times, we don't boast. We don't brag. We point unabashedly to the One who makes it possible. Our eyes are on him.

"Nothing in my hand I bring; Simply to Thy cross I cling,"[9] we sing.

"Dressed in His righteousness alone, Faultless to stand before the throne,"[10] we declare.

"'Twas grace that taught my heart to fear, And grace my fears relieved,"[11] we explain.

Some of us, unlike Peter, never look back.

Others of us, like Peter, feel the wind and are afraid.[12]

Maybe we face the wind of pride: "I'm not such a bad sinner after all. Look at what I can do."

Perhaps we face the wind of legalism: "I know that Jesus is doing part of this, but I have to do the rest."

Most of us, though, face the wind of doubt: "I'm too bad for God to treat me this well. I don't deserve such a rescue."

And downward we plunge. Heavied by mortality's mortar, we sink. Gulping and thrashing, we fall into a dark, wet world. We open our eyes and see only blackness. We try to breathe, and no air comes. We kick and fight our way back to the surface.

With our heads barely above the water, we have to make a decision.

The prideful ask: "Do we 'save face' and drown in pride? Or do we scream for help and take God's hand?"

The legalists ask: "Do we sink under the lead-heavy weight of the Law? Or do we abandon the codes and beg for grace?"

The doubters ask: "Do we nurture doubt by mumbling, 'I've really let him down this time?' Or do we hope that the same Christ who called us out of the boat will call us out of the sea?"

We know Peter's choice.

"[As he was] beginning to sink, [he] cried out, 'Lord, save me!'"[13]

"Immediately Jesus reached out his hand and caught him."[14]

═══════════════

We also know the choice of another sailor in another storm.

Although separated by seventeen centuries, this sailor and Peter are drawn together by several striking similarities:

- Both made their living on the sea.
- Both met their Savior after a nine-hour battle in a storm.
- Both met the Father in fear and then followed him in faith.
- Both walked away from their boats and became preachers of the Truth.

You know the story of Peter, the first sailor. Let me tell you about the second, whose name was John.

He had served on the seas since he was eleven years old. His father, an English shipmaster in the Mediterranean, took him aboard and trained him well for a life in the Royal Navy.

Yet what John gained in experience, he lacked in discipline. He mocked authority. Ran with the wrong crowd. Indulged in the sinful ways of a sailor. Although his training would have qualified him to serve as an officer, his behavior caused him to be flogged and demoted.

In his early twenties, he made his way to Africa, where he became intrigued with the lucrative slave trade. At age twenty-one, he made his living on the *Greyhound,* a slave ship crossing the Atlantic Ocean.

John ridiculed the moral and poked fun at the religious. He even made jokes about a book that would eventually help reshape his life: *The Imitation of Christ.* In fact, he was degrading that book a few hours before his ship sailed into an angry storm.

That night the waves pummeled the *Greyhound,* spinning the ship one minute on the top of a wave. Plunging her the next into a watery valley.

John awakened to find his cabin filled with water. A side of the *Greyhound* had collapsed. Ordinarily such damage would have sent a ship to the bottom in a matter of minutes. The *Greyhound,* however, was carrying buoyant cargo and remained afloat.

John worked at the pumps all night. For nine hours, he and the other sailors struggled to keep the ship from sinking. But he knew that it was a losing cause. Finally, when his hopes were more battered than the vessel, he threw himself on the saltwater-soaked deck and pleaded, "If this will not do, then Lord have mercy on us all."

John didn't deserve mercy, but he received it. The *Greyhound* and her crew survived.

John never forgot God's mercy shown on that tempestuous day in the roaring Atlantic. He returned to England where he became a prolific composer. You've sung his songs, like this one:

> Amazing grace! how sweet the sound,
> That saved a wretch like me!
> I once was lost, but now am found,
> was blind, but now I see.[15]

This slave-trader-turned-songwriter was John Newton.

Along with his hymn writing, he also became a powerful pulpiteer. For nearly fifty years, he filled pulpits and churches with the story of the Savior who meets you and me in the storm.

A year or two before his death, people urged him to give up preaching because of his failing sight. "What!" he explained. "Shall the old African blasphemer stop while he can yet speak?"

He wouldn't stop. He couldn't stop. What had begun as a prayer of fear resulted in a lifetime of faith. During his last years, someone asked him about his health. He confessed that his powers were failing. "My memory is almost gone," he said, "but I remember two things: I am a great sinner, and Jesus is a great Savior."

What more do you and I need to remember?

Two sailors and two seas. Two vessels in two storms. Two prayers of fear and two lives of faith. Uniting them is one Savior—one God who'll walk through hell or high water to extend a helping hand to a child who cries for help.

23

WHY
GOD
SMILES

I HAVE A SKETCH OF JESUS LAUGHING. It hangs on the wall across from my desk.

It's quite a drawing. His head is back. His mouth is open. His eyes are sparkling. He isn't just grinning. He isn't just chuckling. He's roaring. He hasn't heard or seen one like that in quite a while. He's having trouble catching his breath.

It was given to me by an Episcopal priest who carries cigars in his pocket and collects portraits of Jesus smiling. "I give them to anyone who might be inclined to take God too seriously," he explained as he handed me the gift.

He pegged me well.

I'm not one who easily envisions a smiling God. A weeping God, yes. An angry God, OK. A mighty God, you bet. But a chuckling God? It seems too . . . too . . . too unlike what God should do—and be. Which just shows how much I know—or don't know—about God.

What do I think he was doing when he stretched the neck of the giraffe? An exercise in engineering? What do I think he had in mind when he told the ostrich where to put his head? Spelunking? What do I think he was doing when he designed the mating call of an ape? Or the eight legs of the octopus? And what do I envision on his face when he saw Adam's first glance at Eve? A yawn?

Hardly.

As my vision improves and I'm able to read without my stained glasses, I'm seeing that a sense of humor is perhaps the only way God has put up with us for so long.

Is that him with a smile as Moses does a double take at the burning bush that speaks?

Is he smiling again as Jonah lands on the beach, dripping gastric juices and smelling like whale breath?

Is that a twinkle in his eye as he watches the disciples feed thousands with one boy's lunch?

Do you think that his face is deadpan as he speaks about the man with a two-by-four in his eye who points out a speck in a friend's eye?

Can you honestly imagine Jesus bouncing children on his knee with a somber face?

No, I think that Jesus smiled. I think that he smiled a bit at people and a lot with people.

Let me explain with an example.

―――――――――――――

We don't know a thing about her. We don't know her name . . . her background . . . her looks . . . her hometown. She came from nowhere and went nowhere. She disappeared the same way that she appeared, like a puff of smoke.

But what a delightful puff she was.

The disciples, during two years of training, hadn't done what she did in a few moments of conversing. She impressed God with her faith. The disciples' hearts may have been good. Their desire may have been sincere. But their faith didn't turn God's head.

Hers did. For all we don't know about her, we do know one remarkable truth: She impressed God with her faith. After that, anything else she ever did was insignificant.

"Woman, you have great faith!"[1] Jesus stated.

Some statement. Especially when you consider God said it. The God who can put a handful of galaxies into his palm. The One who creates Everests as a hobby. The One who paints rainbows without a canvas. The One who can meas-ure the thickness of mosquito wings with one hand and level a mountain with the other.

One would think that the Creator would not be easily impressed. But something about this woman brought a sparkle to his eyes and . . . most likely . . . a smile to his face.

Matthew called her a "Canaanite woman" and, in doing so, called strikes one and two. Strike one? A Canaanite. An outsider. A foreigner. An apple in a family tree of oranges. Strike two? A woman. Might as well have been a junkyard dog. She lived in a culture that had little respect for women outside the bedroom and kitchen.

But she met the Teacher, who had plenty of respect for her.

Oh, it doesn't appear that way. In fact, the dialogue between the two seems harsh. It's not an easy passage to understand unless you're willing to concede that Jesus knew how to smile. If you have trouble with the sketch of the smiling Jesus hanging in my office, you'll have trouble with this story. But if you don't, if the thought of God smiling brings you a bit of relief, then you'll like the next few paragraphs.

Here's my interpretation.

The woman is desperate. Her daughter is demon possessed.

The Canaanite woman has no right to ask anything of Jesus. She is not a Jew. She is not a disciple. She offers no money for the ministry. She makes no promises to devote herself to missionary service. You get the impression that she knows as well as anybody that Jesus doesn't owe her anything, and she is asking him for everything. But that doesn't slow her down. She persists in her plea.

"Have mercy on me!"[2]

Matthew notes that Jesus says nothing at first. Nothing. He doesn't open his mouth. Why?

To test her? Most commentators suggest this. Maybe, they say, he is waiting to see how serious she is about her plea. My dad used to make me wait a week from the day I asked him for something to the day he gave me his answer. Most of the time, I forgot that I ever made the request. Time has a way of separating whims from needs. Is Jesus doing that?

I have another opinion. I think that he was admiring her. I think that it did his heart good to see some spunky faith for a change. I think that it refreshed him to see someone asking him to do the very thing he came to do— give great gifts to unworthy children.

How strange that we don't allow him to do it more often for us.

Perhaps the most amazing response to God's gift is our reluctance to accept it. We want it. But on our terms. For some odd reason, we feel better if we earn it. So we create religious hoops and hop through them—making God a trainer, us his pets, and religion a circus.

The Canaanite woman knew better. She had no resume. She claimed no heritage. She had no earned degrees. She knew only two things: Her daughter was weak, and Jesus was strong.

The disciples are annoyed. As Jesus sits in silence, they grow more smug. "Send her away," they demand. The spotlight is put on Jesus. He looks at the disciples, then looks at the woman. And what follows is one of the most intriguing dialogues in the New Testament.

"I was sent only to the lost sheep of Israel,"[3] he says.

"Lord, help me!"[4]

"It is not right to take the children's bread and toss it to their dogs,"[5] he answers.

"But even the dogs eat the crumbs that fall from their masters' table,"[6] she responds.

Is Jesus being rude? Is he worn-out? Is he frustrated? Is he calling this woman a dog? How do we explain this dialogue?

Bible commentaries give us three options.

Some say that Jesus was trapped. He could not help the woman because he had been sent first to the lost sheep of Israel. Neat theory, but full of problems. One is the Samaritan woman. Another is the centurion. Jesus had already helped Gentiles and stayed faithful to the focus of his mission. So why couldn't he do it now?

Others think that Jesus was rude. Who can blame him? He was tired. It had been a long trip. The disciples were coming along pretty slowly. And this request was the straw that broke the camel's back.

Like that explanation? I don't either. The one who had had compassion on the five thousand men . . . who had wept over the city of Jerusalem . . . who had come to seek and save ones like this one . . . would not snap so abruptly at such a needy woman.

The most popular theory is that he was testing her . . . again. Just to be sure that she was serious about her request. Just to make sure that her faith was real.

But by insinuating that she was a dog?

I don't think Jesus would do that, either. Let me suggest another alternative.

Could it be that Jesus' tongue is poking his cheek? Could it be that he and the woman are engaging in satirical banter? Is it wry exchange in which God's unlimited grace is being highlighted? Could Jesus be so delighted to have found one who is not bartering with a religious system or proud of a heritage that he can't resist a bit of satire?

He knows he can heal her daughter. He knows he isn't bound by a plan. He knows her heart is good. So he decides to engage in a humorous moment with a faithful woman. In essence, here's what they said:

"Now, you know that God only cares about Jews," he says smiling.

And when she catches on, she volleys back, "But your bread is so precious, I'll be happy to eat the crumbs."

In a spirit of exuberance, he bursts out, "Never have I seen such faith! Your daughter is healed."

This story does not portray a contemptuous God. It portrays a willing One who delights in a sincere seeker.

Aren't you glad he does?

The story is told about the time Napoleon's steed got away from him. An alert private jumped on his own horse and chased down the general's horse. When he presented the reins of the animal to Napoleon, the ruler took them, smiled at this willing private, and said, "Thank you, Captain."

The soldier's eyes widened at what he had heard. He then straightened. Saluted. And snapped, "Thank you, sir!"

He immediately went to the barracks. Got his bags. Moved into the officers' quarters. Took his old uniform to the quartermaster and exchanged it for that of a captain. By the general's word, he had become a private-turned-commissioned officer. He didn't argue. He didn't shrug. He didn't doubt. He knew that the one who had the power to do it had done it. And he accepted that.

If only we would do the same. If only we would have the faith of the private and the trust of the Canaanite woman. If only, when God smiles and says we are saved, we'd salute him, thank him, and live like those who have just received a gift from the commander in chief.

We seldom do that, though. We prefer to get salvation the old-fashioned way: We earn it. To accept grace is to admit failure, a step we are hesitant to take. We opt to impress God with how good we are rather than confessing how great he is. We dizzy ourselves with doctrine. Burden ourselves with rules. Think that God will smile on our efforts.

He doesn't.

God's smile is not for the healthy hiker who boasts that he made the journey alone. It is, instead, for the crippled leper who begs God for a back on which to ride.

Such were the woman's words. She knew that her request was ludicrous. But she also knew that Jesus was Lord.

Daniel's words could have been hers: "We do not make requests of you because we are righteous, but because of your great mercy."[7]

She came, banking on the hope that Jesus would answer her prayer based on his goodness and not her worthiness.

And he did. With a smile.

When I think about the prayers God has answered for me in spite of the life I've lived, I think he must be smiling still.

So I think I'll keep his picture on the wall.

24

THE
SACRIFICIAL
VISITOR

*L*ET ME DESCRIBE A SCENE to you and then ask you to come back to it at the end of the chapter.

An old man walks down a Florida beach. The sun sets like an orange ball on the horizon. The waves slap the sand. The smell of saltwater stings the air. The beach is vacant. No sun to entice the sunbathers. Not enough light for the fishermen. So, aside from a few joggers and strollers, the gentleman is alone.

He carries a bucket in his bony hand. A bucket of shrimp. It's not for him. It's not for the fish. It's for the sea gulls.

He walks to an isolated pier cast in gold by the setting sun. He steps out to the end of the pier. The time has come for the weekly ritual.

He stands and waits.

Soon the sky becomes a mass of dancing dots. The evening silence gives way to the screeching of birds. They fill the sky and then cover the moorings. They are on a pilgrimage to meet the old man.

For a half hour or so, the bushy-browed, shoulder-bent gentleman will stand on the pier, surrounded by the birds of the sea, until his bucket is empty.

But even after the food is gone, his feathered friends still linger. They linger as if they're attracted to more than just food. They perch on his hat. They walk on the pier. And they all share a moment together.

Got the scene? Now put it on the back burner for a few minutes.

Jesus left there and went along the Sea of Galilee. Then he went up on a mountainside and sat down. Great crowds came to him, bringing the lame, the blind, the crippled, the mute and many others, and laid them at his feet; and he healed them. The people were amazed when they saw the mute speaking, the crippled made well, the lame walking and the blind seeing. And they praised the God of Israel.

Jesus called his disciples to him and said, "I have compassion for these people; they have already been with me three days and have nothing to eat. I do not want to send them away hungry, or they may collapse on the way."[1]

This is not the day that Jesus fed the five thousand men; it is the day he fed the *four* thousand. Although the events have much in common, they are different in several respects:

- When Jesus fed the five thousand, he was with Jews. When he fed the four thousand (plus women and children), he was in Decapolis, a Gentile region.

- When Jesus fed the five thousand, he taught and healed them. When he was with the four thousand, there is no record that he taught—only that he healed.

- When Jesus was with the five thousand, he was with them for one afternoon. When he was with the four thousand, he was with them for three days.

And for three days he did a most remarkable thing: He healed them. "The lame, the blind, the crippled, the mute and many others" came to him, Matthew wrote, "and he healed them."

Many times I wish that the New Testament writers had been a bit more descriptive. This is one of those times. "And he healed them" is too short a phrase to describe what must have been an astonishing sight.

Let your imagination go. Can you see the scene?

Can you see the blind husband seeing his wife for the first time? His eyes gazing into her tear-filled ones like she was the queen of the morning?

Envision the man who had never walked, now walking! Don't you know that he didn't want to sit down? Don't you know that he ran and jumped and did a dance with the kids?

And what about the mute who could speak? Can you picture him sitting by the fire late into the night and talking? Saying and singing everything and anything that he had ever wanted to say and sing.

And the deaf woman who could now hear. What was it like when she heard her child call her "Mamma" for the first time?

For three days it went on. Person after person. Mat after mat. Crutch after crutch. Smile after smile. No record is given of Jesus preaching or teaching or instructing or challenging. He just healed.

"The people," Matthew wrote, "were amazed when they saw the mute speaking, the crippled made well, the lame walking and the blind seeing." Four thousand amazed people, each telling a story grander than the other. In the midst of them all is Jesus. Not complaining. Not postponing. Not demanding. Just enjoying every minute.

Then Matthew, still the great economizer of words, gave us another phrase on which I wish he would have elaborated:

"They praised the God of Israel."

I wonder how they did that? I feel more certain of what they *didn't* do than of what they did do. I feel confident that they didn't form a praise committee. I feel confident that they didn't make any robes. I feel confident that they didn't sit in rows and stare at the back of each other's heads.

I doubt seriously if they wrote a creed on how they were to praise this God they had never before worshiped. I can't picture them getting into an argument over technicalities. I doubt if they felt it had to be done indoors.

And I know they didn't wait until the Sabbath to do it.

In all probability, they just did it. Each one—in his or her own way, with his or her own heart—just praised Jesus. Perhaps some people came and fell at Jesus' feet. Perhaps some shouted his name. Maybe a few just went up on the hillside, looked into the sky, and smiled.

I can picture a mom and dad standing speechless before the Healer as they hold their newly healed baby.

I can envision a leper staring in awe at the One who took away his terror.

I can imagine throngs of people pushing and shoving. Wanting to get close. Not to request anything or demand anything, but just to say "thank you."

Perhaps some tried to pay Jesus, but what payment would have been sufficient?

Perhaps some tried to return his gift with another, but what could a person give that would express the gratitude?

All the people could do was exactly what Matthew said they did. "They praised the God of Israel."

However they did it, they did it. And Jesus was touched, so touched that he insisted they stay for a meal before they left.

Without using the word *worship,* this passage defines it. Worship is when you're aware that what you've been given is far greater than what you can give. Worship is the awareness that were it not for his touch, you'd still be hobbling and hurting, bitter and broken. Worship is the half-glazed expression on the parched face of a desert pilgrim as he discovers that the oasis is not a mirage.

Worship is the "thank you" that refuses to be silenced.

We have tried to make a science out of worship. We can't do that. We can't do that any more than we can "sell love" or "negotiate peace."

Worship is a voluntary act of gratitude offered by the saved to the Savior, by the healed to the Healer, and by the delivered to the Deliverer. And if you and I can go days without feeling an urge to say "thank you" to the One who saved, healed, and delivered us, then we'd do well to remember what he did.

―――――――――――――

The old man on the pier couldn't go a week without saying "thank you."

His name was Eddie Rickenbacker. If you were alive in October 1942, you probably remember the day that he was reported missing at sea.

He had been sent on a mission to deliver a message to Gen. Douglas MacArthur. With a handpicked crew in a B-17 known as the "Flying Fortress," he set off across the South Pacific. Somewhere the crew became lost, the fuel ran out, and the plane went down.

All eight crew members escaped into the life rafts. They battled the weather, the water, the sharks, and the sun. But most of all, they battled the hunger. After eight days, their rations were gone. They ran out of options. It would take a miracle for them to survive.

And a miracle occurred.

After an afternoon devotional service, the men said a prayer and tried to rest. As Rickenbacker was dozing with his hat over his eyes, something landed on his head. He would later say that he knew it was a sea gull. He didn't know how he knew; he just knew. That gull meant food . . . if he could catch it. And he did.

The flesh was eaten. The intestines were used as fish bait. And the crew survived.

What was a sea gull doing hundreds of miles away from land?

Only God knows.

But whatever the reason, Rickenbacker was thankful. As a result, every Friday evening this old captain walked to the pier, his bucket full of shrimp and his heart full of thanks.

We'd be wise to do the same. We've much in common with Rickenbacker. We, too, were saved by a Sacrificial Visitor.

We, too, were rescued by One who journeyed far from only God knows where.

And we, like the captain, have every reason to look into the sky . . . and worship.

25

HOLINESS
IN
A
BATHROBE

WHEN YOUR WORLD TOUCHES God's world, the result is a holy moment. When God's high hope kisses your earthly hurt, that moment is holy. That moment might happen on a Sunday during Communion or on a Thursday night at the skating rink. It might occur in a cathedral or in a subway, by a burning bush or by a feed trough. When and where don't matter. What matters is that holy moments occur. Daily. And I'd like to talk to you about the holiest of those moments—I'd like to talk to you about the holiest moment of your life.

No, not your birth. Not your wedding. Not the birth of a child. I'm talking about *the* holiest moment of your life. Those other moments are special. They sparkle with reverence. But compared to this moment, they are about as holy as a burp.

I'm talking about the sacred hour.

No, not your baptism or your christening. Not your first Communion or your first confession or even your first date. I know those moments are precious and certainly sacrosanct, but I've a different moment in mind.

It happened this morning. Right after you awoke. Right there in your house. Did you miss it? Let me recreate the scene.

The alarm rings. Your wife pokes you or your husband nudges you or your mom or dad shakes you. And you wake up.

You've already hit the sleeper button three times; hit it again and you'll be late. You've already asked for five more minutes . . . five different times; ask again and you'll get water poured on your head.

The hour has come. Daybreak has broken. So, with a groan and a grunt, you throw back the covers and kick a warm foot out into a cold world. It's followed by a reluctant companion.

You lean up and sit on the edge of the bed and stare at the back of your eyelids. You tell them to open, but they object. You pry them apart with your palms and peek into the room.

(The moment isn't holy yet, but it's almost here.)

You stand. At that moment, everything that will hurt during the course of the day hurts. It's as if the little person in your brain that's in charge of pain needs to test the circuits before you make it to the bathroom.

"Back pain?"

"Check."

"Stiff neck?"

"Check."

"High school football knee injury."

"Still hurting."

"Flaky scalp?"

"Still itching."

"Hay fever reaction?"

"Achoo!"

With the grace of a pregnant elephant, you step toward the bathroom. You wish there is some way to turn on the light slowly, but there isn't. So you slap on the spotlight, blink as your eyes adjust, and step up to the bathroom sink.

You are approaching the sacred. You may not know it, but you have just stepped on holy tile. You are in the inner sanctum. The burning bush of your world.

The holiest moment of your life is about to occur. Listen. You'll hear the fluttering of angels' wings signaling their arrival. Trumpets are poised on heaven's lips. A cloud of majesty encircles your bare feet. Heaven's hosts cease all motion as you raise your eyes and . . .

(Get ready. Here it comes. The holy moment is nigh.)

Cymbals clash. Trumpets echo in sacred halls. Heaven's children race through the universe scattering flower petals. Stars dance. The universe applauds. Trees sway in choreographed adulation. And well they should, for the child of the King has awakened.

Look in the mirror. Behold the holy one. Don't turn away. The image of perfection is looking back at you. The holy moment has arrived.

I know what you are thinking. *You call that "holy"? You call that "perfect"? You don't know what I look like at 6:30 A.M.*

No, but I can guess. Hair matted. Pajamas or nightgown wrinkled. Chunks of sleep stuck in the corners of your eyes. Belly bulging. Dried-out lips. Pudgy eyes. Breath that could stain a wall. A face that could scare a dog.

"Anything but holy," you say. "Give me an hour and I'll look holy. Give me some coffee, some makeup. Give me a toothbrush and a hairbrush, and I'll make this body presentable. A little perfume . . . a splash of cologne. Then take me into the Holy of Holies. Then I'll make heaven smile."

Ah, but there's where you're wrong. You see, what makes the morning moment so holy is its honesty. What makes the morning mirror hallowed is that you are seeing exactly who God sees.

And who God loves.

No makeup. No pressed shirts. No power ties. No matching shoes. No layers of images. No status jewelry. Just unkempt honesty.

Just you.

If people love you at 6:30 in the morning, one thing is sure: They love *you*. They don't love your title. They don't love your style. They don't love your accomplishments. They just love you.

"Love," wrote one forgiven soul, "covers over a multitude of sins."[1]

Sounds like God's love.

"He has made perfect forever those who are being made holy," wrote another.[2]

Underline the word *perfect*. Note that the word is not *better*. Not *improving*. Not *on the upswing*. God doesn't improve; he perfects. He doesn't enhance; he completes. What does the perfect person lack?

Now I realize that there's a sense in which we're imperfect. We still err. We still stumble. We still do exactly what we don't want to do. And that part of us is, according to the verse, "being made holy."

But when it comes to our position before God, we're perfect. When he sees each of us, he sees one who has been made perfect through the One who is perfect—Jesus Christ.

"All of you who were baptized into Christ have clothed yourselves with Christ."[3]

This morning I "put on" clothing to hide the imperfections I'd rather not display. When you see me, fully clothed, you can't see my moles, scars, or bumps. Those are hidden.

When we choose to be baptized, by lifestyle as much as by symbol, into Christ, the same shielding occurs. Our sins and faults are lost beneath the sheer radiance of his covering. "For you died, and your life is now hidden with Christ in God."[4] Please, don't miss the impact of this verse. When God sees us, he also sees Christ. He sees perfection! Not perfection earned by us, mind you, but perfection paid for by him.

Reflect on these words for a moment:

"God made him who had no sin to be sin for us so that *in him* [emphasis mine] we might become the righteousness of God."[5]

Now read these words in the Phillips translation:

"For God caused Christ, who himself knew nothing of sin, actually to *be* sin for our sakes, so that in Christ we might be made good with the goodness of God."

Note the last four words: "the goodness of God." God's goodness is your goodness. You are absolute perfection. Flawless. Without defects or mistakes. Unsullied. Unrivaled. Unmarred. Peerless. Virgin pure. Undeserved yet unreserved perfection.

No wonder heaven applauds when you wake up. A masterpiece has stirred.

"Shh," whisper the stars, "look at the wonder of that child."

"My!" gasp the angels, "what a prodigy God has created."

So while you groan, eternity gasps with wonder. As you stumble, angels are star struck. What you see in the mirror as morning disaster is, in reality, a morning miracle. Holiness in a bathrobe.

Go ahead and get dressed. Go ahead and put on the rings, shave the whiskers, comb the hair, and cover the moles. Do it for yourself. Do it for the sake of your image. Do it to keep your job. Do it for the benefit of those who have to sit beside you. But don't do it for God.

He has already seen you as you really are. And in his book, you are perfect.

26

THE
CHOICE

W HY DO I WANT TO DO BAD?" my daughter asked me, un-
knowingly posing a question asked by many seekers
of truth. "Why do I do the thing I hate? What is this ape
that gibbers within?" Or, perhaps a more basic question is
being asked. "If sin separates me from God, why doesn't
God separate me from sin? Why doesn't he remove from me
the option to sin?"

To answer that, let's go to the beginning.

Let's go to the Garden and see the seed that both blessed
and cursed. Let's see why God gave man . . . the choice.

Behind it all was a choice. A deliberate decision. An
informed move. He didn't have to do it. But he chose to. He
knew the price. He saw the implications. He was aware of
the consequences.

We don't know when he decided to do it. We can't know.
Not just because we weren't there. Because time was not
there. *When* did not exist. Nor did *tomorrow* or *yesterday*
or *next time*. For there was no time.

We don't know when he thought about making the
choice. But we do know that he made it. He didn't have to
do it. He chose to.

He chose to create.

"In the beginning God created . . ."[1]

With one decision, history began. Existence became measurable.

Out of nothing came light.

Out of light came day.

Then came sky . . . and earth.

And on this earth? A mighty hand went to work.

Canyons were carved. Oceans were dug. Mountains erupted out of flatlands. Stars were flung. A universe sparkled.

Our sun became just one of millions. Our galaxy became just one of thousands. Planets invisibly tethered to suns roared through space at breakneck speeds. Stars blazed with heat that could melt our planet in seconds.

The hand behind it was mighty. He is mighty.

And with this might, he created. As naturally as a bird sings and a fish swims, he created. Just as an artist can't not paint and a runner can't not run, he couldn't not create. He was the Creator. Through and through, he was the Creator. A tireless dreamer and designer.

From the pallet of the Ageless Artist came inimitable splendors. Before there was a person to see it, his creation was pregnant with wonder. Flowers didn't just grow; they blossomed. Chicks weren't just born; they hatched. Salmons didn't just swim; they leaped.

Mundaneness found no home in his universe.

He must have loved it. Creators relish creating. I'm sure his commands were delightful! "Hippo, you won't walk . . . you'll waddle!" "Hyena, a bark is too plain. Let me show you how to laugh!" "Look, raccoon, I've made you a mask!" "Come here, giraffe, let's stretch that neck a bit." And on and on he went. Giving the clouds their puff. Giving the oceans their blue. Giving the trees their sway.

Giving the frogs their leap and croak. The mighty wed with the creative, and creation was born.

He was mighty. He was creative.

And he was love. Even greater than his might and deeper than his creativity was one all-consuming characteristic:

Love.

Water must be wet. A fire must be hot. You can't take the wet out of water and still have water. You can't take the heat out of fire and still have fire.

In the same way, you can't take the love out of this One who lived before time and still have him exist. For he was . . . and is . . . Love.

Probe deep within him. Explore every corner. Search every angle. Love is all you find. Go to the beginning of every decision he has made and you'll find it. Go to the end of every story he has told and you'll see it.

Love.

No bitterness. No evil. No cruelty. Just love. Flawless love. Passionate love. Vast and pure love. He is love.

As a result, an elephant has a trunk with which to drink. A kitten has a mother from which to nurse. A bird has a nest in which to sleep. The same God who was mighty enough to carve out the canyon is tender enough to put hair on the legs of the Matterhorn Fly to keep it warm. The same force that provides symmetry to the planets guides the baby kangaroo to its mother's pouch before the mother knows it is born.

And because of who he was, he did what he did.

He created a paradise. A sinless sanctuary. A haven before fear. A home before there was a human dweller. No time. No death. No hurt. A gift built by God for his ultimate creation. And when he was through, he knew "it was very good."[2]

But it wasn't enough.

His greatest work hadn't been completed. One final masterpiece was needed before he would stop.

Look to the canyons to see the Creator's splendor. Touch the flowers and see his delicacy. Listen to the thunder and hear his power. But gaze on this—the zenith—and witness all three . . . and more.

Imagine with me what may have taken place on that day.

He placed one scoop of clay upon another until a form lay lifeless on the ground.

All of the Garden's inhabitants paused to witness the event. Hawks hovered. Giraffes stretched. Trees bowed. Butterflies paused on petals and watched.

"You will love me, nature," God said. "I made you that way. You will obey me, universe. For you were designed to do so. You will reflect my glory, skies, for that is how you were created. But this one will be like me. This one will be able to choose."

All were silent as the Creator reached into himself and removed something yet unseen. A seed. "It's called 'choice.' The seed of choice."

Creation stood in silence and gazed upon the lifeless form.

An angel spoke, "But what if he . . ."

"What if he chooses not to love?" the Creator finished. "Come, I will show you."

Unbound by today, God and the angel walked into the realm of tomorrow.

"There, see the fruit of the seed of choice, both the sweet and the bitter."

The angel gasped at what he saw. Spontan-eous love. Voluntary devotion. Chosen tenderness. Never had he seen anything like these. He felt the love of the Adams. He heard the joy of Eve and her daughters. He saw the food and the burdens shared. He absorbed the kindness and marveled at the warmth.

"Heaven has never seen such beauty, my Lord. Truly, this is your greatest creation."

"Ah, but you've only seen the sweet. Now witness the bitter."

A stench enveloped the pair. The angel turned in horror and proclaimed, "What is it?"

The Creator spoke only one word: "Selfishness."

The angel stood speechless as they passed through centuries of repugnance. Never had he seen such filth. Rotten hearts. Ruptured promises. Forgotten loyalties. Children of the creation wandering blindly in lonely laby-rinths.

"This is the result of choice?" the angel asked.

"Yes."

"They will forget you?"

"Yes."

"They will reject you?"

"Yes."

"They will never come back?"

"Some will. Most won't."

"What will it take to make them listen?"

The Creator walked on in time, further and further into the future, until he stood by a tree. A tree that would be fashioned into a cradle. Even then he could smell the hay that would surround him.

With another step into the future, he paused before another tree. It stood alone, a stubborn ruler of a bald hill. The trunk was thick, and the wood was strong. Soon it would be cut. Soon it would be trimmed. Soon it would be mounted on the stony brow of another hill. And soon he would be hung on it.

He felt the wood rub against a back he did not yet wear.

"Will you go down there?" the angel asked.

"I will."

"Is there no other way?"

"There is not."

"Wouldn't it be easier to not plant the seed? Wouldn't it be easier to not give the choice?"

"It would," the Creator spoke slowly. "But to remove the choice is to remove the love."

He looked around the hill and foresaw a scene. Three figures hung on three crosses. Arms spread. Heads fallen forward. They moaned with the wind.

Men clad in soldiers' garb sat on the ground near the trio. They played games in the dirt and laughed.

Men clad in religion stood off to one side. They smiled. Arrogant, cocky. They had protected God, they thought, by killing this false one.

Women clad in sorrow huddled at the foot of the hill. Speechless. Faces tear streaked. Eyes downward. One put her arm around another and tried to lead her away. She wouldn't leave. "I will stay," she said softly. "I will stay."

All heaven stood to fight. All nature rose to rescue. All eternity poised to protect. But the Creator gave no command.

"It must be done . . . ," he said, and withdrew.

But as he stepped back in time, he heard the cry that he would someday scream: "My God, my God, why have you forsaken me?"[3] He wrenched at tomorrow's agony.

The angel spoke again. "It would be less painful . . ."

The Creator interrupted softly. "But it wouldn't be love."

They stepped into the Garden again. The Maker looked earnestly at the clay creation. A monsoon of love swelled up within him. He had died for the creation before he had made him. God's form bent over the sculptured face and breathed. Dust stirred on the lips of the new one. The chest rose, cracking the red mud. The cheeks fleshened. A finger moved. And an eye opened.

But more incredible than the moving of the flesh was the stirring of the spirit. Those who could see the unseen gasped.

Perhaps it was the wind who said it first. Perhaps what the star saw that moment is what has made it blink ever since. Maybe it was left to an angel to whisper it:

"It looks like . . . it appears so much like . . . it is him!"

The angel wasn't speaking of the face, the features, or the body. He was looking inside—at the soul.

"It's eternal!" gasped another.

Within the man, God had placed a divine seed. A seed of his self. The God of might had created earth's mightiest. The Creator had created, not a creature, but another creator. And the One who had chosen to love had created one who could love in return.

Now it's our choice.

27

CAUGHT WITH YOUR PANTS DOWN, BUT YOUR HEAD UP

S TEVE LYONS WILL BE REMEMBERED as the player who dropped his pants.

He could be remembered as an outstanding infielder . . . as the player who played every position for the Chicago White Sox . . . as the guy who always dove into first base . . . as a favorite of the fans who high fived the guy who caught the foul ball in the bleachers. He could be remembered as an above-average player who made it with average ability.

But he won't. He'll be remembered as the player who dropped his pants on July 16, 1990.

The White Sox were playing the Tigers in Detroit. Lyons bunted and raced down the first-base line. He knew it was going to be tight, so he dove at the bag. Safe! The Tiger's pitcher disagreed. He and the umpire got into a shouting match, and Lyons stepped in to voice his opinion.

Absorbed in the game and the debate, Lyons felt dirt trickling down the inside of his pants. Without missing a beat he dropped his britches, wiped away the dirt, and . . . uh oh . . . twenty thousand jaws hit the bleachers' floor.

And, as you can imagine, the jokes began. Women behind the White Sox dugout waved dollar bills when he came onto the field. "No one," wrote one columnist, "had ever dropped his drawers on the field. Not Wally Moon. Not Blue

Moon Odom. Not even Heinie Manush."[1] Within twenty-four hours of the "exposure," he received more exposure than he'd gotten his entire career: seven live television and approximately twenty radio interviews.

"We've got this pitcher, Melido Perez, who earlier this month pitched a no-hitter," Lyons stated, "and I'll guarantee you he didn't do two live television shots afterwards. I pull my pants down, and I do seven. Something's pretty skewed toward the zany in this game."

Fortunately, for Steve, he was wearing sliding pants under his baseball pants. Otherwise the game would be rated "R" instead of "PG-13."

Now, I don't know Steve Lyons. I'm not a White Sox fan. Nor am I normally appreciative of men who drop their pants in public. But I think Steve Lyons deserves a salute.

I think anybody who dives into first base deserves a salute. How many guys do you see roaring down the baseline of life more concerned about getting a job done than they are about saving their necks? How often do you see people diving headfirst into anything?

Too seldom, right? But when we do . . . when we see a gutsy human throwing caution to the wind and taking a few risks . . . ah, now that's a person worthy of a pat on the . . . back.

So here's to all the Steve Lyons of the world.

Here's to the Miracles, a choral group out of Memphis, Tennessee, made up of the mentally retarded and the stouthearted. Just see if you can listen to them and still feel sorry for yourself.

Here's to the hero of the San Francisco marathon who crossed the finish line without seeing it. (He was blind.)

Here's to the woman whose husband left her with a nest of kids to raise and bills to pay, but who somehow tells me every Sunday that God has never been closer.

Here's to the single father of two girls who learned to braid their hair.

Here's to the grandparents who came out of retirement to raise the children their children couldn't raise.

Here's to the foster parents who took in a child long enough for that child to take their hearts—then gave the child up again.

Here's to the girl, told by everyone to abort the baby, who chose to keep the baby.

Here's to the doctor who treats more than half of his patients for free.

Here's to the heroin-addict-turned-missionary.

Here's to the executive who every Tuesday hosts a 5:30 A.M. meeting for Bible study and prayer.

Here's to all of you reckless lovers of life and God, who stand on first base because you paid a price to get there.

So what if you forget about pleasing the crowd and get caught with your pants down? At least you're playing ball in the pros.

Most of us aren't even in your league.

28

LEMONADE AND GRACE

*L*EMONADE, *5¢"*
The *e* is larger than the *L*. The *m* is upper cased; all the other letters are lowered. The last two letters, *de,* curve downward because the artist ran out of room on the poster board.

Norman Rockwell would have loved it.

Two girls sit on the sidewalk in little chairs behind a little table. The six-year-old is the cashier. She monitors a plastic bowl of change. The four-year-old is the waitress. She handles the ice. Pours the drinks. Stacks and restacks the paper cups.

Behind them, seated on the grass, is Dad. He leans against an oak tree and smiles as he witnesses his daughters' inauguration into capitalism.

Business has been steady. The Saturday-afternoon stream of patrons has nearly emptied the pitcher. The bottom of the cashier's bowl is covered with thirty-five cents of change. With the exception of a few spills, the service has been exceptional. No complaints. Many compliments.

Part of the success, though, has been due to the marketing strategy.

Our street doesn't get much traffic, so we did a little advertising. As my daughters painted the sign, I called several families in the neighborhood and invited them to the grand opening of our lemonade stand. So all of our clients, thus far, had been partial.

I was proud of myself. I leaned back against the tree. Closed my eyes. Turned up the radio I had brought. And listened to the baseball game.

Then I heard an unfamiliar voice.

"I'll have a cup of lemonade, please."

I opened my eyes. It was a customer. A real customer. An unsolicited neighbor who had driven by, seen the sign, stopped, and ordered a drink.

Uh-oh, I thought. Our service was about to be tested.

Andrea, the four-year-old, grabbed a cup that had already been used.

"Get a clean cup," I whispered.

"Oh," she giggled, and got a clean cup.

She opened the ice bucket, looked in, and then looked back at me. "Daddy, we are out of ice."

The patron overheard her. "That's OK. I'll take it warm."

She picked up the pitcher and poured. Syrupy sugar oozed out of the pitcher. "Daddy, there's just a little bit."

Our customer spoke again. "That's fine. I don't want much."

"I hope you like it sweet," I said under my breath.

She handed the cup to the man and he handed her a dollar. She gave it to Jenna.

Jenna turned to me. "Daddy, what do I do?" (We weren't used to such big bills.)

I stuck my hands in my pockets; they were empty.

"Uh, we don't have any . . ." I began.

"No problem," he said, smiling. "Just keep the change."

I smiled sheepishly. He thanked the girls. Told them they were doing a great job. Climbed back into his car. And drove off.

Quite a transaction, I thought. *We give him a warm, partially filled cup of lemonade syrup, and he gives us a compliment and a payment twenty times too much.*

I had set out to teach the girls about free enterprise. They ended up with a lesson on grace.

And so had I. For all the theologizing we preachers do about God's grace, the kind stranger modeled it better than the best of sermons state it.

Perhaps the story of the stranger who brought grace to our street is a good place for us to wrap up this book. For this story is the story of each of us.

Each of us has seen our ice melt in the July sun of stress. Who hasn't attempted to serve the best, only to find that the best has already been served and that the pitcher needs to be refilled? And there's not a person alive who hasn't wondered what God does when what we promise and what we produce aren't even close to being the same.

Lemonade stands and living life would be high-risk endeavors were it not for the appearance of gentle strangers on our streets. But, thank God, they come.

And, thank God, He came.

For isn't God the stranger who became our friend after looking past the dregs and into our hearts?

And aren't we not much more than surprised children, amazed that what we receive is twenty times, yea, verily a million times, more than what we ask for?

The next time your calm becomes chaos, think of that. The next time you find yourself in a storm and can't see God on the horizon, reflect on the lemonade stand. And if your walking on the water becomes floundering in the deep like Peter's did, lift your eyes and look . . .

A Gentle Stranger may be bringing grace to your street . . . to your life.

CONCLUSION

I JUST DID WHAT YOU JUST DID. I just read this book. It goes in the mail tomorrow. The overnight-express package is on my desk, and the label is typed. The editors and their red pens are waiting. The printers and their presses are expectant. But I wasn't ready to send it off yet. So I sat on the couch with coffee, and highlighter and sipped and read and . . . gratefully. . . smiled.

I liked it. You might find that surprising. You might assume that every writer likes what he or she writes. They should and normally do, I suppose. But I always have that lingering fear that with all the work done, I might sit down to read what I wrote . . . and gag.

But I didn't. I was pleased.

I smiled at the right spots and was warmed at others. It was good to visit the seashore again and see the patient Master touching the people. It was fun to read about the woman who called my bluff on the plane. It did me good to read about the lost contact lens and the recovered vision, Rickenbacker's lost crew and the mysterious sea gull, the impossible stairway and the nameless carpenter.

It was good to be reminded again that this journey is a brief one. That Jesus knows how I feel and that he'd scramble off a mountain and walk through a storm to convince me of that.

It was good to hear God's gentle thunder. I hope it has been good for you. Thanks for reading my book. I realize that it took your time and money. I hope it has been worth both.

And I hope you never forget the last Lighthouse Law: Approach life like a voyage on a schooner. Enjoy the view. Explore the vessel. Make friends with the captain. Fish a little. And then get off when you get home.

Good sailing!

NOTES

Chapter 2 • God Under Pressure

1. Matthew 14:1–13.
2. Luke 9:9.
3. The wording of Matthew 14:1–13 has given rise to some discussion. At the beginning of the passage, it is clear that John the Baptist is already dead because Herod is concerned that Jesus might be "John the Baptist . . . risen from the dead." Jesus withdraws when he "heard what had happened." A fair question is, what news did Jesus hear? Did he hear that John had been killed? Or did he hear that Herod might be after him? Or a combination of both? Those scholars who argue that Jesus retreated solely out of sorrow over the death of John the Baptist suggest that Matthew simply forgot how he began the chapter with a reference to Herod. "[Matthew] . . . has forgotten the parenthetic nature of the story of John the Baptist" (R. Bultmann, *The History of the Synoptic Translation,* ed. John Marsh [New York: Harper & Row, 1963], 48). Other scholars argue that it was the awareness that Herod was looking for him that spurred Jesus' withdrawal. Lamar Cope reasons that Jesus withdrew due to fear that Herod would pursue him next. He writes, "In unpunctuated Greek there were only limited ways to mark off sections of thought" (Lamar Cope, *Catholic Bible Quarterly,* 37:4 [1976]: 515–18). He explains that the Greek indicates that the John the Baptist story was an insert and that the phrase "when Jesus heard" directly refers to Herod's acquaintance with Jesus. Hence Jesus left in peril. Most scholars,

however, are in general agreement that the phrase, "When Jesus heard what had happened," refers to a combination of sorrow and caution. For references see: *A Commentary Critical, Experimental and Practical of the Old and New Testaments; Matthew-John,* ed. David Brown, vol. 5 (Grand Rapids, Mich.: Eerdmans, 1948), 159; J. S. Exell, ed., *The Biblical Illustrator: Matthew* (Grand Rapids, Mich.: Baker Book House, 1955), 267; J. W. McGarvey, ed., *New Testament Commentary: Matthew and Mark,* vol. 1 (Delight, Ark.: Gospel Light Publishing, 1900), 130; Alan Hugh McNeile, *The Gospel According to St. Matthew, Greek Text* (London: Macmillan & Co., 1952), 212; C. E. Montefiore, *Synoptic Gospels* (London: Macmillan & Co., 1909), 60; J. B. Orchard, *A Synopsis of the Four Gospels in Greek* (Macon, Ga.: Mercer University Press, 1983), 30; Adam Clarke, *Clark's Commentary: Matthew-Acts,* vol. 5 (Nashville, Tenn.: Abingdon Press, 1831, 1967), 157; Frederick Dale Bruner, *Matthew: The Churchbook,* vol. 2 (Dallas, Tex.: Word Publishing, 1990), 526, 527; William Barclay, *The Gospel of Matthew,* vol. 2 (Philadelphia, Pa.: Westminster Press, 1975), 98; *The Expositors Bible Commentary,* vol. 8 (Grand Rapids, Mich.: Zondervan Publishing House, 1984), 340, 341; see especially William Hendricksen, *The Gospel of Matthew* (Grand Rapids, Mich.: Baker Book House, 1973), 593, 594.

4. Mark 6:30.

5. Mark 6:12.

6. Matthew 14:21.

7. John MacArthur, *The MacArthur Commentary: Matthew 8–15* (Chicago, Ill.: Moody Press, 1987), 427.

8. Mark 6:31.

9. Ibid.

10. Luke 9:11.

11. Max Lucado, *God Came Near* (Portland, Oreg.: Multnomah Press, 1987), 26.

12. How divinity and humanity could coexist in the same body is not easy to comprehend. Indeed, the paradox of the Incarnation has been a source of tension for theologians throughout

history. Discomfort with the mystery has driven thinkers to relegate the doctrine into one of two extremes, each of which is equally dangerous. One line of reasoning, known as Ebionitism, denies the full divinity of Christ. Those who embrace this position reject the presence of God in Christ. He is presented as a religious genius, a spiritual master, a guru, but not God himself. He was the "perfect religious personality, a spiritual life completely filled by the realization of God who is love." (Walter Rausenbusch, *A Theology for the Social Gospel,* 154, 155, as quoted by Bloesch in *Essentials of Evangelical Theology,* 1:135.) The other approach to the incarnation of Jesus begins with the deity of Christ, but never arrives at his humanity. "Docetism," (which comes from the Greek word *dokeo,* which means "to seem, to have the appearance of"), rejects God as a touchable, reachable human and relegates Jesus to the metaphysical. See Stephen Neill, *Jesus Through Many Eyes* (Philadelphia, Pa.: Fortress Press, 1976), 139. This form of Gnosticism, although comfortable with the overarching pattern or truth that is exemplified in Christ, is unable to endorse the complete indwelling of God in the man, Jesus. Both approaches, Ebionitism and Docetism, strain to exalt one nature at the expense of the other. Both are equally heretical. One leaves you with a good teacher who deceived the world with falsehood and tricks. . . . The other offers a god who simply masked himself in humanity, but never experienced it. The apostles John and Paul have strong words for both. "Every spirit that acknowledges that Jesus Christ has come in the flesh is from God, but every spirit that does not acknowledge Jesus is not from God" (1 John 4:2–3). "For in Christ all the fullness of the Deity lives in bodily form" (Col. 2:9). "In the beginning was the Word, and the Word was with God, and the Word was God" (John 1:1). It was this Word [Jesus] who assumed the human state and "made his dwelling among us . . . full of grace and truth" (John 1:14). Other Scriptures join the chorus. Jesus was "born of a woman, born under law" (Gal. 4:4). He shared in "their humanity" (Heb. 2:14). He "offered up prayers and petitions with loud cries and tears" (Heb. 5:7).

He grew in "wisdom and stature" (Luke 2:40, KJV). Yet, although human, he was divine. He is called "our great God and Savior" (Titus 2:13). He forgave sins (Mark 2:5, 7, 10). He raised the dead; he gave and gives life (John 5:21). He defeated death (2 Tim. 2:8). How do we justify the paradox? How do we explain "the Lord humbled for communion with man and likewise the Servant exalted to communion with God?" (Karl Barth, *The Humanity of Gods,* trans. Thomas Wieser and John Newton Thomas [Richmond, Va.: John Knox Press, 1964], 64). How do we explain that God was equally human and divine? We don't. It is a secret beyond our reach and, consequentially, worthy of our worship. Hence Paul wrote: "Great beyond all question is the mystery of our religion: 'He who was manifested in the body, vindicated in the spirit, seen by angels; who was proclaimed among the nations, believed in throughout the world, glorified in high heaven'" (1 Tim. 3:16, NEB).

13. *More of Paul Harvey's The Rest of the Story,* ed. Paul Aurandt (New York: Bantam Books, 1980), 79, 80.

Chapter 3 • A Mother's Love—A Friend's Empathy

1. Matthew 14:14.
2. Mark 6:34.
3. Luke 9:11.
4. See John 6:15, 26.
5. Matthew 14:14.
6. Matthew 14:15.
7. Matthew 14:16.
8. Mark 6:37.
9. Ibid.
10. Mark 6:41.

Chapter 4 • When Fishermen Don't Fish

1. Mark 6:34.
2. Matthew 14:14.

3. Ibid.
4. Mark 6:34.

Chapter 7 • Thanks for the Bread

1. John 6:1–14.

Chapter 9 • Fending Off the Voices

1. Ann Trebbe and Valerie Helmbreck, "'Ideal' is body beautiful and 'clean cut,'" *USA Today,* 15 September 1989.
2. John 6:14.
3. John 6:15.
4. John 10:3.
5. Revelation 3:20.
6. Matthew 28:20.
7. Hebrews 13:5.
8. John 5:28–29.

Chapter 10 • The Photo and the File

1. Matthew 5:5.
2. Philippians 1:10.

Chapter 11 • Seeing God Through Shattered Glass

1. Matthew 14:22–24.
2. Mark 6:52.
3. Matthew 14:15.
4. Ibid.

Chapter 12 • Two Fathers, Two Feasts

1. 1 Thessalonians 5:9, NEB.
2. Isaiah 57:15.
3. Psalm 74:10; 89:46.
4. 1 Chronicles 29:15.

5. Psalm 39:5.
6. James 4:14.
7. Psalm 103:15, 16.
8. 2 Corinthians 4:16–18.
9. 2 Corinthians 11:23–27.

Chapter 14 • *The Miracle of the Carpenter*

1. Matthew 14:23.

Chapter 15 • *The Woodcutter's Wisdom*

1. Ecclesiastes 7:8.
2. Romans 12:12.
3. Matthew 6:34.

Chapter 16 • *Laws of the Lighthouse*

1. As quoted by Stephen R. Covey, *The Seven Habits of Highly Effective People* (New York: Fireside—Simon & Schuster, 1989), 33.

Chapter 17 • *He Speaks Through the Storm*

1. Job 42:5, TLB.
2. Job 13:4, 5, TLB.
3. Job 33:29.
4. Job 38:2.
5. Job 38:3.
6. Job 38:4, TLB.
7. Job 38:5–7, TLB.
8. Job 38:12, 13, TLB.
9. Job 38:17–21, TLB.
10. Job 40:4, 5, TLB.
11. Job 41:11, TLB.
12. Job 42:5, TLB.

Chapter 18 • Pilgrim Ponderings

1. Matthew 17:1–5.
2. Luke 9:29.
3. Matthew 17:5.

Chapter 19 • Our Storm Was His Path

1. Matthew 14:27.
2. Matthew 14:28.

Chapter 20 • They'd Do It Again

1. Matthew 14:33.

Chapter 21 • Castles of Sorrow

1. 2 Corinthians 7:10.

Chapter 22 • Fear That Becomes Faith

1. John 6:19.
2. Proverbs 9:10.
3. Exodus 14:15, 16.
4. 2 Kings 5:13, 14.
5. Romans 3.
6. Acts 12:6–17.
7. Matthew 14:28.
8. Ephesians 2:8, 9.
9. "Rock of Ages, Cleft for Me," by Augustus M. Toplady.
10. "The Solid Rock," by Edward Mote.
11. "Amazing Grace," by John Newton.
12. Matthew 14:30.
13. Ibid.
14. Matthew 14:31.
15. "Amazing Grace," by John Newton.

Chapter 23 • Why God Smiles

1. Matthew 15:28.
2. Matthew 15:22.
3. Matthew 15:24.
4. Matthew 15:25.
5. Matthew 15:26.
6. Matthew 15:27.
7. Daniel 9:18.

Chapter 24 • The Sacrificial Visitor

1. Matthew 15:29–32.

Chapter 25 • Holiness in a Bathrobe

1. 1 Peter 4:8.
2. Hebrews 10:14.
3. Galatians 3:27.
4. Colossians 3:3.
5. 2 Corinthians 5:21.

Chapter 26 • The Choice

1. Genesis 1:1.
2. Genesis 1:31.
3. Mark 15:34.

Chapter 27 • Caught with Your Pants Down, But Your Head Up

1. "Moon Man," *Sports Illustrated*, 13 August 1990, 58–63.

STUDY
GUIDE

It is my hope that this book has given you encouragement to not only face and survive, but to grow through the storms of life. I hope it has given you encouragement to see Christ standing tall amidst the towering waves and step out toward his holy, helping hand.

This study guide is designed to help you move from encouraging thoughts to daring living in the eye of the storm. If you are reading through this book with a group, you might try to work through one study session a week. (Group leaders, please be sensitive to the personal nature of some of the questions in this guide. Sharing answers with the group should always be optional.)

Whether you use this study guide alone or with a group, I suggest that you have your Bible and notebook close at hand. Write down your thoughts and discoveries. Pray earnestly about how God would have you respond to his promises! Use this guide not as an end unto itself, but as a catalyst for further study—as a tool to further strengthen your faith against the fury of the storm.

SESSION 1

Chapter 1 *From Calm to Chaos*

1. Describe a moment when your life went from calm to chaos. When did it happen? What were the circumstances? Who was involved?

2. Afterwards, how did you feel about that sudden switch from calm to chaos? Did you recover quickly, or do you still bear scars from the trauma?

3. Think about the internal codes you might have used to deal with the chaos. Did you have the right ones? Did you know how to use them? What codes do you need to learn in order to keep cool in the pressure cooker?

Chapter 2 *God Under Pressure*

1. After learning about John the Baptist's murder and Herod's threat, and seeing how tired the disciples were, Jesus called a "time out." He and the disciples "withdrew by boat privately to a solitary place" (Luke 9:9).

When you are dealing with a difficult situation—when you reach your limit of stress, pain, rejection, loneliness—how do you take "time out"? Where do you go? What do you do?

2. The following passages describe some of God's promises that we can hold onto during times of stress: Psalm 33:20; 34:7; 145:18; Proverbs 30:5; Isaiah 41:10; 43:2; Matthew 28:20; John 16:33; Romans 8:17; Ephesians 6:10–17; Hebrews 13:6; 1 Peter 5:10. Select one that is most meaningful

to you and write it down or memorize it so that it will comfort you the next time your world goes from calm to chaos.

3. While Jesus and the disciples were in the boat, peace reigned. Suddenly, when they reached land, the crowd converged on them again and dashed their hopes of having a few hours alone.

Can you relate? Describe a time when what you *sought* and what you *got* were completely different. How did you feel at the time? How did you respond?

4. Read Hebrews 4:15. What is your initial response to the statement, "Jesus knows how you feel"? Is there even the slightest temptation to think, "He knows how I feel most of the time, but he doesn't *really* know what *this* feels like"?

As you review the experiences in your life, is it hard for you to believe that Jesus has fully experienced them? Which ones do you think Jesus may not have fully experienced?

Why do you think it is so hard to truly believe that Jesus knows how we feel? What difference does it make that Jesus shared fully in our experience of temptation—but never sinned?

What experiences and hurts do you need to take to Jesus—your understanding Father and Physician—so that he may heal you?

5. Write down or discuss what the following references tell us about Jesus: Mark 2:5, 7, 10; Luke 2:40; John 1:1, 14; John 5:21; Colossians 2:9; Titus 2:13; Hebrews 2:14a; Hebrews 5:7; 1 John 4:2b, 3a.

SESSION 2

Chapter 3   *A Mother's Love—A Friend's Empathy*

1. Consider this: "Jesus knew the value of people. He knew that each human being is a treasure. And because he did, people were not a source of stress, but a source of joy."

  Could someone make the same statement about you? What do you think makes the difference between seeing people as a source of stress or a source of joy?

2. Try to place yourself in Jesus' position as the crowds surrounded him. Would you have healed all the sick that day, or only certain ones? By what criteria would you have made your decisions?

3. In your daily life, what criteria do you use to determine whether or not you will help someone? How does God's example of helping and healing out of his abundant goodness affect your decisions to help others? Under what conditions are you willing to help people who "have no desire to become Christians?"

4. If you had to list three areas of your life that God "overlooks" when he bestows his love on you, what would you list?

5. Irritated by the crowd, the disciples demanded that Jesus "send them away" (Matthew 14:15). Who in your life have you sent away when you could have meet the need in love?

6. How do you respond to the demands that people make on you? What has God asked you to do that left you

openmouthed and wondering whether or not he was kidding? Why do you think you assumed that God had asked you to do the impossible? Read Hebrews 11:1 and Romans 10:17. What is faith and where does it come from?

7. What has Jesus given you that could enable you to understand how another person feels? Is there someone in your life right now to whom you could reach out with Christ's love?

8. List three areas of your life in which you could use more peace and less chaos. How might the two inner codes— "Jesus knows how you feel" and "people are precious"—change how you handle the chaos?

SESSION 3 —————————————————————

Chapter 4 *When Fishermen Don't Fish*

1. *Compassion* means to feel deep sorrow for a person who suffers misfortune and to desire to alleviate the suffering. Matthew 14:14 says that Jesus had compassion on the people, so he changed his agenda from that of quiet rest to offering healing for body and soul.

Has anyone ever shown this depth of compassion for you? If so, what was it like to be blessed by the compassion of another person?

When have you felt compassion for another person or group of people? What action did compassion prompt you to take?

2. When has God brought hurting people into your world to break the solitude and press you into service? Explain

how you did or did not find perspective when that occurred. Describe the balance between service and solitude that fosters a godly perspective in your life.

3. Read Mark 6:7–12, 30, 31. The disciples flourished when they went fishing, didn't they? They were so excited that the pressing crowd didn't dim their enthusiasm.

When do you flourish? What "miracles" do you do in Jesus' name that get you so excited that crowds don't bother you and you forget to eat?

4. Jesus' words in Luke 6:41–42 illustrate what happens when people stop fishing and flourishing and start fighting.

In practical terms, what steps can you take to focus more of your energy on fishing and flourishing? In what ways do you tend to complain about your friends' stinky socks in the camper?

Chapter 5   *The Joy in the Journey*

1. It's easy to judge people, isn't it? Read the following verses: Leviticus 19:15; Proverbs 24:23; Acts 10:34; Romans 10:12; Galatians 2:6.

When have you made judgments that you shouldn't have made about others and missed what you could have learned from them?

2. When has your journey been interrupted by a lesson you needed to learn? What lesson did you learn? Was it a lesson that you need to be reminded of frequently?

3. How might Jesus' words about an abundant life (John 10:10b) relate to your lifestyle? If you could do three

activities this week just for fun, what would they be? In what ways could you add joy to the routine activities in your life?

SESSION 4 ————————————————————————————

Chapter 6 *Remarkable*

1. After reading this chapter, and its list of "remarkable" things, what remarkable aspects of your life do you tend to overlook? How might your life be different if you recognized more of the remarkable occurrences of everyday life?

2. Read Job 38:4–39:30; 40:9–41:11. How do these images expand your view of the remarkable?

3. Think back to the events surrounding the second most stressful day in Jesus' life (Matthew 14:1–21; Mark 6:7–44; Luke 9:1–17).

What remarkable things do you think the disciples could easily have overlooked on that day? If they had seen those things as truly remarkable, how might their responses have been different?

As you observe these events and the disciples' responses, what parallels do you see in your own life?

4. Read 1 Thessalonians 5:18. For what remarkable things can you now give thanks?

Chapter 7 *Thanks for the Bread*

1. This chapter shares the story of an engineer who took a risk that paid off. When has your life been touched by a person who took the risk to reach out to you?

2. Read John 6:1–14.

Have you, like the little boy, ever stood up and done something that might cause others to laugh at you? If so, how did you feel? What motivated you to do it, despite the risks?

What were the results of your action? If you don't know the results, what do you hope they were?

3. Jesus multiplied the little boy's lunch so that twelve baskets of food were left over. How might this illustration relate to your gifts? Do you believe that God can use you to accomplish great things for him? Why or why not?

4. People often say, "What you believe is fine for you, and what I believe is fine for me. So don't push what you believe on me." What does this chapter say about how God might have us take risks and share our faith with others?

5. Who in your life do you need to thank for taking a risk with you?

SESSION 5 ————————————————————

Chapter 8   *Musings in Minnesota*

1. Who do you call when you "call home" as the author did in chapter eight? What makes calling home so special for you?

2. What do each of the following verses say about Jesus' willingness to listen and answer when we call? Psalm 91:15; Isaiah 55:6; 58:9; 65:24; Jeremiah 33:3; Luke 11:9.

3. When you, like Jesus in Matthew 14:19, face incredible pressure, how do you respond? Get angry? Shoo the crowds away? Take a moment to ask God for help?

Right now, close your eyes and—like Jesus—listen for the familiar, comforting sounds of heaven. Think about what you hear.

How might those sounds change the way you handle things if you were to stop and listen to them the next time the pressure builds?

Chapter 9 *Fending Off the Voices*

1. Tempting voices call out in hotel rooms, from the television, at the office . . . everywhere. Which voices clamor for your attention? What messages do they shout out to you?

2. Note how Jesus responded to the crowd's applause (John 6:14–15). List two temptations you face that on the surface seem positive and uplifting, but that really will lead you toward sin. How do you respond to the clamoring voices and temptations in your life?

3. In John 10:1–5, Jesus talks about how sheep listen to their shepherd's voice. In verses 7–17, he says that he is the Good Shepherd and that his sheep respond to his voice.

What does the voice of Jesus sound like to you? Can you always hear his voice? How can you seek his voice more intently so that you can be led by him?

4. Look up John 5:28, 29. When everyone hears God's voice, what will happen?

Chapter 10   *The Photo and the File*

1. Take a look at the activities you have planned for the coming weeks and months. What do they say about your priorities?

2. If you could make four things in your life a priority, what would you pick?

Now compare these four things to your calendar of events. What does the picture look like? Are your priorities and calendar in balance? What changes would bring your priorities and activities into better balance?

3. Read Philippians 1:9–11. How might these words help you set priorities in your life?

4. When people ask you to do certain things for them—things you are not really sure you should do—how do you typically respond?

Describe the last time someone used guilt and/or pride to try to entice you into making a wrong choice.

Read Matthew 14:22. Have you ever "dismissed the crowd" or said "no" in order to seek God? What did it feel like to make that decision?

5. Who in your life loves you for who you are rather than for what you can do? How does that person (or persons) fit into your priorities?

6. Did the story of the two paddleboats hit close to home? Have you ever won the race but burned the cargo? If so, describe that time.

SESSION 6 ————————————————————

Chapter 11   *Seeing God Through Shattered Glass*

1. Can you remember a time when pain shattered your expectations of God, when he did something that didn't seem right to you or gave you the opposite of what you thought you should receive? If so, how did that experience affect your view of God?

2. Do you have a phrase (or even several) that is always ready to complete this sentence: "If God is God, then . . ."? What is it? How did that phrase develop in your thinking?

3. Read Matthew 14:22–24. Describe a time when you felt alone in the storm—abandoned by God's protection and care. Did you become weary, even exhausted?

  How did you feel about God during that time? In what ways was your heart, like the hearts of the disciples, hardened against him? (See Mark 6:52.)

4. Has God ever used an exhausting, painful, or seemingly impossible circumstance to teach you something about himself or your relationship with him? If so, describe the circumstance and the lesson.

5. In what areas of your life could you trust God more, rather than questioning how he seems to be working?

  When the next storm in your life appears, how can you be better prepared to see Jesus at work in the midst of the storm?

Chapter 12   *Two Fathers, Two Feasts*

1. According to 1 Thessalonians 5:9, what is God's ultimate destiny for your life? In what ways do you prefer to "rest rather than ride" toward the destiny God has for you?

2. When have you found yourself in an unlikely classroom, or on a "decision collision" with God regarding what stops should be made or which way to turn on your journey? Whose itinerary won out?

3. What requests has God said "no" to during your life's journey? Which "nos" were easier or more difficult to take? Why?

4. Reread 1 Chronicles 29:15, Psalm 39:5, James 4:14, and Psalm 103:15, 16. What do these verses say about our journey? About what should be important?

5. What will the eternal rewards be if you allow God to plan your earthly trip? What does "being renewed day by day" really mean? (See 2 Corinthians 4:16–18.)

What makes life's journey worth the hassles? Do you believe that God "will do what is right . . . and best" in your life? Why or why not?

6. As you anticipate the coming weeks, how do you feel? Tired? Strained? Angry? Joyful? Encouraged? What "light and momentary troubles" are you facing right now? In what ways might they be "achieving for you an eternal glory"? (See 2 Corinthians 4:16–18.)

7. Write down three requests that you wish God would honor this next week. Then pray honestly for the strength to follow the destiny he has chosen for you.

SESSION 7

Chapter 13 *Doubtstorms*

1. Jesus' disciples weren't the only ones in the Bible to have doubtstorms. Moses seemed to be plagued with them (see Exodus 3:7–4:17; 5:20–6:12; 6:28–7:6; 17:1–7—just to name a few). The entire book of Job is a doubtstorm. Some of Jesus' disciples faced doubtstorms after he died (Luke 24:13–32).

Can you envision the intensity of these doubtstorms? In what ways did God show his light? Do you think those glimmers of light were expected? Why or why not?

2. Describe your blackest doubtstorms. In what unexpected ways has God shown his light to you in the midst of those storms?

3. What gentle light from God have you seen recently? Did it appear in a way that you expected?

4. Have you ever missed—or almost missed—seeing God's gentle light in the midst of your doubtstorms? How can you train your heart to see his gentle light more clearly?

Chapter 14 *The Miracle of the Carpenter*

1. Write down or share a time when, like the Sisters of Loretto, you or someone close to you faced what seemed like an impossible situation and "ascended the mountain of prayer." Who, or what, did God bring into your life to meet the need?

2. When Jesus faced an impossible day, he took time out to pray. When times get tough for you, what do you do? Do you work harder or pray? Do you get angry or pray? What does it take for you to choose to pray when things get tough?

3. What are the impossible gulfs in your life that you cannot cross alone? Do you believe that Jesus came to span the gap between where you are and where you long to be? If so, write down how you plan to seek God's guidance and power in crossing the gulfs.

Chapter 15   *The Woodcutter's Wisdom*

1. Think about the woodcutter's story for a minute. How would you have responded to the events of the woodcutter's life? Would you have been quick to draw conclusions or content to see what unfolded?

Now consider the ways in which you pass judgment on the storms that blow into your own life. Could you benefit from adopting a perspective more like that of the woodcutter than that of the villagers? Explain your answer.

2. Why do you think it is so easy to pass judgment on life "with only one day's evidence"? What are the dangers of passing judgment too quickly?

3. Describe a time when you made judgments about a specific circumstance without realizing how limited your perspective really was. What was the result of your judgments? Did your judgments stand the test of time, or prove to be only fragments?

4. Read Matthew 6:33–34. What do you think Jesus was trying to communicate to his followers through those

words? How do those words provide perspective for your life?

SESSION 8

Chapter 16 *Laws of the Lighthouse*

1. Building on the Laws of the Lighthouse concept, where do most of your signals come from? Other ships on the sea? Friends on your ship? Lighthouses that shift position with the whims of culture? The time-tested lighthouse of God's Word?

2. Review the list of lights that the author looks for and the signals he heeds. Which ones stand out to you? Why?

Now make your own list. Write down the lights and signals that you believe are vital.

3. How carefully are you heeding the warnings of your lighthouse laws? In practical terms, what can you do to pay more attention to the Laws of the Lighthouse?

Chapter 17 *He Speaks Through the Storm*

1. Describe the most difficult circumstance you've ever faced. Who was involved? What happened? How long did it last?

Did you question or lash out at God during that time? What was the result?

What did you learn through that experience? How did it affect your view of yourself? Of God? Of others?

2. Think about friends who "advised" you during a difficult time. What type of wisdom did they give you? What kind

of advice have you given to others who have faced difficult times?

3. Do you sometimes receive God's unending love with mistrust? Name a situation in which you believed that God's love wasn't in your best interest. What was the outcome?

4. Read Job 1:8–12; 2:3–7. Why did God allow Job's difficult circumstances to occur? How does that knowledge add perspective to what happened to Job? Does that knowledge shed any light on the suffering in your life or in the life of someone you know? If so, explain.

5. The author writes that God is "best heard in the storm." Do you agree? Why or why not?

6. Read Job 38–41. What is God's message to you in his answer to Job's questions?

7. When God finished speaking, Job said, "I had heard about you before, but now I have seen you" (Job 42:5, TLB). What did Job gain as a result of seeing God?

Chapter 18 *Pilgrim Ponderings*

1. Why do you think God the Father spoke to Jesus on the mountain? (See Matthew 17:1–5.)

2. What kinds of experiences make you unbearably weary, leaving you sitting on the mountainside with your face in your hands? What does it take to encourage you during those times?

3. Describe a time when God transformed your desolation and met your need in a specific way.

SESSION 9

Chapter 19 *Our Storm Was His Path*

1. Has God ever used a storm "as his path to come to you"? What were the circumstances? What was the result in your life? In the lives of others around you?

2. What is your usual response when a storm lifts you up and then plunges you into a valley? Do you find it easier to sit in a tossing boat than to step out onto the water and walk toward Jesus? Why or why not?

3. When you have been desperately afraid in your life, and have seen an image coming toward you, have you ever cried out, "Lord, is it you?" If so, what was the answer? Was it as comforting as Jesus' response in Matthew 14:27?

4. Have you ever stepped out in faith like Peter did? (See Matthew 14:28—29.) Why did you do it? What was the result?

5. Write down a time in your life when God responded to your need in a special way and you knew you'd never be the same again. What did you discover about God in that situation that you had never seen before?

6. Most of us tend to look down on Peter's ill-fated walk on the water because he sank at the end. But at least he got out of the boat! In what ways can you take steps of faith and get out of the boat this week?

Chapter 20 *They'd Do It Again*

1. Have you, like the disciples, ever really worshiped God for who he is and for what he has done for you? If so, when? If not, why not?

2. What has Christ done that has touched you so deeply that your response could only be that of worship?

3. What kinds of "crutches" do you turn to when a raging storm erupts? How do they compare with God's strength?

4. At which times in your life have you found it easiest to turn to God when storms hit? Has it ever been difficult for you to worship God even after he has stilled a storm in your life? Explain your answer.

5. What price are you willing to pay for a clear view of God?

SESSION 10

Chapter 21 *Castles of Sorrow*

1. Which of your yesterdays imprisons your todays? What "haunting rooms in your castle" need to be opened to the light of day? What fears, failures, feelings of guilt, or dashed hopes need to be surrendered to God? You may need to work this answer out before the Lord during a special time with him.

2. Contrast the two types of sorrow mentioned in 2 Corinthians 7:10. What are the results of each kind of sorrow? Which kind of sorrow plays the greatest role in your life?

3. What kind of facades do you put up to hide your guilt, failures, or feelings of inadequacy? What hope does the story of Peter's encounter with Jesus on the water (Matthew 14:28–32) offer to you?

4. Read Psalm 1:1–2; Colossians 3:16; Ephesians 1:7; 2:8–9; James 1:22–25; 1 John 1:9; 2:12, 14. What is the foundation of your spiritual house? What can you do to strengthen it?

Chapter 22   *Fear That Becomes Faith*

1. How do you respond when you are backed into a corner? Does your faith flourish or flicker? Do you cling to God or your own self-sufficiency?

2. Would you agree that "faith is often the child of fear"? Why or why not?

What circumstances have produced greater faith in your life?

3. How would you define faith as it is portrayed in this chapter? Compare your answer to the description of faith in Hebrews 11:1, 6.

4. Matthew 14:28–31 tells about Peter's adventure on the water. What parallels do you see between this passage and aspects of your life? Describe a time when you took a small step of faith and were surprised by the way God met your need.

5. Read Matthew 21:21–22; Romans 1:17; 5:1, 2; Galatians 2:16; Ephesians 2:8. When we step out in faith, how does Jesus respond?

Write down three specific ways in which you will practice faith this week—at home, at work, with friends. Share your "faith steps" with a friend or family member.

SESSION 11

Chapter 23 *Why God Smiles*

1. How do you feel about a laughing Jesus? A smiling God? Do you feel comfortable with the idea? Is it difficult for you to imagine a Jesus who is that real? Explain your answers.

2. Think about the events in Jesus' life. In which ones can you imagine him flashing a smile or chuckling with a twinkle in his eye?

3. Jesus said that the woman mentioned in Matthew 15:21–28 had great faith. What, in your opinion, did he find so impressive about her faith? Is it what you would have expected him to be impressed with? Why or why not?

    Read Hebrews 11:4–32. Make a list of other people in the Bible who impressed God by their faith. Is there a person you know whose faith impresses you? If so, what do you notice?

4. Read Matthew 14:23. How did the disciples feel toward the woman? How do you think they felt after Jesus spoke with her and honored her request?

    Why, in our fast-paced culture, is it easy to respond to people the way the disciples did? In light of this biblical example, how might you change your responses to people?

5. Do you find that you prefer to get salvation the old-fashioned way, by earning it? If yes, list the ways in which you have tried to impress God. If not, describe the ways in which God has mercifully chosen to bless you.

Chapter 24 *The Sacrificial Visitor*

1. Matthew 15:29–32 records Jesus' healing of many people and their praise for the "God of Israel." But Jesus didn't preach at them; he just reached out to help them. What does this teach you about what sharing Christ with a hurting world really means?

2. Read Luke's version of this event (Luke 8:1–10). How do Matthew's and Luke's versions differ? In which aspects are they similar? What does Luke's account reveal about the disciples' faith?

3. Read John 3:16; Matthew 1:21; John 10:9; John 1:29; Revelation 5:12; Hebrews 7:26, 27. In what ways have you been saved by a Sacrificial Visitor—Jesus Christ?

4. A miracle occurred in Rickenbacker's life that kept him alive. What miracle has God done in your life or in the life of someone you know?

Rickenbacker gives buckets of shrimp to sea gulls to show his gratitude. What can you give to God to say "thank you"?

5. The crowds were amazed when they saw what Jesus had done (Matthew 15:31). How do you respond when God does something special in your life? Write down four things for which you can praise—or worship—God today.

Chapter 25 *Holiness in a Bathrobe*

1. Were you surprised by what the "holy moment" was? Why or why not?

2. As you read this chapter, did you gain a new understanding of the relationship between *honesty* and *holiness,* the difference between *perfection earned* and *perfection paid*? (See also, Colossians 1:22 and 1 Corinthians 1:8.) Explain your answer.

3. Are you ready to take an honest look in the mirror? If so, what have you been trying to do to make yourself more presentable to God?

Read Hebrews 10:14. How has God made you perfect?

What effect does his love and your perfection in his eyes have on the way you feel about yourself? On the way you relate to others? On how you relate to him?

SESSION 12 ————————————————————————————

Chapter 26 *The Choice*

1. Read Genesis 1:1–26. When was the last time you took time to appreciate God's creation? Which of God's creations amaze you? What do they communicate about the character of God? How does it feel to be the creation that made all of God's creation complete?

2. Why is it so important that God gave Adam and Eve the opportunity to choose? (See Genesis 2:15–17; 3:1–13.) If God hadn't given us a choice, how would that have influenced our relationship with him? Why is our choice as to whether or not we'll love God so important?

What were the consequences of Adam's and Eve's choice? (See Genesis 3:14–19.)

3. What choice did Jesus make to deal with the sins of all mankind?

4. What choice is the author referring to when he writes, "Now it's our choice"?

Chapter 27   *Caught with Your Pants Down, But Your Head Up*

1. How do you think people will remember you? As a person who dove headfirst into life—and perhaps made some memorable mistakes? As a person who cheered from the sidelines? As a person who half-heartedly listened to the game on the radio? Be honest!

2. Read Jeremiah 29:11; Matthew 14:30–31; John 14:12; Romans 10:11. What effect should God's promises have on those of us who are afraid to risk?

3. Have you ever paid a price to "stand on first base"? If so, write down the experience. (If you're meeting with a group, share it with them.)

Would you do it again? Why or why not? How does a person's view of God determine the type of risks he or she will take?

4. Make a list of headlong heroes—those who haven't been afraid to go all-out for what was important to them. How do your heroes inspire you to "get in the game"?

Chapter 28   *Lemonade and Grace*

1. Did the lemonade story remind you of a time in your life when God's grace overlooked your flawed accomplishments? If so, describe what happened.

2. How does God respond to us, even though he knows that what we offer him may turn out to be a gooey mess? (See Romans 8:32, 35; Ephesians 2:4, 5; Hebrews 4:16.)

3. Is it possible, as the author writes, "that a Gentle Stranger may be bringing grace to your street . . . to your life"? In what ways?

Max Lucado is a preacher who writes or a writer who preaches. He is the father of three terrific daughters and the husband of a one-in-a-million wife.

He is convinced that Jesus' tomb is empty, that his promise is not and that the Easter sunrise will never fade. He speaks of this carpenter each week at the Oak Hills Church in San Antonio, Texas. He writes about him in his books. This is his sixth.

Fair Tomorrow

BOOKS BY

EMILIE LORING

THE TRAIL OF CONFLICT
HERE COMES THE SUN!
A CERTAIN CROSSROAD
THE SOLITARY HORSEMAN
GAY COURAGE
SWIFT WATER
LIGHTED WINDOWS
FAIR TOMORROW
UNCHARTED SEAS
HILLTOPS CLEAR
WE RIDE THE GALE!
WITH BANNERS
IT'S A GREAT WORLD
GIVE ME ONE SUMMER
AS LONG AS I LIVE
TODAY IS YOURS
HIGH OF HEART
ACROSS THE YEARS
THERE IS ALWAYS LOVE
WHERE BEAUTY DWELLS
STARS IN YOUR EYES
RAINBOW AT DUSK
WHEN HEARTS ARE LIGHT AGAIN
KEEPERS OF THE FAITH
BEYOND THE SOUND OF GUNS
BRIGHT SKIES
BECKONING TRAILS
I HEAR ADVENTURE CALLING
LOVE CAME LAUGHING BY

Fair Tomorrow

By
EMILIE LORING

GROSSET & DUNLAP
Publishers   *New York*

FAIR TOMORROW

To

LOUISE GORDON HALLET

**WHOSE FRIENDSHIP HAS GLOWED WITH
A LOVELY LIGHT DOWN THROUGH THE
YEARS SINCE WE MET ON CAPE COD**

Fair Tomorrow

Chapter I

———◆———

COATLESS, immaculate white shirt sleeves rolled
above his elbows, red-headed Terrence Leigh
scowled thoughtfully at the gate-legged table set for
two in the sunny window, ceased his muted whistling
to shout:

"Hi! Pam! Which side of the plate shall I put
the cranberry jell?"

In answer a door swung into the room with an
agonized squeak. The sound startled the green and
red parrot dozing on a gilded perch. He lost his
balance, righted himself with a strident:

"Gosh!"

With the opening door came a potpourri of sa-
vory scent: roasting turkey, sage, oyster stuffing,
crisping sausage, onions, spicy mincemeat. Came
also a girl's head with a suggestion of black hair
edging a white Dutch cap, a hint of anxiety in brilliant dark eyes, a flush from kitchen heat on satin-
soft skin.

"Jelly at the right, Terry." Slender, graceful,

her yellow linen frock almost obscured by a snowy apron cloud, Pamela Leigh followed her voice into the dining room. The door swung shut behind her.

"Ooch! That squeak sets my teeth on edge. Wait a minute!" She dashed into the kitchen, returned with a cake of soap. "Rub that on the hinges. The jelly stands up well, doesn't it?"

"Like soldiers."

Terrence soaped the hinges. His boyish smile was humorously one-sided as he swung the door experimentally. "That's all right. Table looks like a million dollars, what?"

His sister's eyes followed his to the maple gate-legged table in front of the long French window which framed a view of a russet-tinged lawn enclosed by a picket fence, guarded by an iron dog whose black and white nose sniffed the salty air. Beyond it blue water stretched to the purple haze of the horizon like a sea of sparkling sapphires streaked with malachite, above it thin filaments of fleecy cloud striped a turquoise sky. Pamela appraisingly regarded the glossy damask, Chinese medallion plates, crystal goblets, molds of cranberry jelly like huge cabochon rubies. Her glance traveled on to the lowboy with its load of cracked nuts, figs, board of cheeses, jug of cider, came back to the table. She rearranged the russet Beau Belle pears, Banana apples, gold and sunburned to a dusky pink, purple and white grapes, in the choice old comport as she agreed thoughtfully:

"It does look well, Terry. I hope that we have provided the right setting. The ad distinctly stated:

"'Wanted: by two persons, old-fashioned Thanksgiving dinner. Anywhere on Cape Cod.' Nature has obligingly furnished the Cape. The dinner is as much like the one Grandmother Leigh used to serve as I could make it."

"Except the price. Five per! You have the nerve of a robber chieftain."

Pamela's lovely eyes, her ardent mobile mouth widened in a laugh. "My instincts are kind but my necessities are urgent. Perhaps the price is a hold-up, Terry, but when Madge Jarvis sent the ad she had clipped from a newspaper, she wrote:

"'Don't give away the dinner, Pam. That advertiser is out for sentiment. Sentiment is the most expensive luxury in which one may indulge, it ought to be taxed. Charge five dollars a cover at least. That might be high for shredded wheat and milk, but it isn't high for a cooked to order meal.'"

Terrence whistled and pulled down his sleeves. "Dinner for two in the wilds of Cape Cod. In the language of Hitty Betts, 'I guess them advertisers like privacy.'" He hummed and cut adolescent antics as he set chairs at the gateleg table. The green and red parrot blinked lidless yellow eyes, jabbered:

"Look who's here!"

Terrence shouted with boyish laughter. "Attaboy! Old Mephisto will add the modern touch.

Cabaret stuff. Hope he doesn't croak, ' Goo'-bye! Goo'-bye! ' in the middle of the dinner. The advertisers might leave without settling. Five dollars per! Zowie! For a hard-boiled female lead me to a college grad and an ex-reporter."

Lightning slashed Pamela's eyes, eyes as dark as eyes may be. "I was never a reporter, Terry Leigh. I did features. That is why I get such a thrill out of the Silver Moon Chowder House. Grandmother called this place The Cottage. Too prosaic. A business like ours needs something with a lift. Silver Moon somehow sets my imagination a-tiptoe. To me each patron means a story. In our English course at college we made diagrams of plots. Mr. A starts for B at the other end of a straight line. Half way he meets C. That contact sidetracks him to D. Contacts represented by dots. Sometimes my Mr. A never reached B."

"You can put that over in a story but it doesn't click in real life."

"Doesn't it? What happened when Father, A, started to visit you, B, at school? Half way he met an actress, C, whose car had broken down. Took her to her home, D. Married her the next month. Never reached you at school, B. What did that meeting with C do to our lives? Tangled them into a snarl, messed them tragically, didn't it?"

"I guess you're right. We'll be in a great old jumble if every person who orders chowder dots our lifelines."

"Let's make a plot diagram for today, Terry. We will call the advertiser who is coming, A, and his friend, B. C is their objective, the house to which they return from here. Perhaps I'll get a story germ. As for my being hard-boiled — somebody must be with Father sick, and those creditors of his sending threatening letters and calling on the telephone — and you having to leave prep school your last year and go to this country academy when you were leading your class in studies and were being groomed for a pitcher, — . Life is just a hideous nightmare."

Terrence cleared his throat. "Brace up, Pam. We'll get out of the woods yet. Remember that poem of Holman Day's I came across the other day about the two frogs in the pail of milk? One gave up and was drowned, the other kicked till he churned an island of butter and hopped out." He patted her shoulder. "Kick, frog, kick! Don't you worry about me. I like the Academy, honest. If you lose courage, 'twill be a cockeyed world." He swallowed hard, brushed his hand over his eyes. "Make that advertiser plank down the cash. Remember the last cheque we took in payment for five chowder dinners?"

Pamela laughed. Not too steadily, not too convincingly, but it passed. Terrence's eyes cleared.

"Remember it? If ever my heart is X-rayed, seared into its jacket will be found the two words written on that returned cheque, 'No Funds.' Hitty

Betts is coming to help clear up. We don't even know the gender of our plot germs. Perhaps A and B are men. If they are, I hope they won't be like the two who dropped in for chowder last week. Their eyes were like gimlets boring into our lovely old pieces of furniture and the Sandwich glass, till I expected to find the maple full of holes and the glass cracked after their departure."

"Perhaps they were antique dealers and knew the real thing when they saw it. A guy wouldn't need a Rhodes scholarship mind to realize that old John Leigh isn't of 20th century vintage."

Terrence and his sister looked up at the portrait above the maple lowboy. A long-gone Leigh as Thomas Sully had seen him. Black coat, white stock, snowy hair, sparse on top, thick and waving over the ears. Speculative blue eyes under bushy gray brows, florid complexion, a hawk nose, which almost met the thin line of clamped lips. A fine hand holding an open letter.

"Goo'-bye! Goo'-bye!" croaked the parrot irritably as he swung head down.

Pamela started for the door. "Thanks for the reminder, Mephisto. One would think I had nothing to do. I hope, Terry dear, that they give you a good tip. If the plot germs, A and B, are men, they will. I'm not so sure about women."

"No two of a kind in it if it's a matter of sentiment, I'll bet my hat."

"I can stand this mess we are in but it seems as if

I couldn't bear it for Terry," Pamela told herself as she entered the big sunny kitchen. The floor was covered with a gray and white linoleum, patterned like tiles. Chairs and tables repeated the color of the pale green walls. The girl flinched mentally even as she approved the charming effect. She had bought the paint and floor covering before she had known of the flock of bills which came flying home to roost soon after the family had moved into the old Leigh homestead.

She shook off the depression which thought of the indebtedness wrapped round her spirit like a smothering cloak and tried to be just. Why shouldn't the creditors clamor for their money? They had supplied the goods. If only she could pay them.

She beat potatoes to swansdown delicacy, added rich cream and seasoning and fluffed again. She struggled valiantly against bitterness as she remembered her last Thanksgiving. Terry had come from school to join her in the city. They had had a grand and glorious time. Twice to the theatre. Lunch and dinner at gay restaurants. She mashed copper-golden squash to delectable lightness as her thoughts trooped on. The financial crash had swept away not only her father's fortune but the money their mother had left to her children. He had gone to pieces physically — so characteristic of him not to brace with all his force to see a difficult situation through. Young Mrs. Leigh had sent for her, had furiously condemned her husband for his lack of judgment; had declared that it was the duty of his two children whom he had expensively brought up — just as if all parents didn't spend money on their children when they could — to look after him now that he was a physical wreck, that she would return to the stage. That night she had departed with all available cash, leaving hotel bill, doctors, nurses unpaid. Pamela's throat contracted as she remembered her dazed bewilderment. Her father had quarreled furiously with Phineas Carr, the lawyer who had been his mother's adviser, who had settled the estate. She couldn't go to him. She had sent for Terrence. Together they had worked out the plan to take their father to the Cape Cod farm house which Grandmother Leigh had left to her with all its contents, with acres of shore land, a short time before. She had given up newspaper work to become home-maker and nurse. The legacy had included fine diamonds. Those had been sold to pay hotel, nurses and doctors. How it had hurt. She adored jewels. She had been glad to get away from the city, with its reminding shop windows glittering with gems.

An automobile! Stopping? She slipped a pan of oysters — with pink strips of bacon between their rough shells — into the oven. Excitement rouged her cheeks. If she made good this time the two advertisers would recommend the Silver Moon, and its fame would spread and spread and spread. Once established, she would make a specialty of chowders, lobster, clam, fish, corn, egg, the variety was end-less. Pies for dessert. Her friend Madge Jarvis had put the idea into her mind.

"Of course you can earn money at home. Think up something different for people to eat and your fortune's made, Pam. The path worn bare to the door of the mythical mousetrap man won't be in it with the path to yours. Grandmother Leigh en-dowed you with something of infinitely more value than house and lands and jewels, when she taught you to cook. Your lobster chowder would make the mouth of that iron dog on your lawn water; as to your pie-crust—"

Terrence banged open the door. His eyes sparkled with excitement. "They've come!"

Spoon in hand Pamela tiptoed forward. Whis-pered in her turn: "What are they like?"

"Man and girl. Classy roadster. Black with wide brilliant red stripe, stainless steel wheels, red morocco upholstery. It's a bird! She's little and blonde, swanky fur coat. He's big and strong."

"Young?"

"So-so. Ready?"

"Will be when the glasses are filled."

Pamela pulled the pan from the oven. Big, plump oysters with crisp curls of bacon, sizzled in their own juices as she arranged six of the hot shells around a frilled half of lemon rosy with pa-prika, on a doily covered plate. She sniffed. Done to a turn. Luscious smell.

Would A and B be too absorbed in one another

to notice the maple chest, the Sully over the lowboy, the Queen Anne mirror, the Sandwich glass in the corner cupboard, the Lowestoft punchbowl? She still had those. She would work her fingers to the bone before she sold them. To what extent was she morally responsible for her father's debts? Good grief, wasn't serving the dinner enough without getting those on her mind?

"Let's go, Pam!"

Terrence in a white coat followed his excited whisper into the sunny kitchen. He picked up the plates of oysters from the porcelain-top table, kicked open the door and disappeared. Pamela listened, caught the murmur of voices, a laugh that sent a faint vibration through her heart which had seemed numb these last nightmarish months.

What sort of girl would a man with a laugh like that care for, she wondered as she surrounded the delectably browned turkey with crisp sausages, sunk cranberries deep in the curled greenness of garnishing parsley for a bit of color.

"Hi!"

The sepulchral whisper came from the other side of the swing door. She pulled it open, admitted Terrence with a plate in each hand.

"Crazy about the oysters, A, the man, is. Take it from me, B, the girl couldn't be crazy about anything. She's a snappy number, though," he admitted before he disappeared with the hot dinner plates.

He was back in a moment for the turkey. As Pamela held the door wide for him she glanced at the dining room mirror to glimpse the paying guests. She gazed straight into reflected amused eyes, a man's eyes. They set her heart, which she had thought numb, to quick-stepping. She let the door swing shut with a suddenness which caught Terrence in the heels with a bang. She heard Mephisto's explosive,

"Gosh!"

"A's as pleased as a kid with an all-day sucker, that he has a turkey to carve," Terrence confided, as he picked up a dish of fluffy potato and one heaped with squash of feathery lightness.

"He can't get any come-back from the girl, though," he continued when he returned from serving the onions, white, bursting from tenderness in the yellow of melted butter — the giblet gravy, smooth, brown, piping hot in its silver boat. "First she found fault because there wasn't any soup. I explained in the grand manner that we never served soup before turkey, thought it killed the hanker for the national bird. Then she fussed because he hadn't provided cocktails. If you ask me, I'll say he has a rocky road ahead if he has that ball and chain fastened to him for life."

"Cocktails! Grandmother Leigh always served sweet cider! Thought that was as important with a Thanksgiving dinner as the turkey," Pamela protested. She whisked French dressing with the eggbeater before pouring it on the salad, pale green lettuce and perfect segments of chilled grapefruit, with a fig stuffed with a fluffy mixture of cheeses on the side of the plate. As she added a pink flush of paprika to its delicate yellowness she glanced at the clock. Mehitable Betts would arrive soon to help with the dishes. After Terry had taken in the dessert and coffee she would carry her father's dinner up to him. She dreaded his caustic comments. He was bitterly opposed to the Silver Moon idea, though he had no constructive money-producing plan to offer in its place.

She marked the pies in generous portions. Apple, baked in an oblong tin, the four corners lusciously candied with molasses which had been used for sweetening in place of sugar; mince pie; pumpkin pie. She stopped to look at the world outside. Two snow birds were busily pecking for their Thanksgiving dinner in the rusty grass, in front of the cottage which had once housed the farmer and his family. Purple shadows from drifting clouds cast curious patterns on the sand dunes. A rising breeze was kicking up white caps, which looked as if the sparkling blue and green sea had acquired a passion for lace ruffles. Marvelous afternoon. The dining room door swung under the urge of a vigorous kick. Terrence dodged in holding the pewter platter. He deposited it on the table, whispered:

"B's name is Hilda. Hilda Crane."

"Tender?"

He reached for a tempting sliver of white meat. "Hilda? Anything but—"

"Silly, I mean the turkey."

"I'll say it was. The joint fell away almost as the knife touched it. Made my mouth water. A said, 'Cooked to a turn!' She didn't eat fifty cents', let alone five dollars', worth, glory be." He returned to the dining room. When he came back with the plates he whispered:

"A's name is Scott Mallory."

"Mallory! His letter was signed, 'Cryder.'"

"Secretary, maybe."

With the dishes of vegetables, he contributed: "She's all excited because he insisted upon 'dragging' her to the country for Thanksgiving, she thought she was going where there would be music and dancing. She said: 'I hate sentiment—' then he crashed in, explaining that he hadn't had a real old-fashioned dinner since he went to South America, two years ago, that all the while he was away he kept dreaming about one. He's been back a month. Wanted a Thanksgiving dinner on the Cape. Advertised. Can't make out whether they're engaged or he's teetering on the brink of a proposal. He'd better Stop! Look! Listen! before he plunges. She's the kind who'll try to make him sit up, roll over and play dead dog. Salad looks grand," he approved as he picked up the green crystal plates.

When he came back with them empty he encouraged: "The snooty Hilda made no crack at that."

"Thank heaven, she has liked something. Clear the table. Put on the dessert plates and come back for the pies."

"Boy! Those smell good!" Terrence sniffed upon his return. He munched a flaky bit of crust. "A's getting colder and colder. That B has taken the fun out of his party. He was jolly and talkative when he came. She makes me think of the second Mrs. Leigh."

Pamela stood on one foot and then the other, to relieve the tired ache in them, as she poured steaming, dark amber coffee into a squat silver pot.

"That's the type which catches the big strong men. They like 'em little and grafting."

She prepared a tray for her father. Slipped a pan of oysters into the oven. Terrence came out with the pie-plates.

"B wouldn't touch hers. A's white with fury. He was saying something when I went in about intending to see this dinner through. He stopped short. And she said hateful like — wanted me to hear, I'll bet — 'See it through then! I shan't.' How I hate rows. Just as if life in this house wasn't enough of a trail of conflict with Father upstairs seeing things battle-ship gray, without having 'em brought in by our customers."

"Clientele, Terry. Clientele, it is less commercial," Pamela corrected with an attempt at gaiety.

"Bring out the pies. Then put the nuts and rasins on the table. Let the snappy Hilda pour the coffee. I will get Father's dinner ready."

As she removed the oysters from the oven she struck her hand against the door. The contact left an angry red burn across her fingers.

"Ooch! That smarts!"

She covered the turkey and vegetables with a hot plate, added crisp celery and cranberry jelly to the tray.

Harold Leigh, in a deep chair by the sunny window, frowned as his daughter entered his room. A table in front of him was strewn with postage stamps and a loose-leaf book. Sunshine accentuated the whiteness of his hair, turned his skin to the color of old wax. How old he looked, yet he was only fifty-five, Pamela reminded herself. His nose seemed about to hook into his upper lip. His resemblance to the portrait in the dining room was startling. He tapped the arm of his chair impatiently.

"Always the last one to be thought of. It's an hour past my usual dinner time."

"Sorry, but I couldn't bring it before." She pushed the stamp-laden table aside and pulled up another for the tray. Eagerly he lifted the top of one of the shells. Plump, juicy, the oyster yielded an appetizing aroma. He frowned, picked up a strip of bacon.

"I hope what you served downstairs was crisper than this. I suppose anything will do for me."

Pamela opened her lips, closed them. Why retort? She would say something for which she would be sorry later and this was Thanksgiving Day. Why take away his grievance? He would have nothing to talk about. She swallowed the lump which always rose in her throat at his irritation with her. With the assurance that she would bring the dessert later she left the room.

Curious that her father still had power to hurt her, she thought, as she went slowly down the stairs. As a child she had adored him; he had been gallant and gay, her Prince Charming. One look of affection, one tender word from him, would set little wings on her feet as she ran about to serve him. As the years passed he had grown more and more indifferent to his children; she had been rebuffed whenever her love for him had bubbled to the surface — she had been such a buoyant, bubbly sort of person in those days. His indifference had hardened her toward all men. If she hadn't laughed, she had shrugged at protestations of love. A mental hygienist, doubtless, could explain in scientific terms just what had happened to her heart; she knew only that her father's indifference had smothered something beautiful within her which had glowed.

As she entered the kitchen Terrence burst in from the dining room. His eyes, so like his sister's snapped with excitement; his red hair was rampant; his hoarse voice choked:

"Your plot germs have skipped!"

"Skipped! Terry! Not without—"

"You've said it! Without paying. That girl, Hilda, was opening up, high, wide and handsome because Scott Mallory wouldn't take her home at once. I guess I went goggle-eyed—I'm not used to women who row—for he told me to bring more coffee. Had to heat it a little. When I went back they had gone."

Chapter II

PAMELA crushed down the memory of the amused eyes which had met hers in the mirror. She laughed, a bitter little laugh.

"Managing the Silver Moon is just one disillusioning experience after another, isn't it? Dash after them in the fliv, Terry. If you catch them hang on until you get our money. If—"

Terrence was out of the room before she could finish the sentence. As she collected the plates, wherever she looked the clear, darkly gray eyes with the light of laughter in their depths seemed to meet hers. Never before had she met a man whose eyes had plunged into her heart and warmed it. And now he had run away! Of course, a person such as she had thought him wouldn't chance into the threatening, terrifying world of debt and disillusionment in which she was living.

A resounding knock shook the old door of the kitchen. Pamela glanced at the clock. Too early for Mehitable. Creditors? Their shadows were ever at the heels of her imagination. They couldn't be so inhuman as to come collecting on Thanksgiving! A yellow Ford station wagon had stopped outside. She opened the door. One of the men who had bored into her maple furniture with his gimlet eyes the other day confronted her. He touched his hat as if grudging the courtesy, scowled, demanded truculently:

"Does Harold Leigh live here?"

"Yes. But you can't see him. He is ill."

He called over his shoulder: "All right! This is the house!"

He pushed by Pamela into the kitchen. His hat on the back of his head revealed a forehead which appeared to have no terminal.

"What do you want?"

With cocky condescension he thrust one hand deep into his trousers pocket, waved a sheaf of bills in the other.

"I've come to collect on these."

"Don't shout. You will disturb Mr. Leigh."

"Oh, I will! Well, take it from me, that's what I'm here for. He hasn't answered letters, I'll see if I can get action this way."

He sniffed. His eyes dilated, his nostrils quivered like a rabbit's as he sighted the tempting remains of the turkey, one appetizingly browned side uncut. He stretched out a not too clean hand, seized a piece of white meat with a dangling strip of crisp skin. He had the succulent morsel half way to his mouth when Pamela rapped his knuckles smartly with the silver serving spoon.

"Drop it!"

He dropped it. Her eyes were brilliantly, angrily black, her face colorless as she picked up the scrap between thumb and forefinger, lifted a range lid, flung the white meat into the heart of the red-hot wood embers. The intolerable smart of her burned fingers added fuel to the flame of her fury. The man blustered:

"Treat me like that, will you? Now you'll get what's coming to you. The county sheriff is on the truck outside. I have orders to seize all the antique furniture in this house on account of these bills. See this?"

He threw back the lapel of his coat and revealed a badge of sorts. Pamela looked from it to the man at the wheel of the yellow truck. He was a stranger. She remembered now that the new sheriff was from a town at the other end of the county. No help from him. The collector laughed. Pamela restrained a furious desire to crack his knuckles again. As he took a purposeful step toward the dining room she backed against the swing door.

"You can't go in there."

He stuck his repulsive face close to hers. Shouted, "Can't I?"

The door behind her was jerked open. She fell back against someone, caught a coat lapel, steadied herself.

"He has come to seize the antiques for the creditors. Don't let him take them, Terry! Don't let him take them!"

"Not a chance of his taking them," assured a strange voice.

With a gasp of amazement Pamela looked up into the fine, lean face of a man, into the eyes she had met in the mirror, not amused now, but keen, determined. A! The advertiser! He had returned. Had Terry dragged him back? She didn't care. He had come. He stood behind her like a rock, broad of shoulders, bronzed of face. The rich green of his tie accented the soft grayness of his suit. He was a man one could take on trust, a man one could like immensely, she decided. Doubtless, by the same token, a man about whom many girls and women had thought the same. He stepped into the kitchen. The door swung shut behind him.

"What's going on here?"

The collector swept his finger along the sheaf of papers, thrust out an aggressive chin. "Got a sheriff outside to attach the antique furniture here on these bills. I know it's genuine, brought an expert here for chowder last week and he gave it the once-over. You can take it from me I'm going to get it."

"What's your name?"

"S. Linsky."

"Where's your writ, Slinsky?"

"S. Linsky! S. Linsky!"

"Well, S. Linsky, where is your writ?"

"Here. Think I'd come without it? Take me for a boob?"

"I wouldn't take you on any terms." A—Terrence had said that his name was Scott Mallory, Pamela remembered—examined the writ. "You are attaching the furniture in this house on account of bills owed by Harold Leigh and his wife, Cecile?"

The door behind him swung. Framed in the opening stood almost the prettiest blonde Pamela ever had seen in quite the most stunning fur coat. The girl was gowned with exceeding smartness in blue with a matching hat. With her came a faint scent. *Nuit de Noel. Parfums Caron.* Paris. Pamela recognized it. In the dear dead on-her-own days, she had plunged recklessly to the extent of an ounce of the perfume. The "snappy Hilda" of course, who else? Curling ends of fair hair gleamed from beneath the brim of her hat. Her lips were a brilliant bow, an undertone of angry red flushed her rose-leaf skin, her violet eyes were set in delicately blackened lashes, her arched brows met in a deep line of annoyance. She demanded petulantly:

"Scott! What are you doing? Surely it hasn't taken all this time to pay your bill. You dragged me back when you remembered it although I told you that a mailed check would do just as well." She frowned at Pamela, drawled with acid innuendo: "Perhaps you really came back to say 'au revoir' to the cook. I understand now why you brought me to Cape Cod. It wasn't entirely because of Thanksgiving dinners you had had here as a boy, as you so carefully explained. Cut the farewell short. I want to go home."

Pamela marvelled at Scott Mallory's self-control. Only his darkening eyes and loss of color betrayed his emotions as he apologized:

"Don't mind Miss Crane. She is apt to forget her manners when she loses her temper." He pulled open the swing door. "Wait in the dining room until I come, Hilda."

The girl flushed furiously at his reproof, set her head at a supercilious angle.

"I won't wait a moment. You are to come at once or I go — at once."

Pamela caught Scott Mallory's arm. "Please go. Don't bother about my affairs. I'm not afraid of Slinsky, really I'm not."

"S. Linsky!" The collector growled correction.

Mallory looked down at the angry burn which streaked the fingers on his sleeve, at the bald-headed man smirking satisfaction at the situation. His face was a mask as he demanded:

"Let me get this right, S. Linsky. You are attaching the furniture in this house on account of bills owed by Harold Leigh and his wife?"

Hilda Crane stood like a girl of stone. There was an instant of prickling tension before Mallory repeated his question. Was he as unaware as he seemed of the vicious bang of the swing door behind her as she dashed from the room? Linsky swelled with gratified importance, like a puff pig when its stomach is scratched.

"That's the stuff."

"You are sure that it is his furniture?"

"Sure. Didn't she say he was upstairs too sick to come down?"

Mallory looked at the papers in his hand. Demanded of Pamela:

"Are you Cecile Leigh? Wife of Harold?"

"No! I am his daughter."

"Does the furniture in this house belong to Harold Leigh or his wife?"

The side door opened. Pamela's heart thumped madly. The sheriff? Come for her old maple and the Lowestoft bowl? She sighed relief. It was Mehitable Betts looking more like a gaunt grey wolf than ever. Darn! She would spread the news of the sheriff's visit all over town before night. Mallory reminded:

"You haven't answered my question. To whom does the furniture belong?"

"To me. Every piece of it."

He held out the writ. "That settles that, S. Linsky."

The collector bristled like a hedgehog charging. "Settles it! How do you get that way! Of course she'd say it belonged to her. That girl wasn't born yesterday." He rubbed one hand over the reddened knuckles of the other.

"Well, then, I say it's hers!" Mehitable Betts, skin and thin hair as drab as her skimpy dress, jerked her steel bowed spectacles back to the bridge of her nose before she folded her arms across her flat breast. Bony hands gripping her elbows, she belligerently confronted the doubter. " I lived with old M's Leigh goin' on twenty years, on and off. I signed my name at the bottom of her will a few days before she died. And when lawyer Carr carried it away she says to me, ' Hitty,' she says, ' I'm leavin' this house and everything in it to Pamela,' she says. ' That hoity-toity stage woman Hal's married is not our kind of folks, she wouldn't know old maple from pine kindlin',' she says, ' she'd sell it. Pamela'll hold on to it for her children and her children's children.' "

Scott Mallory suggested : " That's all, S. Linsky. There isn't any more."

The collector's already high color took on a purplish tinge. " Ain't there? Perhaps not just now but I'll be back for that fake sick man upstairs."

" Better get after his attorney."

" Do you think we haven't tried? He hasn't one and his wife's skipped. I knew the girl wasn't her. He couldn't pay the price of an attorney."

Mallory presented a business card. " I am his attorney. I am acting for Miss Leigh, too. You will find me at that address."

Linsky scowled at the bit of pasteboard. There was more than a hint of awe in his voice as he inquired :

" Are you the Mallory who's trying that big case against those South American fellas? "

" The same Mallory."

With an inarticulate growl S. Linsky slouched

out. Pamela watched him climb aboard the Ford truck. He was gesticulating angrily as it turned down the road. She looked up at the man beside her.

"I can't begin to thank you for saving my lovely old maple. Knowing absolutely nothing of legal procedure, I might have bitten and scratched to keep it and in the end let it go to pay my father's debts."

"Don't let anything go. I owe you an apology for tearing off without paying my bill. I was so boiling mad that not until I reached the village did I remember. Then, in spite of — well, I came back."

"You didn't meet Terry?"

"Terry? Is that your brother's name? No, I didn't meet him. Was he after me to collect?"

His smile lighted even the closed garden of her heart into which she had locked her ambition to make good in her profession. He suggested:

"Come into the dining room. I am sure that I can help. You will let me, won't you?"

The impatient tinkle of a bell came from the floor above. "Good grief, I've forgotten Father's dessert." Pamela seized a plate. Mehitable Betts grabbed it.

"Give me that! Had any dinner?" The girl shook her head. "Hmp! Thought not. Go right into the dining room and set. You're beat out doing the cooking. Ought to have put vinegar on your burned fingers. I'll bring you something to eat and then I'll tend to your Pa. I'm not afraid of any man living. Folks is sayin' he'd be a sight better if you didn't coddle him, if he got out and found a job 'stead of hivin' up in his room licking his wounds. You and your beau go into the dining room."

Pamela snatched off her white cap, slipped out of the voluminous apron. She pulled down the sleeves of her yellow frock as Mallory pushed open the swing door. As they entered the sunny room she put a hand to her flushed cheek.

" Don't mind Hitty's conclusions. To her, every man is a potential beau; that is her word, not mine. Why — where is Miss Crane? S. Linsky was so upsetting, I forgot about her. She must be waiting in the living room. Please, please don't bother about me any more."

Hands in his gray coat pockets Mallory stood at the window. "I suspect that Miss Crane is now speeding toward home in my roadster. It's gone."

" Gone to C!"

He swung round to face her. "Gone to sea in a roadster?"

" C, the letter, not s-e-a. It is part of a plot diagram Terry and I imagined. You, the advertiser, were A. Your friend was B. C was your objective when you left the Silver Moon. My affairs dotted your life-lines and sent each of you off at a tangent. I'm sorry. Miss Crane hated everything about the place, didn't she?"

Mallory shook his head, explained slowly as if he were thinking the situation through: "It was not

the place, it was the man. Curious how a person **can**
change. Perhaps it isn't the person, perhaps it is
one's point of view. Hilda Crane was on the boat
coming up from B. A. She was the first American
girl I had played round with in two years. She was
good fun. Gradually she suffered a land-change. I
wouldn't believe that I could be so mistaken in a
person, have always thought I was a wonder at reading character. I hoped that if we had an old-
fashioned Thanksgiving dinner together — I hadn't
told her that we were not going to a gay place, my
mistake — shows what an incurable nineteenth century romantic I am — the girl I had imagined her to
be might return. She didn't, so, that's that."

He laid money on the table. "Sorry, I forgot it.
The dinner was perfect. My secretary, Jane Cryder,
selected your answer to my advertisement from
among fifty others. None of my friends are old-
fashioned enough — perhaps New England enough
— to serve the kind of dinner I remembered. I
wanted to spend the day on the Cape. I craved a
whiff of the country in which I was born, wanted to
come back to it, if only for a day, with a fresh appreciation of what it had meant to me as a boy. Miss
Cryder selected your reply because she loved your
name, Pamela Leigh. Isn't that like a woman's
reasoning? I will admit that in this case it was intuition. Suppose I talk with your father about those
bills while you are having your dinner?"

"Will you? The hounding creditors are such

a nightmare." The eagerness departed from her eyes and voice. "But, we have no money with which to pay a lawyer."

"I haven't earned a fee yet. After all, you don't know anything about me. Why should you trust me? That's merely a rhetorical question. I hope you will. Here is my card. Put a Bertillon expert on my fingerprints, if you wish."

Pamela looked down at the bit of pasteboard in her hand, up at the gray eyes watching her.

"I trust you without the expert."

"Thank you."

Gaunt Mehitable Betts with a plate in each hand kicked open the swing door. The parrot broke into a wheezy chuckle. "Look who's here!" he croaked sardonically.

Pamela hastily averted the tirade she knew would follow. The woman and bird were ancient enemies.

"Hitty, will you show Mr. Mallory to Father's room?"

Miss Betts set down the plates with a bang. "Sure I'll show him up. Like's not he'll show him down, quick, but he looks as if he could stand it."

Her father had not shown Scott Mallory down, Pamela rejoiced, as an half hour later she arranged the table silver in the drawer of the maple lowboy. She could hear the rumble of voices overhead. Terrence poked his red head into the room.

"The plot germs came back all right, didn't they? Saw the roadster beating it this way just as I was shooting through the village. Mr. Mallory'll lose his train if he doesn't get a hustle on. Just asked me to take him to the station. I'll say that the girl had nerve to go off in his sporty roadster. He gave Hitty and me each a fat tip. I returned mine. Hurt like the dickens to let it go but I wouldn't take money from him when he has offered to help Father. But Hitty — boy! When she realized what she had in her hand — Miss Betts lugged out pail and brush, flopped to her knees and began scrubbing the kitchen floor. Listen to her hymn of praise." From the other side of the door rose a rough voice hoarse from disuse.

"'Praise God from whom all blessings flow
    Praise Him all creatures here below
    Praise Him above ye —'" the song cracked and rattled into a gurgle.

"Poor Hitty. Life hasn't handed her many tips. You'd better remind Mr. Mallory of the time."

Eyes on the shifting color values of sea and shore Pamela stood at the window. A far off white sail flashed against the dusky horizon like a bit of mother-of-pearl. Beyond the orchard stretched a forest of scrub oaks and stunted pines through which at intervals white birches gleamed like swaying ghosts. Rose tints in the blueness of the sky deepened to claret. What a day! Scott Mallory appearing like a modern dragon-slayer at the exact dramatic moment. The relief, the inexpressible relief of knowing that there was someone of whom she could ask advice. Should she allow him to help

when she couldn't pay him? The same old obstacle
bobbed up to confront her at every step. Money!
Money! Money! She turned as Mallory entered.
Terrence hovered impatiently in the background.

"Your father has authorized me to represent
him. I have a list of his securities — somewhat of
a misnomer — and debts. I hope to pull enough out
of the lot to settle up, stop this nightmare, as you
call it. If a creditor appears or phones refer him
to me."

"We haven't any money to pay — "

"Don't think of that. Let me help." On a
breath of laughter he suggested, "I'll collect my bill
in chowders. How's that?"

"Ready to go now, Scott?" From the hall
threshold Hilda Crane asked the question. Her
pleading violet eyes seemed too big for her small
face, her painted mouth too red. "Did you think I
had run away? I wouldn't leave you. Been poking
round the antique shops in the village waiting for
you to finish your important business." Her voice
was honeyed.

Her tone, her pouting lips, her provocative eyes,
set off little fiery pinwheels in Pamela's mind.
Giving an imitation of the charming girl of the
steamer, was she?

Scott Mallory's voice was as grim as his lips.
"My business is finished, Hilda. You have ruined
this day, and by rights you should be sent home by
train, but, when I start out on a party with a girl
I see it through. Go on."

She hesitated.

"Goo'-bye! Goo'-bye!" croaked the red and green parrot testily.

Terrence camouflaged a chuckle in a racking cough. "Sorry! Have these attacks occasionally." He patted his sister's arm before he left the room. His song drifted back.

> "'The fool frog sank in the swashing tank
>   As the farmer bumped to town.
> But the smart frog flew like a tug-boat screw,
>   And he swore he'd not go down.'"

Pamela choked back a nervous giggle as she sensed his reminder to her. Hilda flung her a furious glance before she sauntered into the hall.

Mallory caught Pamela's hands in his. "I'm coming back — tomorrow. Dinner for two."

Aware that Miss Crane was observing them, Pamela explained gaily: "Second-day party, we call it on the Cape. Like warmed-over turkey?"

"Mad about it."

"Then come. There are dozens of questions I want to ask you about Father's business."

He spread the burned fingers gently on his palm, looked down into her gallantly smiling eyes.

"Sweet child!" He cleared his voice. "When I have answered them I have one or two to ask you."

"Scott!"

"Coming Hilda."

Chapter III

◆

WITH a growl like the distant rumble of thunder
the Belgian police dog in his smart breast strap
sprang at his double standing near the curb of the
sidewalk before the post-office in the village. The
challenged one laid back his ears, snarled, bared
his teeth invitingly. Pamela Leigh's dark eyes dilated with concern even as she caught the challenger
by the collar, tried to drag him back.

"Stop it, Babe!"

"Drop him! Good God, drop him!" shouted
a man who was leaping down the steps of the brick
building three at a time. The girl had a confused
sense of brown hair, blazing eyes, brown skin, curiously blanched, a mustache like a third eyebrow, impeccable sports clothes, the faint, far drone of a
plane beating like a rhythmic pulse in the air, before
she tightened her hold. She twisted the leather
collar, choked the aggressor back upon his haunches.
The man snatched at the tail of the other Belgian,
yanked him away. He deftly caught the dog's collar, face ashen, demanded:

"Don't you know better than to mix up in a scrap

like this?" He turned at a shout behind him, glared at the man in an army coat belted with a rope who was running toward them. "This dog yours, Eddie Pike? Grab him. What the devil do you mean by letting a fighter like this loose?"

The breathless, unshaven man, with a mouth designed on codfish lines, caught his charge by an upright ear, glanced apologetically at the girl who still clutched the collar of the challenger.

"Sorry, Miss Pamela." He scowled at his accuser. "Why shouldn't I let him loose? 'Twant him started the trouble. There ain't no law 'gainst exercising dogs here, are there? Come along, Bozo."

He snapped on a leash. With a rumble and a savage glare in the direction of his adversary Bozo obediently started off at his keeper's heels.

Now that the late unpleasantness was over Pamela's knees wobbled treacherously, her heart pounded deafeningly. Under pretense of adjusting the Babe's breast-strap she dropped to the steps. A vision of the picture the contending factions had presented set her a-quiver with nervous laughter. The man protested with a hint of arrogance:

"What's the joke? Can't see the comedy in taking a chance on getting chewed to pulp."

Pamela made a valiant effort at control, explained in a voice still shredded with mirth: "When you grabbed that horrid dog's tail—I thought—I thought even as I choked the Babe—sup-suppose it sh-should come off? After that your technique was su-superb." The sentence ended in a spasmodic gurgle.

"Pull yourself together. I don't wonder you were frightened. You'll have hysterics if you don't watch your step."

"I never had hysterics in my life." Indignation brought Pamela to her feet. She met his concerned eyes defiantly, even as she admitted to herself that she had been frightened, she never had been in the ring at a dog-fight before.

"Beg pardon for yelling at you when I butted in on the little party, but your recklessness frightened me stiff."

"But not dumb."

He laughed. She liked his laugh.

"I'm sorry. May I get your mail?"

She looked from him to the dog who had dropped to the sidewalk, whose throat rumbled as with a retreating thunder-shower.

"If you will. The Babe is as popular in the post-office as an ice-storm in an orange-grove. The R.F.D. man collects from the box at our gate in the early morning as he passes. Delivers at noon. We come for the afternoon mail. Box 52. I'm Pamela Leigh." Did he look startled as he turned away or was it merely her imagination?

She sank to the steps. The vicious line-up of the two dogs had left her limp as a de-sawdusted doll. Catch her bringing the Babe to the village again.

Babe! Anything but. Soon after that memorable Thanksgiving dinner for two, Scott Mallory had asked them to board the dog. He had tried to keep him in his apartment, much to the detriment of the furniture which he had a playful habit of chewing, and the indignation of neighboring tenants. Who was the man who had come to her rescue? A native son home for the week-end? He was about twenty-eight. Nothing so young in males had crossed her path since she had come in June to live in Grandmother Leigh's house.

Perfect afternoon. Lavender-winged gulls soared and dove above the sand dunes which were patched with the shadows of drifting snowy clouds. The out-going tide pitilessly exposed their sea-weedy, tin-can strewn gums; trailed fringes of white foam as it ebbed in curling amber-green waves. Beyond stretched an indigo sea, amethystine where it met the horizon. The sun dropped behind the highest dune, splashed the sky above with lovely color. Pamela felt its beauty like a tangible thing. Crimson, lemon, green, orange, fluffs of mauve, scarfs of rose. Lavish splendor! The afterglow tinted the roofs of the sedate old houses which bordered the main street, gilded the black bands on their white chimneys, transformed windows into molten sheets of brass and copper. Columns of smoke from wood fires spiraled and spread. The air was soft, salty, with an indefinable hint of spring. Pamela filled her lungs with it. This wasn't much like a February afternoon in New York City. One couldn't go about coatless in a green jersey frock there, at this time of year.

She watched the villagers trickling out of the post-office. She knew them all. One couldn't live in an old house which one had inherited in a Cape Cod town without being the object of speculation, the cynosure of every eye when one appeared in public, especially when every living inhabitant above ground—and perhaps some under—knew of the creditors who had hovered like vultures to collect the bills which her father and his wife had lavishly contracted before the crash.

Had hovered! Since the day Scott Mallory had offered to help straighten out the mess, she had not heard from one. Had he in some miraculous way managed to quiet them? Whatever had happened it was a respite for her. She no longer suffered the nausea of apprehension and humiliation when she answered door or telephone bell.

The man who had barged into the dog fight approached with a handful of white envelopes and newspapers.

"Looks as if you would be submerged in a greeting-card blizzard."

She dropped the mail into a basket woven of gay colors. "Thanks lots. Tomorrow will be my birthday. Everyone I ever knew has sent a greeting this year. I suspect that as they posted them my friends sighed.

"'Poor Pam! Marooned on Cape Cod.' Come Babe."

The dog rose leisurely, stretched one hind leg after another, yawned, wagged his tail.

"Mind if I walk with you? Our house is at the foot of the hill. I am Philip Carr."

Philip Carr! Son of Grandmother Leigh's legal adviser with whom her father had quarreled furiously! Quarreled because the lawyer had urgently advised him to carry out his mother's expressed wish, that he settle a sum of money on each of his children. Had the senior Carr had a premonition of what was to happen, had he lacked faith in Harold Leigh's judgment? Whichever it was, it was a pity he hadn't won out.

Philip Carr, about whom the townspeople conjectured, romanced, gossiped and whispered not too kindly! Several years before, his father had restored the house of his paternal great-grandfather for use a few months of the year. "Spoiled, terrible spoiled and a born lady-killer," Hitty Betts had described the son. He seemed more like a grown-up boy out of tune with the world, whose brown eyes sparked defiance, whose full red lips below the slight mustache curved in a suggestion of contempt. In spite of what she had heard in disparagement, she liked him.

"Well? Does my request require so much wrinkled-brow consideration? Say no, if you don't care for what you've heard about me. Our neighbors here are a sturdy little band of knockers.

They've told you probably that I spend most of my time about theatres. I do. Not because I'm crazy about actors as people, but because I want to design stage-settings. You may feel that we have not been properly introduced. Have I made a social blunder? Perhaps I should not have spoken to you until a third party had shouted above the growls and barks of the contending factions: ' Miss Leigh, allow me to present Mr. Carr.' "

She ignored the bitterness of his voice. " Introduced! Don't be silly! I have no aversion to theatres — I'm mad about them — or actors " — " except one actress," she added under her breath.

She saw the color steal to his hair, caught the instant's unsteadiness of his boyish mouth. Evidently he had been hurt. Nothing in the world was more cruel than small-town gossip. Often she had seen Mehitable Betts clamp her lips, before she opened them to preface a bit of scandal with:

" Folks is sayin' — "

Philip Carr shifted step to suit hers. " How long have you had that scrapper? "

" He isn't a scrapper. Usually he is beautifully mannered. He's just temperamental like some humans. You can't be expected to like every dog you meet, can you, Babe? " She patted the head of the Belgian who was walking sedately beside her. " He doubtless had an attack of indigestion and took it out on someone else — as do the majority of his sex."

"Not a high opinion of mortal man, have you?"

"You have guessed it. We are taking care of the Babe — we, means Terrence, my brother, and me — for our legal adviser." The last phrase induced a sense of financial solidity.

They approached a big Colonial house in a setting of spruce hedges. Pamela caught a glimpse of an old-fashioned garden in the rear tucked in for the winter. She approved enthusiastically:

"You have the loveliest home in the village. We are all so glad to have it open again."

"All right to have it open if you are not expected to live in it. Father and Mother hurried home from Europe to be sure the cold frames were started so that plants for the garden would go in early. So they say. I suspect that he is pawing the ground in his eagerness to get back into court. He says that he is through with legal battling, but he never will be so long as he finds a case which interests him. It's in his blood. Did you meet my people before they went across?"

"No. I haven't seen your father since he and my father clashed over the settlement of Grandmother Leigh's estate."

"Montague and Capulet stuff?" His smile was boyish. "That wouldn't make any difference to Mother if she liked you and she will. How did anything so vivid as you get caught in this Cape Cod tidepool? This is my third visit since the house was opened. I can't stand it more than twenty-four hours at a time."

Pamela remembered Hitty Betts' comment on the son and heir of the town's plutocrats. "Folks is sayin', that Phil Carr will bring the gray hair of his parents in sorrow to the grave. He goes with a fast lot of young folks, movie and theatre crowd mostly."

Of course, the natives would think him on the moral toboggan slide if his ideas of propriety differed from theirs. Their views on matters theatrical were strictly seventeenth century, Puritan. She met his friendliness with a swift explanation of her presence in the "tidepool." Added gayly:

"Seeing more immediate returns from cooking than from writing I turned Grandmother Leigh's old home into the Silver Moon Chowder House. Silver Moon because of the roses with mother-of-pearl petals and golden hearts which climb over the walls in June. Making money feeding people is stodgily pre-Lindbergh, isn't it? Since that epoch-making flight, girls are going in for all sorts of aviation angles, radio announcing, business management, banking, posing for commercial photographs, anything which isn't tarred with domesticity. I had to make money at home."

"It's sporting of you. I know your place. Used to go there with Father. While he conferred with your grandmother, the farmer's wife filled me up with milk and cookies in her cottage. Do you make the Silver Moon pay serving only chowders?"

"The point is well taken. As I'm not an Alice Foote McDougal yet, while I'm building up the business I give patrons what they ask for. Someone phoned for a reservation for six tomorrow and ordered young pig. Ever seen a young pig ready for roasting? Rear view it looks so like a plump fair-skinned baby that I salted it with my tears, figuratively speaking. I will sidestep and make Mehitable Betts put it into the oven." She was aware of his cynical regard.

"You don't impress me as being tender-hearted. There is a frozen quality in your voice which makes me a little afraid of you."

"Ever had your feet so cold at a football game that you wished they would hurry up and get numb so they would stop hurting? I am hoping that my heart will freeze so that it will stop feeling. Being a house-owner seems to be just one repair after another. Terry reported this morning that the roof of the farmer's cottage — which you remember — was leaking like a sieve. I wish the building would consume itself before the taxes consume it." She went on lightly: "Forget the sobbie. Don't think that I dislike my business venture — perhaps adventure; I love contact with people, even if I do hate having them wandering all over the house and patronizing, ' Nice little place!' Feeding them is just one problem after another."

"Are you the cook?"

"I am. At this stage of the enterprise I can't afford to have even one guest find anything wrong."

"You don't care a little bit about yourself, do you?"

" Crazy about Pamela Leigh," she attested gaily. "Oh, there's your mother! I met her once years ago but she probably does not remember me."

A woman in a smart gray gown was waiting at the gate. Her hair was surprisingly white in contrast to her youthful skin. Her eyes were as brown, as eager as her son's. She held out her hand.

" Miss Leigh, I am so glad to see you again. I have been wondering how soon I might run up to call. I wanted Phil to meet you but apparently he has accomplished that pleasure without my help. Won't you come in for tea? "

Had the son wirelessed that suggestion to his mother? "Thank you, but I must hurry home. We have a full day tomorrow. Has Terry brought the eggs you ordered? When I left he was in the poultry house mumbling incantations over the hens. With that utter disregard of the timely so characteristic of the species, they have gone on strike just as you have opened your house."

" You don't mean that you run a poultry farm as well as the Silver Moon? "

" The poultry is my brother's enterprise, Mr. Carr. I wouldn't go so far as to say that he runs it. At present it is running him — ragged. However, as we have adopted for our coat of arms two green frogs, a milkpail rampant, with Kick Frog! Kick! illumined on a silver field, we should worry."

The blaze of admiration in his eyes brought warm color to her face. The drone of a plane overhead almost drowned his boyish wheedle. "Mother, ask the little girl if your little boy may play with her."

Mrs. Carr regarded him with smiling adoration. "Phil's unprecedented shyness takes my breath. May he call? I should be happy to have you friends."

"I would love to have him come after business hours, but you are witness to my warning, I am dull company at the end of the day."

"I'll risk that. Do you good to go for an airing in my roadster. I'm a safe non-skid driver warranted steady at the wheel. Here comes the omnipresent Milly! Wouldn't you know it? The fairies who presided at that girl's advent into this old world scrimped on her chin and spread themselves on her bump of curiosity. How can you stand her snooping, Mother?"

"Because she is an excellent waitress, prefers to remain near her brother, and while she spends every cent she can get on clothes she hasn't the city urge. What is it, Milly?"

The girl in a pink linen frock with dainty white collar and cuffs and apron, who had run down the path, was slightly breathless. Her pale blue eyes were interrogation points as they shifted from face to face, her mouth was a trifle pinched, her light hair waved close to her head, her skin suggested the tint and texture of a magnolia blossom. If she had a trifle more chin and a suggestion of soul in her make-up, she would be beautiful, Pamela decided.

She took an instant dislike to her. Untrustworthy.
Philip Carr was right. She had prying eyes.

"Mr. Phil! Long distance call."

"Must be my client." He chuckled. "Why are
our offices crowded?"

Mrs. Carr's eyes were starry. "Phil! Have
you a client? Did you get the theatre contract?"

Her son reddened, laughed. "Mother! Why
reveal the humiliating fact that this is my first?"
He pointed his question by a glance at the maid who
with jaw slightly dropped was staring at him. "See
you tonight, Miss Leigh," he called back as he
started for the house.

"M's Carr, please may I go down to the field to
see the airplane? I've never seen one close," pleaded
Milly Pike.

"Run along, but be here in ample time to serve
dinner."

The girl raced away. The street, which had
seemed under the spell of an afternoon siesta, suddenly came alive. Men and women boiled out of
houses to hurry in the direction of the field.

Pamela's fingers tightened on the Babe's leash.
"I'd better get back to the Silver Moon. There
were no reservations for the afternoon so I left
Hitty Betts in charge while I ran away for an hour.
She won't be able to resist the lure of that plane."

Mrs. Carr's eyes were luminous. "My dear,
you will never know until you have a son of your
own how glad I am that Phil met you. It was tact-

less of me to betray the fact that he has not been overworked. He took up architecture against his father's wishes — my husband wanted him to be a lawyer — and studied abroad. Now he has opened an office in New York. Too much leisure is a menace to any man. I don't like the young people with whom he has associated since he came from Europe, their idea of twentieth century liberation seems to be to acquire habits which shackle them with steel. Not but what they are decent enough," she hastened to assure loyally, "but they don't bring out the best in Philip. You will." With which declaration of faith she turned away.

Chapter IV

———◆———

PAMELA absentmindedly returned greetings of villagers as they passed on their way to the store. Terrence, buoyant with the zest of living, his auburn hair glinting red-gold in the late sunlight, dashed by with a basket.

"Got to deliver these — eggs — going to see the plane," he shouted as he passed.

Her thoughts returned to her meeting with Philip Carr. Had she been too friendly? After but five minutes' acquaintance she had practically told him the story of her life. Would she ever learn to be reserved with strangers? If she liked a person at all she was too ready to credit him or her with all the virtues. She must have inherited her Virginia mother's friendliness along with Grandmother Leigh's New England conscience.

What would young Carr's father think of their friendship? He had been Grandmother Leigh's adviser for years. Her husband had willed half of his large estate to his son, Harold, half in trust to his wife, the income to be hers, at her death the principal to revert to their son. He had given no thought to protecting the interests of his grand-children. Immersed in important legal battles as Carr was, he had found time to attend to his elderly client's business.

Her faith and dependence upon the advice of her attorney, the fact that she had appointed him sole executor of her estate, had maddened her son. He had been insultingly antagonistic to Phineas Carr's suggestion that he settle even a small amount of money on his children. That he would provide for them generously had been his mother's hope and prayer. The lawyer had steadfastly continued his duties until the estate was settled. He had turned it over to the heir with a few vitriolic comments which had sent Harold Leigh home white-lipped. The remembrance of her father's version of the interview had kept Pamela from consulting her grandmother's old friend when she needed advice. What would he think when he discovered that his son was friendly with the daughter of the man whom he must heartily dislike!

Mehitable Betts met her on the threshold, a shawl flung over her thin drab hair, was drawn severely down across her high temples.

" Land's sake, Pamela, what you thinking 'bout so hard? Look's though you'd been to a funeral. Thought you'd never come. I just got to see that plane. Everything's ready for tomorrow, so I won't come back. You don't need me. 'Most forgot to tell you, while you were out a girl phoned and asked if Mr. Mallory had reservations here tomorrow. I wa'n't born yesterday. So I told her I didn't know and I wouldn't tell her if I did. The way girls nowadays follow up the boys beats me. Milly Pike, who works down at M's Carr's — Carrs are the only folks in town who keep two hired girls — says that the minute Phil arrives for a week-end, the telephone begins to ring. Must keep her busy trying to find out who's calling. Never have seen anyone beat that girl for curiosity. She finds out things and then she tells anyone who'll listen to her. Fortunate Phil Carr doesn't come much or she'd never get her work done."

"He is at home now. I met him."

"Is he? The village will hear all about it from Milly Pike. He and his father don't jibe. The boy was set on being an architect — always drawing houses in his school-books — they say he planned all the decorating inside when the old house was done over — but the Judge — that's what folks call a lawyer round here — tried to badger him into the law. Didn't succeed. Driving a square peg into a round hole isn't being done so much as it used to be. Phineas Carr thinks his wife is spoiling the boy. I guess she is, too. She'd get the moon for him if he cried for it. M's Carr's a quiet appearing woman but when once she sets her lips there isn't no use trying to budge her. She's rich in her own right which condition helps a female to be independent more'n all the amendments you can cram into the

Constitution. I'd better start if I'm going to see that plane."

Pamela's eyes followed her as she hurried away. She did need her. She had planned to have her prepare supper and wash the dishes while she took things easy in preparation for a strenuous day to-morrow. No use trying to stop her. Hitty considered the service she rendered in the light of a favor. She had to handle her with gloves, nice, soft plushy gloves. Who had phoned to inquire about Scott Mallory? Hilda Crane? Her name had not been mentioned between them since Thanksgiving day. He had come to the Inn in the village almost every week-end since. He had held business conferences with her father, had carried her off for drives in his roadster. Week-ends were more than week-ends at the Silver Moon. Fridays and Saturdays were a steady procession of meals. Sunday evenings he took her out for supper and a long drive before he went back to the city.

He had old-fashioned ideas about being at his office early Monday morning. Grandmother Leigh would have liked that, he would have been decidedly "our kind of folks." She had had a theory that one morning hour was worth three of the afternoon for accomplishment. She would have liked everything about him, his tolerance of the opinions of others; his sympathetic understanding which was almost divination; the standards he steadily maintained for his own conduct; his unaffected courtesy;

his eyes, most especially his eyes; his smile which warmed one's heart; his good looks and his clothes. Grandmother Leigh had liked men. Once she had said: "You'll never know how drab life can be, Pam, till you live in a house with only women, with no men coming home at night."

As Pamela entered the living room of the old house the burning logs in the fireplace sputtered a welcome. The flickering flames accentuated the sheen of the pine paneling, brought out copper tones in rug, damask hangings, chair and couch coverings. They sent shadows flitting over the bookshelves like ghostly fingers searching for an old time favorite among the volumes, lighted little flares in the Spanish topaz on the neck of the Lady Claire in the portrait above the mantel. From the radio in her father's room came the high, shimmering chords of a violin.

The Babe flung himself to the hearth rug with a boisterous sigh. Pamela opened the white envelopes in her basket. Birthday greetings. She would be twenty-five tomorrow. Dear of her friends to remember her in the rush of their busy lives. College and newspaper days seemed a million or two light years away. She had been on her toes with the zest of living, had laughed away any approach to sentiment; time enough for that when she had made good in her profession. Not for a moment had she expected continuous smooth sailing, exemption from problems and disappointments. She had tried to acquire a fulfillment-may-be-waiting-round-the-next-curve philosophy which would steady her through swift water, she had meant to take the breakers of life on the surf-board of gay courage. Now that each day was a hectic struggle to evade the reaching claw of debt she found it increasingly difficult to practice her creed. The birthday cards were responsible for her depression. Each greeting had set a tiny fibre of memory vibrating. Philip Carr's suggestion that she was caught in a Cape Cod tidepool hadn't helped. Caught! She was tied hand and foot. She couldn't marry. She must take care of her father. What man would shoulder that burden? She wouldn't permit it if one wanted to. Was self-sacrifice always so tragically lacking in allure?

The greeting cards fell in a white drift as she sprang to her feet. "What's the big idea sitting here stiff with fear of the future?" she demanded of the looking-glass girl who frowned at her. "Didn't Scott Mallory lift a crushing load from your shoulders when he took over the liquidation of your father's affairs? Isn't the business of the Silver Moon growing? Can't you be patient?"

The mirrored eyes which gazed steadily back were the velvety richness of black pansies as Pamela answered her own question.

"I hate being patient. I want to get behind and push. Grandmother Leigh used to say:

"'Never pray for patience, Pamela, pray for courage to keep on keeping on, to march straight up to the firing line.' I must crash through the barriers which lack of money conjures in front of me whichever way I turn." She wrinkled her nose at her reflection. " You won't do much crashing if you waste time thinking about your troubles, woman."

She ripped the wrapping from a newspaper and glanced at the headlines. Scott Mallory's picture! What had he done? The printed caption marched in eye-filling type across the head of a column.

SCOTT MALLORY WINS $1,500,000 SUIT AGAINST SOUTH AMERICAN DEALERS. MASTERLY PREPARATION AND CONDUCT OF CASE HAS SET PARTY LEADERS A–TIPTOE. GUBERNATORIAL MATERIAL?

Scott had won! Pamela rejoiced for him. Gubernatorial material! Would he become a politician? He would be an ideal candidate for any office. Fearless, unshakable in his principles but — what would become of his law practice? Hilda Crane would regret now — the thought dragged a comet-like tail of light through her mind. A possible governor! First Lady of the State! Would she let him go? Never. Evidently she had telephoned as soon as she had seen the paper.

Her father's bell! Pamela flung her soft green hat to the couch and ran up the stairs to his room. He was at the window in a wing chair looking at the crimson sky above the sand dunes through which one brilliant star was twinkling. An open letter lay on his shawl-covered knees. A letter from his wife? What was she after now?

"Want me, Father?"

His eyes were dull and clouded as they met hers. He looked as a man might who had received a stunning blow. Pamela had an instant of inexplicable panic.

"I — I've had a letter from Cecile."

She dropped into a low chair beside him. Something in his tone took the stiffness from her knees. She tried to keep her sense of apprehension from showing in her voice.

"How is she getting on? Still in the same show?"

He cleared his throat. "She has had to leave. She is in New York. She isn't very well. She writes that she needs money for hospital care."

Pamela clasped her hands hard to steady them, stared unseeingly at the stain on the wall whose outline suggested a cat done in the modernist manner. Why should the fact that young Mrs. Leigh had to go to an hospital shake her? Surely it was not affection. She cordially detested the woman if she was her father's wife. She tried to answer sympathetically, laid her hand over his, cold and supine on his knee.

"Don't worry, Father. Perhaps she thinks that you have money which you are holding out on her?

She would better page Mr. Mallory and learn the truth. She has a mother and sister to help her. She has been acting for eight months. Hasn't she saved anything?"

Harold Leigh stared out at the purpling sand dunes. "She's due for an operation, a very delicate operation on her foot. She has had a wonderful chance in a revue offered her, she thinks it will make her reputation. She hasn't signed up yet because she can't walk."

The world crashed about Pamela's ears. A vision of white-clothed surgeons, starched nurses, bare, but expensive hospital rooms, burgeoned. Curious that she didn't feel a prick of sympathy for the patient. Was she contracting hardening of the emotions? Through the turmoil of her senses she heard her own voice mocking:

"Another redskin bit the dust."

"What do you mean by that? Are you quite devoid of sympathy?" Anger accentuated the hook of Harold Leigh's nose.

"I'm sorry. I went goofy with surprise, perhaps a touch of despair, that's all." Pamela's mind cleared to practicalities. "Where is the money coming from to pay the bills? Have you thought that out?"

"Mallory has my securities. He will have to realize on those."

"Securities! Mostly insecurities. It will take those and more to settle your debts — one third yours and two thirds Cecile's."

" The money must go to her instead. I will talk with him. She wants it within forty-eight hours."

Pamela regarded him through narrowed eyes. Within forty-eight hours! A fast worker, Cecile. Why hadn't she told him before? She must have known that the operation was hovering in the offing. Did he still love the woman? Could he after her desertion of him at the moment of his illness? She had married him for his money; when that had taken wing she had hastily departed. Apparently he had not missed her, but perhaps humiliation, heartache, were at the bottom of his irritation. She must be more tender with him, but — where, where was the cash coming from to meet this expense?

"If we can't get money from the securities, you must raise some on this house, Pamela. It is free and clear."

"Mortgage Grandmother Leigh's home to pay Cecile's expenses? Have you forgotten that all my jewels went to settle the hotel and doctor's bills which you two contracted? Mortgage this house? How do you think we would meet the interest? All Terry and I can do now is to squeeze out taxes and insurance." She rose in perturbation. Her father looked up at her with shrewd eyes.

"You've always been jealous of Cecile. She knew it. Used to say that you would separate us if you could."

"Be fair, Father. I've not been so jealous of her as she has been of me. You know that she was speechless with rage when she discovered that Grandmother's jewels came to me, not to you, for your wife."

"You're right, Pamela. I—I would have done more for you and Terry if—what's the use looking back! The money must be procured for Cecile somehow."

"How much?"

He looked at the letter. "She says that she ought to have a thousand dollars, but she will try to get along with eight hundred if she can come here to convalesce. She will be unable to walk for two months."

"Eight hundred!" Pamela giggled. Caught her breath in a sob. Good grief, was she cracking-up? She set her teeth in her lips to steady them.

"What price operations! It is time for your supper. Better not think of the money any more tonight or you won't sleep."

She patted his hand, smoothed his hair before she turned on the light on the table beside him. She ran down the stairs. Hands clenched, she stood in the middle of the fire-lighted living room. Eight hundred dollars! Mortgage the place! Never. Of course, Cecile would have to come to the Silver Moon until she could use her foot. That would save a few hundreds. The Ancient Mariner with the albatross hung round his neck had nothing on Pamela Leigh. Would any man want to marry her? "Marry me, marry my family." She was not enchanting enough to swing that.

"Hi! Pam! I'm sunk!" Terrence dashed into

the room. "What do you think's happened now? The duck eggs in the incubator have exploded! Laugh that off!" He patted the head of the dog, who sensing excitement, sprang to his feet. "Keep your breast-strap on, Babe. This isn't your funeral."

"Terry! Those expensive eggs! What have you done wrong?"

"Starting in the poultry business, I guess."

Pamela sank to the couch, dropped her head in her two hands. Her laughter was punctuated with tearing gulps of emotion. Terrence shook her shoulder.

"Cut that out! You'll be having hysterics. Everything's going to be all right! What's so funny about the duck eggs?"

"It isn't the eggs, Terry. It's—it's—life—so tangled, so confused—and Cecile. Her foot is to be operated on, and—and you and I must produce the money for it!"

Terrence went beet-red. "Honest, Pam?"

His sister nodded. "Father just told me. Cecile wants a thousand dollars. She will try to get along with eight hundred if she can come here until she can walk again."

Terrence dropped to the corner of the table desk. "Eight hundred *dollars* for an operation on her foot! They ought to take off a leg for that. Sure it's only eight hundred? Might just as well have asked for eight thousand. Someone's knocking!"

"Answer, Terry. If it is a patron for the Silver

Moon, say that it is closed for the evening. I just couldn't serve anyone tonight."

She listened as Terrence opened the door.

"I wasn't expected until tomorrow, but I have won my case! Couldn't stay in the city another minute. The Cape road tempted me — and — here I am. Where is your sister?"

Scott Mallory! Almost before he had finished speaking he was in the room. He looked from her to Terrence.

"What is the matter? Something gone wrong with the Silver Moon?"

Pamela shook her head. Terrence answered.

"Nothing — much. A prospective addition to the family, that's all."

Mallory's face went white. He caught the girl's hands in a grip which hurt. "Does that mean that you are to be married, Pam?"

She wrenched herself free. All the bitterness of the last months welled to the surface, the futility of plans for herself, the sense of a crushing load to carry, her father's self-absorption, and lately — the deep and insistent demand of her heart for love.

"I married! I hate men! I wouldn't marry an angel from heaven were he to lay his halo at my feet." With which pronunciamento she departed for the kitchen.

Chapter V

———◆———

PAMELA'S anger cooled as she commenced prepara-
tions for supper in the green and white kitchen.
Why had she allowed her temper to blow-up?
Her cheeks burned. Xanthippe! Scott Mallory's
assumption that she was engaged had been unbearable when she knew that a husband was the last
thing on earth she was likely to acquire — or want.
She had not said a congratulatory word about his
legal victory. After that outburst he would put
her in the class with Hilda Crane. So much the
better. He would stop coming.

She turned the faucet with a force which sprayed
hot water over the front of her green jersey frock.
What a mess! Served her right for letting her
temper get the better of her. She fastened an en-
veloping apron about her neck. If she didn't watch
her step she would get as drab and crabbed as
Hitty Betts. That thought didn't help either.
Scott Mallory pushed open the swing door.

"Terry has told me about it, Pam. He will look
after your father while you come out for supper
with me."

Pamela's spirits soared like a captive balloon let loose. She had not realized before how deadly tired she was of preparing meals. Nevertheless, she hugged her chains.

"Can't. Too much to do."

"That's bunk and you know it. Everything is ready for tomorrow, isn't it? Be honest."

"Yes — but —"

His fingers against the back of her neck as he unbuttoned the apron sent a quiver feathering along her veins. He had charm, he had tact, he had distinction, but she sensed steel under his easy friendliness. He would be a difficult person to combat.

"No 'but' in this party. Get your coat and hat. You said that you wouldn't have a minute to celebrate on your birthday, we'll break loose tonight." As she hesitated, he added, "You and I ought to talk over this demand of young Mrs. Leigh's before I discuss it with your father. We are likely to be interrupted here."

She shed the apron. "You are right. I begin to suspect that you are always right. I'll go. Don't think that I am not thrilled by your legal victory, I am. Read of it in the paper just before you came. Thought of telephoning you, then Father's news crashed in. Congratulations — Governor Mallory!"

Color stole under his bronzed skin. "Now I know what paper you read. The man who wrote that stuff will get fired, if I'm not mistaken. No politics in mine, thank you."

"I had supposed that the practice of law was the world's best stepping-stone to politics."

"It is, but my ambition doesn't point that way. I'll put all there is in me into my profession and then, 'Beyond the Alps lies Italy!' Ever hear of the Supreme Court of the United States?"

"You mean that you want to be—"

He reddened darkly. "I don't mean anything. Forget it! The decision of that case in favor of my client has gone straight to my head. Just because I know how Christian felt in Pilgrim's Progress when the burden loosed from his shoulders, I'm talking like a wild man. I've got to celebrate —with you. Come on!" He caught her by the shoulders.

"Just a minute! You wouldn't have me go hatless, would you? I—" She answered the ring of the telephone.

"The Silver Moon. . . . Here. . . . Yes, I know you did, Mr. Carr, but you mustn't lose that client. . . . Next week Sunday? Supper with your mother? I should love it. . . . The farmer's cottage? . . . Move it to the shore! *I* suggested the idea! I never have thought of it. . . . An income from it! Four thousand dollars will remodel it? Sounds as visionary as a rocket to the moon. . . . Sunday week at six? . . . Thanks lots. Good-bye."

Pamela hung up the receiver. Her eyes felt like over-developed stars.

"That was Philip Carr."

"So I gathered. Who is he and where did you meet him?"

"He and I refereed a dog-fight this afternoon. He had said he would call tonight. He phoned that he had to get back to New York. In the excitement of Father's news and your victory I had forgotten him. What do you think he suggested?"

"Something stupendous. You look as if you were ready to hit the ceiling. What was it?"

"He proposed that we move the farmer's cottage to the shore. I had told him that it was being consumed by repairs. That gave him the idea, he says, to make a few additions and rent it. It would be a marvelous location. He will draw the plans. Hitty says that he's a born architect." The light of enthusiasm waned in her voice and eyes. "It sounds wonderful, but as bristling with impossibilities as a trip to Mars. Up bobs the same old Jack-in-the-Box, Money! Money! Money! He is sure that it can be done for four thousand dollars. I wonder what Philip's father will say when he discovers that his son is advising a Leigh."

"What's wrong with advising the Leighs? I'm doing it."

Pamela paid an instant's tribute to his smile. "Nothing generally. Only his father, Phineas Carr, was Grandmother Leigh's—"

"Phineas Carr! Carnation Carr! Always wears a white pink. His florist had orders to forward them to him wherever he was trying a case.

If the flower was late in arriving he would fidget and wait until it came. He's a colossus in his profession. He the Leigh attorney! Did I butt in on *him* when I offered to straighten out your father's affairs?"

"No! No! Don't look so aghast. Father had quarreled with him. He has not seen him since the estate was settled."

"I feel better. Do you like this Carr boy?"

The curt question sent the color to Pamela's hair. Indignant with herself, inexplicably angry with Scott Mallory, she answered flippantly.

"Mad about him. I know now what Hitty Betts meant when she said he was a born lady-killer. What a profile lost to the cinema! What an answer to a director's prayer! Speaking of irresistible males, reminds me, a girl called on the phone this afternoon, inquired if you were expected here over the week-end. Someone to congratulate you on your success, doubtless."

"Doubtless. What did you tell her?"

"Don't scowl. I didn't talk with her. Hitty, who keeps a keen, if glum, watch over the love-life of our patrons, told her that she didn't know and wouldn't tell her if she did, and sourly reminded me, 'I wasn't born yesterday!'"

"I owe Miss Betts a season's talkie money for that. I will let that 'love-life' thrust, pass — for the present. Let's go. We'll celebrate first. Not a word about business until we start for home. Then we will talk things over. Your outlook will be different after a change of scene and something to eat."

He had been right, Pamela admitted, as tucked into the roadster beside him she looked up at the stars which spread like an intricate pattern of gold lace over the dusky blueness of the heavens. The air was cool and clear, soft as transparent velvet against her face. They had driven miles for a delicious supper. Now they were homeward bound. She nestled back with a contented sigh. If only she could go on and on. Dreading to go home was getting to be a habit. It wasn't the work which mattered, it was the conflict.

She shook herself mentally. If this was the effect of breaking loose from care she would better keep everlastingly on the treadmill. Better get back to realities at once by tackling the Cecile proposition. If she had learned nothing else in these last perplexing months she had learned that the sooner one faced a problem the sooner one got it behind one. She sat straight. Her determination was reflected in her tone.

"Mr. Mallory."

"My friends call me Scott."

"In spite of the fact that it dates my bringing-up, I wouldn't dare be that familiar with so august a personage as my legal adviser." She could see his eyes narrow, the muscles of his jaw tighten.

"Glad you are properly impressed with my authority. You will get a lot of it from now on. Just what did your father tell you about his wife, this afternoon?"

Pamela repeated the conversation. He listened without comment. That was one of Scott Mallory's comfortable traits, he never interrupted. As she talked, the roadster slid smoothly forward over the shining black asphalt bordered on one side by shrubs and scrub-oaks, on the other by sea-drenched sand over which a white scalloped tide advanced and retreated for all the world like a dainty lady trailing her laces back and forward in the measures of a dance. The car swerved sharply to avoid a pair of emeralds in the road.

"Lights must have mesmerized that cat." Mallory slowed the pace to a crawl. "When did Mrs. Leigh leave your father?"

"The first of June. The date is seared into my memory, as well as the picture of the Silver Moon roses which were rioting all over the old house the day we brought Father down."

"And this is the middle of February. How long has he known that she had serious trouble with her foot?"

"If he knew before he received that letter, the stage has lost a star; he seemed stunned by surprise. When she left us stranded in New York she went directly to Hollywood. We haven't seen her since. She was in musical comedy when Father met her. I suppose she thought him a millionaire, though to be just, he can be charming when he likes, and he really didn't look more than forty. Mother left him a fair fortune and he inherited from his father. Grandmother Leigh had the income from a trust fund which passed to him unconditionally at her death. She told me before she died that she had tried to save a little for me, with which to carry on this place, but, she loved beautiful things and traveling — she and I were abroad together for a year — so there were only a few hundred dollars.

"Mother, who was an F.F. of Virginia, died when Terry was a little boy. We made our home with Grandmother Leigh, summers. She gave us an emotional, an intellectual outlook, a sense of confidence and stability, which we never would have acquired at the schools we attended. As a little girl, I adored my father. One tender word or look from him now and I fling my heart at his feet. He must have had a sizable income. He never took his children into his confidence as to the amount. Mother left Terrence and me each fifty thousand dollars, the income to be used for our education, the principal to be paid when we were twenty-five. It was in Father's hands, was swept away in the financial cloudburst. Hope you enjoy biography."

"I do. Yours. And you will be twenty-five tomorrow. Tough luck. If your father had no business what was his interest? He must have had something."

"He traveled a lot. He had only one hobby — that I know of — collecting stamps."

"Stamps!"

"Why so explosive?"

"Nothing. I was interested because like every other boy in the world I collected stamps for a while; it's the healthy, normal interest of the human male to collect something. My book is kicking round somewhere now. Did his wife know of his hobby?"

"I can't believe that she didn't know everything about him before she married him although when he told Terry and me that he was to be married — we had one day's notice of the coming event — he asked us not to mention his stamp complex to Cecile. He said:

"'She thinks collecting — anything but jewels — a symptom of senility. I shall sell the few specimens I have at once, anyway.'

"I supposed that he had done so and was surprised when he produced a book of them after we came here. Terry and I hailed it with delight. It has kept him more or less interested. I suspect that he amuses himself trading duplicates. He sends and receives letters from a stamp concern."

"He does! Interesting but it doesn't get us anywhere. To return to a subject of more importance — he suggested that you mortgage your property to pay his wife's bills?"

"Yes. Scott, do you think I ought to do it?" Not until his eyes met hers did she realize that she had scrapped formality.

"No. Make no move without talking it over with me first, promise."

"I promise, though it makes me feel that I'm a spineless leaner."

"If women would lean a little more before they walk blindly into a fool complication, they wouldn't have to be derricked out."

"Haven't an overwhelming respect for the female of the species, have you?"

"Not for the average when it comes to her judgment on legal matters. Men aren't so much better. Remember, my job is to untangle complications which need not have been tied into a hard knot if advice had been asked before, instead of after the blunder. It is like pulling teeth to get the whole truth out of people. That client is a menace who, before trial, wilfully or in ignorance withholds facts from his lawyer which are brought out in cross-examination. It is like advancing through sharp-shooters' sector. You never know where the next crack will come from. Tell me something of Mrs. Leigh. Try to be impartial. I know that you don't like her, but, has she any qualities which you do admire?"

"One. Her ability to think quickly. She is a so-phisticate. I would be willing to wager the Lowe-stoft bowl that two minutes after Father had come to her rescue in the road, she had determined to marry him. Within twenty-four hours after she learned of his financial crash, realized his physical collapse, she was off on her own with every bit of cash available. Now she demands money within forty-eight hours. She has a hair-trigger mind and she dislikes and distrusts me. Our spirits buckled on their armor the first time our eyes met."

"She is in New York?"

"Yes. Her mother and sister live there."

"Is she pretty?"

"Beautiful. Blonde, with provocative eyes — when animated. When in repose they are sullen, broody, always made me think of a darkening sky before a tempest. Her frocks are ultra chic, but she herself isn't, if you get what I mean. Rather mussy. She never looks quite smart."

"Does she use her married name on the stage?"

"Neither there nor anywhere else. Father sends his letters to Miss Cecile Mortimer — that was her maiden name. When I inadvertently picked up an envelope he had so addressed, he explained elaborately that she had more chances professionally if she were known as Miss. I can't make him out. Part of the time I think him numb from the shock of the loss of his fortune and his wife. At other times when I enter his room I surprise a swift look of cunning in his eyes. I have the curious feeling that he is concealing something. Yet, what would he have to conceal? He hasn't been in business for years, can't be complications of that sort. I wonder what he will say to Philip Carr's real estate proposition. Coming from that source he will probably turn his thumbs down hard."

"That summer-cottage idea is good. I think you'd better do it."

"Where would I get the money, Scott?"

"I know someone from whom you could borrow a building loan."

"Not you!"

"Don't be so shocked. Not I. It would mean putting up a part of your property as security."

"Suppose I have to borrow on that for Cecile."

"You will not borrow on it for Cecile. Get that straight, Pamela."

"I wish I might feel as sure as you sound. Once I would have forged ahead, had the farmer's cottage moved before you could say 'Hands up!' Now, I stop to consider the risk. That is what this last year has done to me. The nightmare of those pursuing creditors lingers in the offing like a thick fog threatening to roll up and envelop me again the moment I depart from my pay-as-I-go policy."

"This is a different proposition. The element of risk is inseparable from any business enterprise, but there is such a thing as open-eyed risks. If one never embarked on a project for fear it might turn out a failure, one never would get far. Have you a plan of your land?"

"Yes, a blueprint. In the safe in my room. Grandmother had the plan made. She was born with business sense, she wasn't one of the average whose intelligence you scorn."

"Something tells me that you resent my conclusions. Let me have the blueprint tonight. I will go over the land tomorrow, then we'll get down to cases. I'm sold on the idea of making over that cottage. If it is to be done it should be started at once. No bookings for Sunday?"

"No. I am hanging on by the teeth but I have managed so far to resist the lure of profitable patrons on that day. Grandmother was a pillar of the church. I can't give money so I play the organ. Trying to live up to her standards is the least I can do to show my appreciation of what she did for me. Besides, if I didn't go to church, Terry wouldn't."

"Isn't there something in the Bible about the Faithful Steward? To return to real estate. Trust me enough not to commit yourself to Carr about moving the cottage until you hear from me?"

"Would that be fair when it was his suggestion and we think we may put it through?"

"We will make that up to him later. There are reasons why the fact that you are considering borrowing should not leak out until the title has been looked up and the mortgage is nailed."

"Oh, you lawyers! Always laying a smoke-screen of caution. You think that Father would oppose it. He would. Anything which Terry or I might suggest."

He concentrated upon passing a line of trucks which were chugging along like prehistoric monsters. When once more the road stretched clear and shining and black ahead he said gravely:

"Perhaps we should be more charitable to your father. Irritability is often the last resort of the defeated. His wife's desertion must have cut deep."

"I realize that, Scott — though there are moments when I wonder if it was not a relief. Every morning I wake with the determination to be patient, tender with him, tenderness is so different from kindness, but by noon my endurance is worn to a frazzle. What right has one person to take the joy out of life for everyone else in the house? He is not the only member of the family who has been disappointed."

"Do you hate your life here so much?"

"I don't hate it at all, but, Philip Carr was right when he said I was caught in a tidepool."

"Darn Philip Carr!"

The soft, succinct exclamation was death to conversation. Withdrawn and silent, Mallory brought his roadster to a stop at the door of the old Leigh homestead, followed Pamela into the living room. From the radio above came the sound of strings and wood instruments in the music of Beethoven's Pastoral Symphony. It served as a faintly harmonious background for the charm and light and color of the old room.

Terrence looked up from a book on the table desk. His red hair, shot through and through with gold in the lamplight, had been furrowed by his fingers till it stood on end. His fine eyes so like Pamela's were black from concentration, his handsome face was flushed. He stretched long arms, clasped his hands behind his head, balanced his chair on its hind-legs at a breath-snatching angle.

"Miss Crane phoned you, Mr. Scott."

"Here?"

"Yep. Said your office told her you could be reached at the village Inn. Nothing doing there so she tried the Silver Moon. She wants you to call her house tonight. Important. She said to tell you that Belle was in difficulties again. Suppose you know who Belle is? Sounds like a horse or cow to me."

"Belle is her sister. A rich woman who spends her income before she gets it and is everlastingly being sued by creditors."

"God have mercy on her soul," sympathized Pamela fervently.

Mallory laughed. "Don't pity her. She brings it all on herself."

Terrence scooped up his school books, yawned prodigiously. "And so to bed. Everything's locked up, Pam, but the front door and Father. He pulled his usual line about being neglected, but, he managed to eat a square meal."

"Thanks lots for looking after him, Terry. I am all rested and refreshed for the big day tomorrow."

"I'll say you are; I could light a cigarette at your eyes, they shine so. Good-night, Mr. Scott. Good-night, Pam." His whistle, musical, muted, drifted back from the stairs.

Mallory laid his hands on Pamela's shoulders. "Take off your coat." She slipped out of the soft camel's hair garment. As she curled up in a corner of the couch she asked:

"Isn't it time now to advise me what to do about the eight hundred dollars for Cecile?"

He backed up to the fire. "I will talk with your father about that tomorrow morning."

"He may be furious that I have told you."

"Why? He has retained me as his attorney. As I intimated before, the client who withholds information from his legal adviser is just naturally looking for trouble. Will you get the plan of the land?" She started for the door. "Just a minute. Think you can find the address of the stamp firm with which your father corresponds?"

She paused on the threshold. "I believe you have contracted a touch of stamp fever, from hearing about his small collection. I've heard that it is as contagious as any of the other children's diseases, the longer and harder the search for a treasure the more acute the attack. Look out, little boy, or you will be having measles next."

She smiled to herself. Somehow she couldn't imagine Scott Mallory being interested in stamps; he would be more likely to collect books, or fine prints. She hummed as she snapped on the electricity in the room which had been her grandmother's and now was hers. For some inexplicable reason she felt absurdly light-hearted and young. Getting out of the rut of daily living had done the trick. She must beware of mental staleness. From now on she would try to slip away from the Silver Moon more often. Better to have fewer patrons and keep her viewpoint normal.

Even her room took on fresh charm. The four-poster with its snowy canopy and valance, the hooked rugs with their impossible roses and less possible fruits, the white Staffordshire dogs on the mantel with their red ears and tails, had occupied the same places as far back as she could remember.

The little safe against the wall had been a more recent acquisition. On her knees before it Pamela twisted the knob till the door swung open. As she pulled out the plan for the land an envelope fell to the floor. She didn't remember putting it in. She looked at the name in the upper left-hand corner.

" Brown of Boston."

That was all. It was addressed to her father. He had asked the combination of the safe explaining that he had an important paper he wanted to keep there.

Brown of Boston. What was that curious sound? Someone choking? She looked up. Her father was braced against the door-case. His face was ashen. In his lounge robe he looked gaunt and abnormally tall. His lips trembled, his voice shook as he demanded:

"What are you doing with my papers?"

Chapter VI

———◆———

PAMELA regarded him with honest incredulity. "Your papers! I came for the plan of the land and this envelope fell out." She remembered Scott Mallory's warning to say nothing about the cottage proposition. "If I am to borrow money on the place I must have something to show the extent of the property."

She sensed his relief. "That's all right. Saw you with the envelope in your hand, thought you might be—might be watching my correspondence. I will take that letter."

Still on her knees Pamela handed it to him. "If it is important enough to put in the safe once, shouldn't it be kept there? However, that is your business." She closed the door and rose.

"Where are you taking that plan?"

"Downstairs to Mr. Mallory."

"How long has he been here? Why didn't he talk with me?"

"He is to be at the Inn until Sunday night. He said he would see you tomorrow."

"Did you tell him about Cecile?"

"Of course. I must have someone to advise me."

"What did he say?"

"About raising money? He asked to see the plan."

"Hum! Well, he should have conferred with me." Harold Leigh shuffled toward his room, the heels of his worn slippers flapping. His daughter watched him out of sight. He had been brought to the Cape in an ambulance in June. For months he had not left his room. Now he was walking about. He must be much stronger. However, nothing made him quite so furious as to be told that he looked better.

Mallory stamped out his cigarette as Pamela entered the living room, pulled a wing chair nearer the fire, now a bed of red coals stabbed through and through with flashes of flame. The Babe flopped a languid tail in greeting before he relapsed into noisy slumber.

"Sit here." As the girl sank into the comfortable depths he pushed a stool under her feet. "That better? Did I break it?" he demanded in consternation as it shed a foot.

"No. It isn't a break. It's a habit." She leaned back and looked at him with solemn eyes. "I adore my old furniture, Scott, but it is always going maimed. When I achieve my best-seller I will live in an apartment — I am sold on the penthouse idea — furnished in the contemporary manner — *Salon des Artistes Décorateurs* — lots of color, simple lines, sharp contrasts of dark and light. Perhaps a black mirror-top table in the dining room to repeat the gleam of silver and the sparkle of glass. A silver wall, egg-shell lacquer, somewhere.— That's my dream."

"And mine is to own a summer home on Cape Cod. A house with a black-banded white chimney, a picket fence and an old-fashioned garden." His voice, which had sent little curleyques spiraling along Pamela's arteries, was back to normal as he asked: "Where were we when the casualty occurred? I remember. Did you get that plan?"

He settled himself in the Hong Kong wicker chair which had been brought from the Orient in one of great-grandfather Leigh's ships. Pamela held out the roll of blueprint. He thrust it into his pocket.

"I will examine that later. I heard you talking with your father. Hope that you didn't bother him with my request for the name of the stamp concern."

"I forgot it. When I opened the safe, an enve-lope addressed to him with 'Brown of Boston' in one corner — just that, nothing more — fell out. While I held it, speculating about a person who could be of sufficient importance to print his name like that, he appeared. I felt that he suspected me of undue interest in his correspondence, though he didn't accuse me of it. He cooled down when I told him that I was there for the plan."

"Did you tell him why I wanted it?"

"Hadn't you warned me not breathe a word of the remodeled cottage proposition? Would I dare disobey my legal adviser?"

"Good child. 'Brown of Boston.' Seems to me

I've heard that combination before. I won't keep you up any longer. I will see your father in the morning. I'll be here at nine o'clock tomorrow evening to take you for a drive."

"We are to have a tremendous day. I shall probably be so tired that I'll go to sleep with my head against your shoulder."

He bent over her. "All right with me. Ever think how temptingly sweet you are, Pam?" The roughness of his voice startled her. He straightened abruptly. "Don't get up. Good-night."

Pamela sat curled in the big chair long after he had gone, eyes on the dying fire, his disturbing voice echoing through her consciousness, the feel of his hands still warm upon her shoulders. She heard Terrence close his door and bang open his window. The house stilled. A board squeaked in the stairs as if a light foot had pressed it. The coppery tints in the room gleamed in the soft light. The Hong Kong chair creaked as if relaxing strained muscles after holding a man's weight. A dried vine tapped eerily at the window. Pamela jumped to her feet. What price air-castles! The Babe whined and twitched in his sleep. She tenderly pulled his ears.

"Wake up, old boy. Dreaming of that dog you almost knocked out today?" Today! Was it only this afternoon that she and Philip Carr had separated the fighting dogs? In her concern over Cecile's demand she had completely forgotten the poor little rich boy until he telephoned. She would be willing to wager that he wasn't bad at all, village gossip spread like the downy contents of a pillow flung on the air. No one ever took time to chase the feathers and put them back. Had she been wise to accept the invitation for supper before she knew whether the head of the house would welcome or resent her presence? Perhaps Phineas Carr would forget that she was her father's child and remember only that she was his old client's dearly loved granddaughter. She would adore seeing the inside of his home. She had heard that it was a treasure-house of priceless antiques.

There would be nothing more charming than the portrait of the Lady Claire. She looked up at the picture above the mantel flanked by carved Sheraton candlesticks with tall tapers. Chestnut hair piled high on a haughty head, eyes the velvety brown of pansies, magolia tinted shoulders and throat, their delicacy accentuated by a necklace of Spanish topaz set in medallions of intricately carved gold. Long matching earrings hung from the shell-like ears, bracelets girdled the arm, a massive ring was on the patrician hand which held a soft yellow rose at the point of the low-cut brown bodice.

Pamela sighed enviously. She could picture herself in that set of topaz. She would be twenty-five tomorrow! The birthday upon which she would have received the legacy from her mother, had there been any legacy left to receive. Twenty-five! A quarter of a century!

She set the brass screen before the smoldering

fire, snapped out the lights. From the threshold she looked back at the dear, familiar room. Through the interstices in the plant window she could see the lawn. Snowing! Flakes as big as half dollars were drifting down casually. And she had thought that spring had come. Just as she had thought her anxiety about the debts was over when Scott Mallory had offered to stand between. Now, along came this demand for money from Cecile.

Suppose Cecile were bluffing? Pamela was brushing her hair before the triple mirror on her chintz-hung dressing table when the thought came to her. Suppose the second Mrs. Leigh were trying to get money for a different project? It had been done. The face reflected went quite white. Had Scott thought of that? She reached for the telephone. An extension set in her room was the one luxury she allowed herself, it saved countless minutes and miles of steps. She would pass her suspicion, more of a hope, on to him at once. Her hand dropped to her lap. No. He might at this very moment be talking to Miss Crane. He was attorney for her sister. How old was the irresponsible Belle? Did he still care for the soulless Hilda? He never mentioned her. He had gone darkly red at the little gibe about his love-life; there had been a biding-my-time glint in his eyes, but he had let it pass.

"Ever think how temptingly sweet you are, Pam?" She must forget the shaken question. He had probably said the same thing to other girls. Hadn't he brought Hilda Crane to the Silver Moon for a Thanksgiving dinner for two? A man didn't do that sort of thing unless he was quite mad about a girl. What possible difference could it make to her whom Scott Mallory loved or did not love? She must not let herself care for him. It would be tragically easy. Hadn't she a father to support? Suppose Cecile were telling the truth and had to be cared for at the Silver Moon to save money?

She brought the brush down on the waves of her already satiny hair with a force which started tears of pain. She admonished the girl in the mirror.

"That's crossing a bridge before you come to it, my dear."

A breeze blew in cold and clear as she raised the window softly that she might not disturb her father. What a night. A light snow covered fields, powdered trees. Moonlight tranformed the sand dunes into silver domes. Fair tomorrow. How still the world was. Not a creature stirring — not a creature — but a long purple shadow at the entrance of the drive by the mail box. Curious, she never had noticed that before. It was walking! Coming up the path stealthily. A burglar after the old silver?

Unmindful of the frosty wind fluttering the delicate pink crêpe of her pajamas, she knelt by the window. How slowly the person came. Kept stopping as if for breath. Was he shrouded in a shawl? Now he was at the steps. Would she better call Terry? Was that the front door opening? Excite ment tightened her throat. She stole to the threshold of her room. Listened. The old house quivered with cautious sounds, its aged joints creaked. Someone coming up the stairs! Coming heavily, with labored breathing. The hall was kept dimly lighted in case the invalid rang in the night. Whoever it was was making a clumsy attempt at caution. The banister groaned as if a heavy weight had lunged against it. Each stair squeaked a protest. Almost at the top! Pamela opened her door an inch wider. Peered out. Closed it soundlessly. Her father!

She leaned against the wall, breathless from surprise. He had been to the mail-box. Why the secrecy? The R.F.D. man picked up the mail as he went by at six o'clock in the morning. Had he sent a letter? To Cecile? Of course. To assure her that the money for hospital expenses would be forthcoming? Perhaps this was not his first surreptitious midnight trip. Perhaps Tinker, the postman, left letters for him. As boys, the two had fished the surrounding ponds together. She remembered Hitty Betts' comment, "Folks is sayin' he'd be a sight better if you didn't coddle him."

Ooch! It was cold. Shivering, she snapped off the light. "I'll investigate in the morning before Tinker comes," she told herself as she snuggled down under the bedclothes. "I wouldn't care about Father's mail ordinarily but when mortgaging this house is at stake it is time someone knew what was going on."

Tinker had come and gone when she awoke. She had an instant of self-castigation for oversleeping before the day's activities swept her into their vortex. When Scott Mallory came at nine in the evening she demurred against going out in the roadster.

"I am all in. I should be a dumb companion. Now that the rush is over, my mind feels as cramped as a stowaway in an airplane."

"Come for an hour, Pam. It will rest you to get away from the house and your problems."

At the word "problems" the memory of her father's midnight pilgrimage shot to the surface. " I had forgotten. I'll go. I have something curious to tell you."

For the first half hour she drifted in a Nirvana of relaxation. Mallory drove slowly. A dusky amethyst veil, vague as her own thoughts, blurred the horizon. Little white clouds chased one another across the deep Ionian-blue sky like a flock of woolly sheep. From a field came the distant clank of a cow bell, the drowsy purl of running water on its leisurely way to the sea. Lights on the highway blinked like nocturnal owls caught in a glare of searchlight. A line of red, Cyclopean eyes was dimming into the salty gloom of the night. Pair after pair of green yellow orbs approached, "whooshed " by and were gone. Rested, refreshed, she straightened in the seat.

"Anything the matter with my shoulder?"

She looked up, startled out of her preoccupation. Mallory was smiling. She remembered.

" Nothing doing in shoulders tonight. You were right about coming out. It has rested me. I am all made over. I have much to tell you."

" Shoot."

To the accompaniment of the soft purr of the engine she told him of her father's trip to the mailbox. " I didn't know that he had been downstairs for months. It gives me a plot for a story, MID-NIGHT MAIL MYSTERY."

" You miss your writing, don't you? "

" Frightfully — when I have time."

" Cheer'o! All of these problems and disappointments are providing material for later work. You can put more emotional color into the portrayal of an episode, deepen it and broaden it, if you have experienced its meaning even to a slight degree. Cold comfort but it is true. To return to your father. You can think of no one to whom he would write surreptitiously except his wife? "

" No one. But why surreptitiously to her? I never have commented on his letters."

" Has she ever before proposed coming back to him here? "

" Only once that I know of. He read me part of a letter in which she wrote that she was not well, that the doctor said that she should be where she could relax and be waited on for a month or two."

" What answer did you make? "

" What answer could I make but one? She had left us high and dry when Terry and I didn't know which way to turn. We had just started the Silver Moon enterprise. It took every moment and every cent we could scrape together to keep things going. Waited on! Had I thought that Father really wanted her here I would have managed to take her in somehow, but, he didn't. He said she would tire him. I told him to tell her that she must find some other place in which to rest. She has a mother and sister."

" Did he? "

"I suppose so, he never mentioned the subject again. Oh, I didn't leave it all to him. I wrote and told her what I thought of her desertion, told her I wouldn't have her in my house, that I was sure he would be happier, get well faster without her."

" Good Heavens! "

Pamela stared up at the man at the wheel. His profile looked cameo clear in the dusk.

" What did you say? "

" Did I say anything? Did you keep a copy of that letter? "

" A copy? I didn't even keep it in the house a minute after it was written for fear I wouldn't send it. I am apt to compose a red-hot masterpiece, think it over until my fury has cooled, then tear it up. I meant that to go while it sizzled." A troubled note crept into her voice. " Perhaps had she come this foot trouble wouldn't have developed. But — but — I don't believe there is anything the matter with her! I believe it is a touch for money. I almost phoned you last night when that blinding suspicion flashed into my mind."

" Why didn't you? "

" I thought probably you were telephoning Miss Crane."

She met his direct gray eyes, eyes that saw much, much beneath the surface of things she was sure. Had the miracle of mind-reading come to pass? Did he know what she was thinking, know that she was wishing that a polite, gentlemanly typhoon would catch up Hilda Crane and swirl her into matrimony?

" We'd better talk over the Cecile and cottage business now," he announced with a curtness which confirmed Pamela in her suspicion that he was a mind-reader. " I shall not be here next week-end."

" Not coming! " She was hotly aware that the words wailed.

" Why should I? You will be at the Carrs', won't you? "

" But only for supper, Sunday. Did you talk with Father about the money for Cecile? "

" Yes. I will hold off the creditors and give her some of the cash from the securities I've sold — if she is telling the truth."

" Then you doubt her too? "

His smile almost drew her head to his shoulder. " In the language of Hitty Betts, 'I wasn't born yesterday.' "

Chapter VII

———◆———

PAMELA squeezed a few drops from the almost juiceless half of a lemon on the fluted layers of the plump oyster in the half-shell. She shut her eyes in gastronomic ecstasy as the cool, salty morsel, not without some difficulty slid down her throat.

" That was luscious, Cap'n Crockett."

The small eyes in the short man's face which was weather seasoned to the color and consistency of the dark boards of the walls of the shack behind him, twinkled in their setting of fine lines. " Kinder reckon that one was big enough for you. You're always sayin' the bigger the better, Miss Pam-ee-lia."

" If it had been one millionth of an inch larger or fatter or juicier it wouldn't have slipped down."

" Have another? "

Pamela looked from the rough shell into which he was about to thrust a short dull blade, to the pile with purplish eyes dotting their mother-of-pearl linings, on the board before her. She shook her head, and wiped her hands on the handkerchief she pulled from the pocket of the green jacket of her sports suit.

"I'd love it but I have had ten now. Why is it oysters never taste so good as they do here?"

Cap'n Iry Crockett dried his brawny, hairy-backed hands on his blue denim apron. "'Cause they're right out of the water. How many you takin' in bulk today?"

"A bushel."

"Guess trade's hummin'."

He lifted a rake, its iron tines curved in a semicircle, from a hook on the wall, caught up a burlap bag. Pamela followed him into a dusky compartment, sat on a box while he scooped oysters from dark depths. The place smelled of brine and seaweed.

"Yes. Business is growing. Not long now before I stop serving oysters. Why don't people eat them in the months without an r, Cap'n Iry?"

He shook a rake full of rough shells into the burlap bag which Pamela held open. "They spawn in May and June round these parts — they're right prolific — an' they're not so good eatin'. There, guess that's a bushel. Sure 'twill be enough? Beats all how you know how much of things to lay in."

"I don't, always, but most of our patrons order ahead, then after school Terry can hop into the old fliv and get shell fish in a few minutes. It isn't as if I served meats and steaks."

Back in the outer room he tied up the bag. Pamela paid him. " I'll lug this to the car for you."

She followed him from the floating shack, across

the swinging bridge that rose and fell with a tide which reflected the clear blue of the sky, to the sandy road. He lifted the dripping bag into the shabby flivver.

"Those ought to last you for a while. They tell me the Inn's fillin' up early this spring."

"I am glad of that, it will mean a hungry horde for the Silver Moon. People like a change of eats even if the table is good." The sunlight struck a metal disc partially concealed by the strap of his overalls. "What's the decoration, Cap'n Iry? Been made the High Ruler of something or other? If you have, make the Town Fathers give you a decent road here."

He touched the badge with a gnarled brown, finger. "That? That means I'm deputy sheriff."

A flash-back of the man in a yellow truck waiting to seize her antique furniture set Pamela's heart thumping uncomfortably before she remembered that the creditor-haunted days were over, thanks to Scott Mallory. They were unless he had had to take money due on bills to send to Cecile. She was aware of Cap'n Crockett's thoughtful regard. He must wonder why she was sitting staring at the wheel. She started the car, nodded to him.

"Thanks, Cap'n Iry. See you soon. Bye-bye!"

The Inn truck passed laden with trunks, a score of them, sets of smart luggage, smooth tweed hat-boxes and suitcases. The season was beginning early. That meant business for the Silver Moon.

She must engage someone to wait on table. It was getting to be more than Terry could do alone. Perhaps one or two of the Academy boys would be glad to earn extra money. She liked to deal with boys better than with girls. She drew a long breath of the salty air. Glorious day.

Highty, the postmaster, lumbered down the steps as she neared the brick office. He waved a letter. She drew up to the curb.

"Special delivery for you, Miss Pamela. Guess whoever sent it didn't stop to think that you live more'n a mile from the post-office. I was hoping some of your folks or neighbors would be going by to take it up to the house."

His second chin quivered; his small eyes, sunk in pouches, twitched nervously. His spotted waistcoat, which never had been even a collateral of his baggy trousers, displayed an imposing array of fountain pens. He looked at the letter before he lingeringly relinquished it.

"Never've seen that writing before in your mail."

Pamela tucked the envelope into her pocket. Neither had she. She started the car. Above the protesting groan of the engine she suggested:

"Better not try to follow my mail, Mr. Highty. I'm always getting letters in regard to reservations."

His chin quivered over a flagged question, his mouth hung open, he blinked furiously as after a preparatory lurch or two the car started. Pamela had a curious feeling that the letter in her pocket was not from a prospective client. It broadcast magnetic currents. In sudden determination she turned down the rough lane which led to the shore, her shore. She had heard nothing more from Scott Mallory about raising the money with which to move and make over the farmer's cottage; neither had she heard from Philip Carr. Why should she? She was to have supper at his mother's house Sunday night. He would tell her his plan then. Much more satisfactory to talk it over than to write.

She stopped the flivver. Her spirit quickened to the beauty of the sparkling water, only a degree bluer than the cloudless sky above. Gulls sunned themselves on the silver dunes, which were beginning to show tufts of coarse grass; two marsh hawks sailed above them. Far off on the horizon floated a faint haze of smoke which meant a steamship Europe bound. A great cloud, gilt-edged, sailed along like a proud ship. Cranberry bogs showed faintly green. This shore was an ideal location for summer cottages.

She pulled the letter from her pocket, frowned over the post-mark. New York. Couldn't be from Scott, he lived in Boston. A man's writing. Perhaps it was from Philip Carr. Club stationery. She tore open the envelope and looked at the signature. Scott Mallory! What was he doing in New York and why write to her? She pulled off her close hat, settled back in the seat. The salty breeze ruffled her hair as she read.

NEW YORK CITY

DEAR PAM —

You were right in your suspicion. The operation yarn was a hold-up for money. I wasn't satisfied myself so came over here at once to investigate. Invited a man named Latimer who was in my class in college, and is now making a name for himself on the stage, to dine with me at the Club. Thought he might know your stepmother and I would get a line on her from him. Over smokes I asked him if he had met a girl in his profession named Cecile Mortimer. He said:

"Curious you should ask that. She's all but engaged for a show in which I'm cast. Never've seen her but hear that she's one of those pink and blonde perils — and some little plunger in the market. I am asked to meet her tonight."

It wasn't difficult to extract an invitation to go along. It was to be a party, I discovered, where half the guests were unknown to the hostess and were likely to remain so. I went. I met Cecile Mortimer, "the second Mrs. Leigh." She is beautiful. I recognized what you meant about her clothes. Her gown was smart but crushed. We danced together several times. Each time I waited for her to stop because of a troublesome foot. Not so much as a fraction of a flinch. It was a noisy party, an exceedingly wet party. Young ex-marrieds, ex-marrieds not so young. Wild women, lit ladies by the giggling score; swashbuckling gents, even if they were arrayed in the latest word in dinner clothes, they were swashbucklers just the same. She grew talkative but made no mention of her past. I asked her no questions — I had found out the one thing I wanted to know — neither of her two feet required surgical attention — had they, she couldn't have danced so incessantly. I don't drink. Perhaps because of that I sensed her suspicion. Her animation waned. Her eyes smoldered, "sullen, broody." There was a tempest brewing, I felt it in the air. When Latimer swayed up and suggested — you see, I'm giving you all the sordid details — " Want a divorce or two put through, Miss Mortimer? Now's your chance, darling. One of the brightest lights of the Massachusetts Bar is at the present moment eating out of your hand."

" Massachusetts Bar! "

Her repetition was a whisper. I remembered what you had said about her hair-trigger mind. She sprang to her feet, caught Latimer's arm, repeated:

" Massachusetts Bar? "

" Sure. Boston. You know Boston. The place where the censors come from. That's good — "

Cecile Mortimer was not interested in his wise-cracks. Her face blanched, her eyes narrowed to pin-points. She said under her breath:

"How could I have been such a fool." She caught Latimer's arm. "I had begun to suspect that your friend didn't belong at this party. You are an actor as well as a lawyer, Mr. Mallory; you are showing just the right amount of incredulity — you're good, but not good enough."

She walked away. I left without saying good-night to the hostess whom I had not met. That was an hour ago. Ever since, Latimer's words, "and some little plunger in the market," have been milling round in my mind. Where does the money come from with which she plays the stock market? I am writing to you at once that one burden may be speedily lifted from your shoulders — no money will be needed for an operation — would that I could dispose of others so easily. I have written you in detail first because I want you to know all that happens, second because it seems to bring me near you, as if I were talking to you.

Better say nothing of all this to your father. I will be down on Saturday. Have secured the loan on your land. We can push ahead on the cottage. Will be off again before your party at the Carrs'.

Sincerely,
SCOTT MALLORY.

"Sincerely." Pamela made a little face at the word. New England granite. As an antidote she re-read — "It seems to bring me near you, as if I were talking to you." That had some warmth.

She admonished herself sharply. Ungrateful person, sitting here criticizing Scott when she should be giving loud thanks that there was no need of raising eight hundred dollars. How had Cecile dared! She must think the Leigh family an easy mark. Why not? Hadn't they allowed her to walk away with everything cashable at the time of her husband's breakdown? Where was she getting money to invest? How like her to jump to the conclusion that Scott Mallory was shadowing her to make certain that her claim was valid.

It wasn't, glory be! What would she try next? Perhaps even now she was preparing another coup. How could she think that there was money to be had from the Leighs? The raw grinding of gears as she started the flivver was an outlet for Pamela's emotions. She was still pondering the question as she drove up to the kitchen door.

Mehitable Betts hurried out, thinner, gaunter, drabber than ever. "Get the oysters, Pam? Seem's though the whole world's gone crazy 'bout your oyster chowder. Three parties, four each, phoned for supper tonight." She picked up the still dripping burlap as if it were a five cent bag of popcorn and carried it into the kitchen. Mentally cal

culating a problem in liquid measure, Pamela
followed.

"Three fours — twelve — fourteen —"

"For the land's sake, what you mumbling 'bout?"
Miss Betts emptied the oysters into a pan, perched
on a green enamel stool, jerked her spectacles in
place, inserted a dull blade into a tightly clamped
shell, with unbelievable economy of motion.

Pamela studied the reservation pad with wrinkled-
brow intentness. "I don't recognize any of these
names, Hitty."

"They said they were new, told who the folks
was who'd recommended them, but I couldn't be
bothered taking that down. My, isn't it warm for
this time of year? Folks is sayin' that the rooms
are taken at the Inn from now till clear through
October."

A shadow fell across her busy hands. She looked
up. "Eddie Pike, what you stealing up like that
for? Might's well kill a body as scare her to death."

The loose jointed man in a rope-belted army overcoat, with barnyard mud on his boots, a stubby
young beard sprouting from his round face, surveyed her with big, vacant, light blue eyes. In the
drive an aged white horse hitched to a top-buggy
drooped in harness. He drawled:

"Terry asked me to come up an' kill them chickens fer him. I couldn't come tomorrer 'cause I
have to pump water for Kelley-the-miser. He's apt
to take a bath round the end of the week."

Pamela consulted the reservation pad. "The squabs for Saturday. Six. All right, Eddie, come out to the poultry house and I will show you where to find them."

Pike rubbed his hand up and down his unshaven cheek. The sound resembled nothing so much as an able-bodied young buzz-saw in operation. His loose mouth twitched.

"Squabs! You mean pigeons? I couldn't kill a dove, Miss Pamela."

Knife in one hand, oyster shell in the other, Mehitable Betts stared at him. "Eddie Pike! How long since you've got so sensitive? You trap and hunt and fish all the year round, open season or not open season, and now you——"

"They are chickens, not pigeons, Eddie." Pamela stemmed the caustic torrent of words. "Squabs is a term applied to small chickens. Come on."

He shuffled along beside her, a burlap bag in his hand. She led the way to the poultry house. Long rows of buildings with tidy yards only a few of them inhabited, were enclosed by a galvanized wire fence. A great white Leghorn rooster, wattles and comb like coral carvings, flew at the netting in a vain attempt to attack. Pike shrank away.

"Gee, that fella's a fighter."

"Yes. He's a terror, he flies at anyone who comes near him. Terry has named him the White Hope. Here are the chickens to be dressed." As a

dozen or more plump, small, yellow feathered cock-
erels flew and fluttered in the coop in the expectation
of food, she added hastily, "Don't take them out
till I get into the house. I — I — hate this part of
the poultry business."

She was conscious of his grinning regard as she
dashed away. She slammed the kitchen door to shut
out the sound of frightened chirping and wildly
flapping wings. "That's that!" she sighed in relief.

Mehitable Betts sniffed. "Open that door again,
Pam. Room smells like a barnyard. Folks is sayin'
Eddie Pike sleeps with the old white horse. 'Tisn't
hard to believe. That's better. What do you know
about his being so sensitive about dressing pigeons?
Pity he isn't more tender-hearted some other ways."

"He is fond of his sister, isn't he?"

"If you call it being fond to suspect every man
who looks at Milly Pike of wanting to run off with
her and lead her astray. He's got a twist that way.
There's your father's bell. I'd like a dollar for
every time he jingles it. I wouldn't have to work
much longer."

Pamela answered the impatient summons. Her
father was in the big chair by the window, eyes on
the cloudless blue sky and the shimmering sand
dunes. There was a book on his knees, the stamp-
laden table had been pushed aside. He looked up
as his daughter entered. His face seemed rounder,
his eyes clearer, his voice stronger than it had been
since he came to the Cape.

"When is Mallory coming again?"

"Saturday."

"Has he sent Cecile the money?"

"If he has, he hasn't told me."

"I don't like him, he's — he's so unflinching."

"Father!" Pamela disciplined her indignant voice, said more calmly: "After all he has done to help you! How ungrateful. Had he not been unflinching we might be sitting on packing boxes instead of on choice old maple chairs. We haven't paid him a cent for the time he has given to our pesky problems."

"He offered to help, didn't he?"

"And did it."

He stared out of the window again. Color crept under his waxen skin. He cleared his throat. The cords on his forehead stood out.

"I didn't wait for him to send the money to Cecile. I got it for her myself."

Pamela's world whirled, steadied. He had sent Cecile money! She had lied to get it. Where had it come from? Was that the explanation of his midnight trip to the mail-box? She tried to keep her voice steady.

"I thought that Mr. Mallory had charge of all your securities?"

"I realized on an antique a — friend held for me. I — you have done so much — I wouldn't let you mortgage your property for us."

Pamela blinked furiously to keep back a sudden,

unexpected rush of tears. He did care a little for her! What a child she still was about her father!

"Cecile wrote that if I didn't send the money she would come here. We couldn't have that. I told her that you had convinced me that she and I never could be happy together again."

"Father! I never have advised you about your wife!"

"I had to say something to prevent her coming. We don't want her, do we? My nerves wouldn't stand the excitement of having her around."

His nerves! Indignation dried even Pamela's long, drenched lashes. "Don't worry, she won't come now that she has the eight hundred. You might have saved your precious antique. Cecile fooled you. That operation story was a try-out for money."

The knuckles of his hands strained white as he clutched the arms of his chair.

"How do you know?" The question was sharply incredulous.

"A friend saw her at a party in New York. She danced and danced and danced. She wouldn't do that, would she, if she were slated for the hospital?"

Harold Leigh's face was colorless. His eyes were wide with fury, his voice hoarse.

"Fooled me, did she! I'll make her pay for that, even if she is a woman who never pays for anything, but just digs, digs, *digs!*" His chin quivered like a hurt child's. "My mint block! My mint block!" The last word was a wail.

Chapter VIII

———◆———

SCOTT MALLORY laid a paper on the desk in the living room. Pamela smiled radiantly.

"I am so glad you came. You said you would not be here this week."

His face and eyes were as noncommittal as his voice. "Wanted to get this loan through. I stood over the title-examiner with a club — figuratively speaking — to be sure he pushed ahead. Work should be started on the cottage at once or it won't be ready to rent this season. That would mean a loss to you. Read the mortgage before you sign."

Under the light of the lamp Pamela dutifully scanned the printed words.

"Perhaps sometime I will understand legal terms. This seems a muddle of whereas and whereupon and grantor and grantee to me. However, the gist of it is that I am placing a mortgage for four thousand dollars on thirty acres of shore land. Who is this trusting person who is willing to plunge to that extent?"

"A friend of mine. We could have borrowed from a bank but I wouldn't take a chance at the news of the loan leaking out until the deal was consummated. Hurried it up on that account. Sign here —and here."

He laid a note on the mortgage. She wrote her name on both. He witnessed her signatures and stamped the document with his Notary's seal.

"I understand that this leaves the house, the cranberry bogs and the rest of the land clear. Am I right, Scott?"

"Correct. Here is your cheque. The first six months' interest has been deducted. By the time the next comes due the cottage should be finished, rented, and an advance payment made. When you get a tenant I'll draw the lease and make sure it is water-tight."

"It won't be your fault if I am not an efficient business woman." Pamela looked at the pink slip of paper. "What shall I do with it? Deposit it with the money I keep for current expenses?"

"Better not. Better open an account in a Boston bank."

She tapped the desk with the end of her pen as she looked up at the man looming above her.

"Scott, of what are you afraid?"

"What do you mean, 'afraid'?"

"Don't fence. You are afraid that Cecile will try to get that money, aren't you? How could she? Why should she?"

"If it once occurred to her as a lucrative possibility, she might attempt it. You never know what

the power of suggestion, combined with the tendency
of the human mind to see and believe what it wants
to see and believe, can accomplish."

"I still can't see why she should try to get money
from me. Have you paid her any?"

"No. I wrote why."

"Father sent her some."

"Where did he get it?"

"Don't shoot questions at me like that and please
sit down."

"Come over here on the couch." He caught her
hand, seated himself beside her. Spread her fingers
on his palm. She doubled them up.

"Inky, aren't they? I despair of ever domesti-
cating a fountain-pen. Just as I think I have one
well-trained it leaks."

He laughed. "I'll send you one that won't. I'll
put a spell on it so that it always will write to me the
things I want to hear. Tell me what has happened
since I have been away."

The fire snapped accompaniment as she repeated the conversation with her father. "When
he said that he wouldn't let me mortgage this property for Cecile and himself, my incurable romanti-
cism vaulted to the saddle, I — I almost hugged him,
I was so touched by his consideration. Luckily I
remembered in time that he hates demonstration.
Later, when he said that his 'nerves' wouldn't stand
having his wife about, I flung the truth at him, told
him that she had been lying to get money. I thought

for an instant her deception had killed him. He looked ghastly, then furious, then threatened to make her pay, crumpled and wailed:

"'My mint block! My mint block!'"

"That meant nothing to me. Do you suppose he owned a rare block print—if there is such a thing? Had he said mint-bed, it would have been within the scope of my practical ken. There is a marvelous patch in Grandmother Leigh's herb-garden, you can smell it a mile away—almost."

"What a good little sport you are, Pam. Your sense of humor will buoy you in the roughest water." Head back, Mallory blew smoke rings at the ceiling, repeated thoughtfully, "'My mint block!' I wonder if he has more treasures up his sleeve."

"If he has it seems frightfully unfair that Terry and I should be worried to a frazzle trying to make both ends meet. It isn't the work I mind, but it is this everlasting counting pennies. A dime assumes the proportions of a gold piece when I consider parting with it. Shall I get so niggardly that I shall forget how to spend?"

He laid his finger lightly between her brows. "That pucker is adorable, but don't worry about forgetting how to spend. The knack will return, you'll be surprised. I can't bear to see you working so hard. Who the dickens is that?" Pamela waved him aside when he would have answered the telephone.

"Probably someone to make a reservation." She

spoke into the transmitter. "Silver Moon. . . .
Right here. . . . Mr. Carr! . . . Of course I am
coming tomorrow. All excited about it. . . . You
have. . . . I'm crazy to see it . . . I have the
money! My legal adviser approves. . . . You will!
Marvelous. . . . No, don't come for me. Terry
will drive me over. . . . Of course, you may bring
me home. Good-bye."

Pamela returned to the couch. Her eyes shone,
her cheeks were pink from excitement.

"That was my poor little rich boy. He has a
cardboard model of the cottage as it will look made
over. I am having supper at the Carrs' tomorrow
night."

Arm on the mantel Mallory met her eyes. "I
have not forgotten."

"Why so solemn? You don't disapprove of a
little change of scene for me, do you?"

"No. I would pack your days full of pleasure if
you would let me."

Pamela swallowed her heart which had soared to
her throat at the emotion in his voice. She steeled
herself to say practically:

"You are doing something for me all the time,
Scott."

He took a step toward her. Put his hands hard in
his pockets. "I am going back to town tonight.
Can't you come to the city one day next week? You
really ought to deposit the cheque, and open an account personally."

"To town! I haven't been away from this house for a day since I came here in June. It sounds heavenly. It would have to be Thursday. I could get everything planned ahead for the week-end. I am sure of Hitty Betts that day and Terry has a light schedule. He would be here. I could buy the new machines."

"What machines?"

"A big tricolator and an electric ice-cream freezer. We have been making coffee, four cups at a time, and freezing ice-cream in small lots. We have saved money enough to get big ones."

"All right, Thursday. Come to my office first. I will take you to the bank, then we'll have luncheon and go to a show. It will be a talkie, no real theatre on that afternoon. Couldn't make it Wednesday, could you?"

"I couldn't. Taking Thursday is a risk and we will cut out the matinée. I should lose the last train down."

"Forget the train. I'll drive you home. Don't say 'no.' Good-night."

He was gone before she could answer. Was he afraid that she might change her mind about going to Boston? She was not so heroic. Now that she had had a vision of what a day in the city would mean she would grab the pleasure though the heavens fell. Lucky she had the excuse of the purchase of the tricolator and freezer as a sop to fling to her New England conscience.

A sense of anticipation glowed in her heart during

church the next morning. It was difficult to keep her mind on the service, keep from visualizing shops and crowded streets and luncheon with Scott. The downpour of rain dimmed her vivid imagination not at all.

At home as she changed her green crêpe to a simple print in which to prepare dinner, she frowned at the sleeve. Thin on the elbow? What would she do for clothes when her present supply gave out? She and Terrence had planned to put every cent they didn't need for living into equipment.

She was still pondering the question as she fastened her belt at the window. A dingy day. From horizon to horizon the sky was spongy with formless clouds. A pair of drenched birds snuggled close in a bend of the eaves, kept up a monotonous, Cheep! Cheep! Water rivuleted down the shingles, dripped in a platinum fringe from the roof, settled in pools which looked like fragments of a shattered mirror on the sodden lawn which showed a tinge of green in its russet. Little mists hung above the hollows. Village chimneys were darker blurs against the drab sky, the church spire was of no more importance than the cupola of the little red schoolhouse. Rain, like a gauze curtain, turned all color to a neutral gray. The smell of the sea stole into the room. An open car chugged up the drive. Cap'n Ivy Crockett's! Why was he coming? She hadn't ordered oysters. Who was with him? Someone in yellow oilskins.

She stared incredulously as the sou'wester blew

back from a blonde head. Cecile? Her father's wife! Here!

Pamela flew down the stairs. The Babe, roused from a doze in front of the living room fire, joined her as she opened the door, his hair bristling. He dashed to the porch, stopped for an instant to regard the oilskin figure picking its way from stepping-stone to stepping-stone, then, with a growl, charged.

The woman screamed as he snapped at her yellow slicker, tore at it. For a stunned instant Pamela felt turned to stone. Cecile here! Why? Had she come for more money?

"Pamela! Pamela! How dare you set him on me!"

The scream unlocked the girl's muscles and tongue.

"Babe! Babe!" She had the dog by the collar. With all her might twisted it. A growl gurgled in his throat as she dragged him back.

"Run for the house, quick, Cecile! Run!" she gasped.

The woman took a step forward, sank to the ground, panted through livid lips:

"I knew you hated me! You've turned your father against me! You'll pay for this! What beastly luck that my attorney isn't with me!"

"Cap'n Crockett! Come! Help!" Pamela called as the dog almost pulled her arms from their sockets in his attempt to reach the yellow slickered figure.

The Captain in his black rubber coat, which glistened with rain, puffed up.

"What in tarnation's that pup raising such a row about? Ain't he notional!"

"Never mind! Never mind! Help her into the house. Quick! I can't hold him much longer. Come along, Babe! Come!"

Spanking, pulling, pushing, Pamela dragged the infuriated dog toward the barn. Devoutly she prayed that the collar would not give way under the strain, fervently she hoped that Cecile was safely in the house, she didn't dare turn to look. Why, of all days in the year had one of the Academy teachers selected this one to invite Terrence to dinner? The barn at last!

At the girl's tempestuous entrance a Jersey cow stopped chewing her cud to gaze with ruminative eyes; an old horse neighed a welcome; a hen flew down from the loft and with a frenzied cackle scurried into the rain; a mouse which had been feasting on chaff scuttled into its hole. She pushed the dog into a box stall, slammed and fastened the door. White, breathless, shaken, she leaned against it outside. She shut her eyes tight to keep back tears of relief, set her teeth into her lips to steady their nervous twitching, clenched her hands to control her shaking body.

Cap'n Crockett poked his head into the barn. "The lady's all right, Miss Pam-ee-lia. She wasn't so hurt as she seemed when she tumbled to the

ground. Ain't surprised she was frightened.
Thought when you an' that pup burst out of the
house you was settin' him on her. Guess she'll wish
she hadn't pestered me to death to bring her."

With an effort Pamela steadied her voice.
"Where did you pick her up, Cap'n Iry?"

"She was in a mighty han'some sedan stuck near
the oyster shack. A real natty man come to my door
and asked if I would take a lady up to the Leigh
place.

"'But I haven't got nothin' but an open fliv,' says
I. 'Just cruise along nor'-east, an' glimpse up toward
the hill an' you'll see the house, find it yourself,'
I told him. 'My car's stuck. Haven't you a slicker
you can lend her?' says he. 'She's my client, she's
got to get there. I'll have this thing tinkered an'
you can bring her back to the Inn.'

"I didn't want to do it but he pestered me so
I fetched the slicker and sou'wester an' brought
her along. She was pleasant-speakin'. Asked me
a lot about you an' the old Leigh place. I gave
your family a great setting out, Miss Pam-ee-lia.
Told her that the Leighs had been the first family
here since the place was settled, that they was awful
proud of their record, never'd been a breath of
scandal or a charge of dishonest dealin' against one
of them in all the years they'd lived here. I forgot
for a minute your father owed a lot of money folks
couldn't collect. Guess I bragged some. Told her
your grandma left you most a peck of di'monds,
that she'd refused a fortune for her land. I wasn't

goin' to let her think 'cause you run one of those new
fangled eatin'-places that you wasn't just as good
as any city folks as might come here. She seemed
terrible interested. Said she thought that this might
be a pretty place when the sun shone, she might like
to spend the summer here, she hadn't been very
well."

Consternation slashed a zig-zag course through
Pamela's mind. Evidently the " real natty man " was
Cecile's attorney. They had been on their way to
the Silver Moon. Why? In all good faith Cap'n
Iry had set forth the value of the Leigh property.
His reference to the " peck of diamonds " must have
been a flick on the raw; Cecile had been wild to
have them. Would she take advantage of the information? Try to get more money? Hadn't
Scott said that it might occur to her as a lucrative
possibility?

Pamela was aware of the oysterman's dropped
jaw as she flashed past him. She dashed into the
house. Stopped at the living room door. No one
there. No sound but the snap of the fire. Voices in
her father's room! His bell. Why should she
answer it? Why should she be dragged into a row?
The bell again, an irritated protracted ring. With
a little grimace of distaste she slowly mounted the
stairs.

Cecile, the color high in her fair skin, her green
eyes sullen, her small rouged mouth unbecomingly
twisted, turned as Pamela entered the room.

"I told Harold that you set the dog on me. He

laughed. Was it his plan as well as yours to keep me out?"

Pamela looked at her father standing behind the arm-chair, his hands gripping its back. He raised warning brows. What did he mean by that wireless? Her anger flared as she looked at the woman who had married him and deserted him at the first sign of adversity. She struggled to keep her voice coolly amused.

"Don't be an idiot, Cecile. Of course I didn't set the dog on you. Think I'm looking for more trouble? Just why are you here?"

"Why am I here! My attorney brought me."

"Where is he?" Harold Leigh's waxen face lost the bit of color it had acquired from the surprise of his wife's arrival.

"His car is stuck in your beastly, wet Cape Cod sand. We missed the main road and landed at an oyster shack. I came to demand an allowance from you, Harold."

"An allowance! That is almost funny, Cecile. You know that I have nothing left."

"Then where did that money come from you sent me?"

He set a little back-fire. "You lied to get it, lied about the operation, didn't you?"

Cecile blazed. "So, that lawyer was sent by you! I knew it!"

"Lawyer?" The surprise in her father's voice closed Pamela's lips. She had been about to defend him. He had not known that Scott Mallory went to New York to check up on Cecile. He may have suspected who the "friend" was who had reported back, but he had asked no questions. She would better say nothing.

"You're good, but not good enough, Harold. It didn't take me long to realize that your Mr. Mallory was there to shadow me. He was as out of place in that party as Galahad in a speakeasy. As for the lie—as you call it—nothing hackneyed about that. I might have claimed that an appendix was clamoring for removal, or high blood pressure. The foot operation was much more original." Her flippant voice hardened. "I was advised to make the test. I knew that you and your daughter had money cached somewhere. I suspected that you would sacrifice your last treasure rather than have me here for a few weeks. Now I know it."

Pamela noticed in her father's eyes the furtive look which had puzzled her before. "My last treasure! I have nothing left except a few lame ducks I picked up in the stock market."

"I'm not so sure. If you did not send Mallory—"

"Send Mallory! Would I have sent you that money had I doubted your word? The Leigh women don't lie, Cecile."

"Oh, don't they! *You* and your family! I was glad of the excuse to break away when you were ill. It wasn't all lack of money. I was fed-up with your talk of what your ancestors had done. You! You sitting back and spending what they had made and never trying to make more. *You,* one of those millions of the living who are already dead! You don't know the first letter of the word ambition!"

Her voice lashed. Harold Leigh winced. Pamela's love for him flamed as a gray coal blazes into red light when blown upon. She tucked her hand under his arm, comforted as she had when a little girl:

"Never mind, Dad, never mind!"

His clammy fingers clutched hers as he answered his wife. "Didn't try to make more! My God, when I did try what happened?"

"You crashed, you being *you.* I suspect now that you didn't crash. I know that you and your daughter have money. I shan't sue for a divorce, I should cut myself off from inheriting my share of your property. I don't want to marry again, not a chance. I have been advised that I am entitled to an allowance. I came to talk with you amicably. As usual Pamela steps between us. I suspect that the loss of fortune was your way of getting rid of me, Harold. I —"

"Would I give up the work I love, come here and run a chowder house if we had anything?" Pamela interrupted stormily. "You are crazy!"

Cecile recovered her voice with the convulsive swallow of one whose determination to riot and revel in an orgy of tirade had been blocked suddenly.

"Really! Before you came upstairs your father had confirmed what he had already written, that you had persuaded him that I was not necessary in his life. The old man who brought me here told me that the Leighs had been the first family since the place was settled, that they were 'awful proud,' never had had a breath of scandal. I'll show them! I will start proceedings for an allowance, but before that—" With a nice sense of theatric values she paused on the threshold to hurl her bomb— "I will drag you into court, Miss Leigh!"

She was out of the room before the smoke of battle had cleared sufficiently for Pamela to sense the threat. Drag her into court? Why? She would make her tell before she left.

She flew down the stairs. The yellow slicker was crackling out of the front doorway. She followed. Stopped on the porch. Philip Carr was smiling at Cecile as he shook hands.

"Hulloa! Thought you hated the country. What are you doing here?"

She shrugged. "Merely calling upon my husband."

His surprise was funny if one could see anything funny in this outrageous situation, Pamela thought. He demanded:

"Do you mean that you are Harold Leigh's wife? The wife who deserted him? I didn't even know that you had been married."

Cecile's lips whitened and tightened. "That

needn't make any difference in our — friendship, need it?"

Carr put his hands hard into his pockets. "Sorry, but it will. Miss Leigh is my friend and — my client. I don't care for the way you ditched her and your husband when they were in trouble. A poor sport! I've heard about it from my father. That's that."

He spoke to Pamela standing rigid on the top step. "I came to confirm measurements of the cottage. I'll get them now. See you tonight."

Cecile followed him with her eyes. Said acidly: "In love with you, isn't he? You have a fatal charm, haven't you? I pulled every wire I could to meet Philip Carr. He is backing a revue, and now he has turned me down for you. Believe me, you'll need his friendship before I get through! *Au revoir!*"

Pamela tried to protest, but her throat contracted, shut off her voice. She watched her stepmother as she picked her way along the wet stepping-stones. Retort after scathing retort flamed in her mind. Why hadn't she thought of them in time to hurl them at Cecile. Why hadn't she told her that she had met Philip Carr but once before? A lot of help, these after-the-fight flashes of invective. She watched Cap'n Crockett's shabby flivver chug down the drive to the accompaniment of a lugubrious horn, till it was but a drab blotch in a gray curtain of rain.

Her father's bell rang as she entered the house. Darn! Her conception of Hades was a place where one would be sentenced to forever answer the imperative tinkle of a bell, she told herself, as she went slowly up the stairs, reluctance in every step. When she reached his room he was leaning back in his chair, his brows wrinkled thoughtfully.

"Has she gone?" His voice was agitated.

"Yes."

"Even in that slicker she was beautiful, wasn't she? I had forgotten. I've been living in a haze." He brushed his hand across his eyes.

Pamela regarded him incredulously. How could he see anything lovely in a woman who had slashed at him as had Cecile? Should she tell him that his wife was trying for a revue which Philip Carr was backing? Better not. The name of Carr was anathema to him. She hadn't told him of the plan to move the cottage yet. Besides, Cecile might be lying. She disagreed passionately:

"Beautiful! Not to me. Cecile won't seem so to you when she begins proceedings for an allowance."

He picked up a newspaper. "What can she get? I have no money. Mallory will stand between and handle the matter for me."

"You wouldn't ask him to do more for nothing?"

"Why not? Lawyers, like doctors, do a certain amount of work for which they are not paid. You'd better get in touch with him, better tell him of Cecile's threat to you before you worry about me." He looked up from his paper to add significantly:

"You own this place. You have more to lose than I have."

Chapter IX

———◆———

PAMELA caught a reassuring glimpse of her amber-frocked self in the great gold-framed mirror in the hall of the Carr house. Her hair was still black. After the fright the Babe had given her this morning it ought to be streaked with white. Suppose the dog had bitten Cecile! But, he hadn't. What a coincidence that she should have been trying for an engagement in the revue in which Philip Carr was interested. But it wasn't coincidence. She had admitted that she had pulled every possible wire to meet him. A maze of crossing life-lines; would it ever straighten out? For what cause would the second Mrs. Leigh hale her stepdaughter into court? But, of course, that had been merely an angry threat. Suppose she did? More annoyance for Scott Mallory on her account? Never. Why had she let him step into her life that first day? Let him? How could she help it? His smile and eyes had gone so straight and deep into her heart, his voice had been so steadying, his mouth so clean, his eyes so clear, and she had been so hungry for a nice man to talk to. Suppose Cecile did sue her? What

could she get? Forget it! Wasn't this a party?
She would much better spend thought on the brand
of greeting she would receive from her senior host.
She met Philip Carr's eyes in the mirror. Laughed.

"Not too bad."

"Look swell to me. By the way, better not mention the fact that I know your stepmother. I'll explain why later," he added in a low voice before
he led the way through the hall.

Pamela paused on a threshold. What a room!
The walls were of cypress to a height of six feet,
warmly brown, paneled like an ancient vessel's cabin.
Behind glass panels reposed the most comprehen-
sive, rare collection of books on ships and shipping
to be found in the country, she had heard. The
plaster above was tinted blue, the blue of the sky
on a windy day at sea. Ship models on the shelves
which topped the book-cases were arranged with a
nice attention to artistic and chronological relativity.
There were ships of wood, metal, bone, ivory, glass.
There were ships with bellying sails, ships with guns,
ships rich with decoration. There were man-o'-war
models, whaling models, models of Chinese and
Japanese junks, of Spanish and Dutch ships, of
Greek coasting vessels, of Viking galleons. There
were models of ships which had helped make American history. There was the clipper ship *Flying
Cloud,* nearby, the packet *Massachusetts*. Ships
pendant from the ceiling held cunningly concealed
bulbs in their hulks the light from which shone softly

down through glass bottoms. A tall Willard clock in the corner, topped by three brass balls which reflected the firelight, showed on its face a scudding barque about to dip below the horizon.

After the involuntary pause Pamela stepped forward to greet her hostess whose delicacy might have materialized from a fan of the Louis the Fourteenth period. Her gown was a blend of violet and flesh color, the latter no more delicate than her rosepetal skin. Her hair, white and soft as the silk of a Scotch thistle, was arranged to show the charming contour of her head. Her eyes were lovely, but, for all her apparent sweetness her mouth had a stubborn line when in repose. The value of her string of pearls would have reinstated a deposed ruler in the king business, supposing, of course, his subjects wished him reinstated. Her hand clung to the girl's.

"This marvelous room stampeded my manners, Mrs. Carr. I'm sorry!"

"You will win my husband's heart if you like his ships, Miss Leigh. Phin!"

There was a note of appeal in her voice. Was she afraid of him, Pamela wondered. She had met women before who handled their soul-mates as if they were high explosives. Must be wearing to live with a man of whom one was afraid. The tall one looking into the fire turned. Since the settlement of her grandmother's estate she had seen Phineas Carr in the distance only, his long arms, swinging as he strode, giving the effect of a walking-beam. Her

eyes met his. Her heart broke into a quickstep.
She had a flashing premonition that this man would
ineradicably change her future. That silly plot-construction stuff again! She would better get it out of
her system, it dramatized even the most common-
place events of life for her. There was power in
his black eyes, inflexibility in his stern mouth. His
thick hair, streaked black, white and gray, had the
lustre of smoked pearl. His arm seemed abnormally
long as he extended his hand.

"Glad to see you here, Miss Leigh. I admired
your grandmother. She was a wonderful woman.
Hope you have inherited her grit and her sunshiny
philosophy. It was always, 'Fair tomorrow', with
her. Hers was not a shallow optimism but a deep
and abiding faith in the ultimate victory of the
dragon-slayer."

His gruff voice was kind, his smile whimsical.
He was not holding her responsible for her father's
sins of omission or commission — whichever they
were. Thank heaven! Pamela sensed the relaxation of his wife and son. What had they expected?
Was he a martinet? The villagers spoke of him
with mingled awe and affection. "A hard man but
a just one, the Judge."

If the dining room was an example of Philip
Carr's taste she was all for it, she told herself, as
he drew out a chair for her at the beautifully appointed table. It was in dark and light burgundy
shades with dark rose and light rose, vivid thrusts of

gold, mauve and tender green.   Rose brocade on the seats of the mellow wood chairs; rose brocade at the windows, across one of which were shelves holding up pink Opaline against the light; vases; bottles; curious flagons with touches of gilt in their rims. A rich burgundy carpet covered the floor.   Mirrors on opposite sides of the room amplified the proportions, gave back the rose and burgundy tints, gave back also the pale amber of her gown which was like a shaft of sunlight.   The house had an up-to-the-minute atmosphere.   She loved it.

She was conscious of tension throughout the delicious supper — a compote of fruit, sea-food newburg on crisps of toast which made her wish she might keep on eating forever — a hot-house tomato salad, ice-cool, to accompany it — fluffy rolls and fresh unsalted butter — a baked Alaska which was a perfect thing of its kind — served by pink-frocked Milly Pike.

Mrs. Carr and her son kept the conversation-puck within bounds.   Perfect teamwork between them.   Was it because of the presence of the maid with her over-developed bump of curiosity or were they afraid of an outburst from the stern, silent man at the head of the table?   It was abundantly evident by the way he looked at his wife that he adored her; it was equally apparent that he disliked — no, that wasn't the word — distrusted Philip.   Once when discussion evidently neared thin ice, the mother swept it to safety again.   Pamela caught a sardonic gleam in the senior Carr's eyes. He was aware of her tactics, indubitably.

It was a relief after supper to escape to Philip's work-room. He swept a pile of drawings from a small drafting-table and placed a chair in front of it.

"Sit here, Miss Leigh." He ran his fingers through his hair. "Gosh! This place is a mess. It isn't Mother's fault, really, I turn the key on it when I go away."

The room was large and exceedingly dusty. Tall rolls of paper, cardboard and tracing-cloth there were, a corner full; portfolios, a fat and bulging collection; paints, crayons, brushes, squares, triangles, scales, by the battered score; a desk crowded with ruling pens and inks in bewildering variety. On the wall, drawings in frames, plans thumbtacked; bits from colorful gardens; a drypoint or two; the fragment of a peristyle; gateways; antique façades; a water-color of marvelous Taj-Mahal. A guitar lay on the window-seat.

Pamela's eyes returned from their voyage of observation. "I believe that you really work — or — is this clutter for artistic effect?"

He took her seriously. "Of course I work. I'm doing some stage settings for a revue. To nail the chance I had to help back the show. That's how I ran into your — Cecile Mortimer. Mother knows what I'm doing — Mother always understands — but we don't want Father to hear of it until I've made good. He wouldn't see it at all. Get me? That's the reason I warned you in the hall. This is my play-room. I fool with plans when I come home. I've worked like a dog this last week in New York that I might have something to show you."

From an alcove he dragged a large table on wheels. On an expanse of green paper, to simulate a lawn, was a cardboard model of the farmer's cottage. Dormers had been let into the roof, a porch faced a shellac shore sprinkled with sand, which edged a scrap of brilliantly blue painted sea. Pamela regarded it incredulously.

"How could you copy the cottage so perfectly?"

Philip Carr perched on the arm of her chair. His eyes were boyishly eager. "I told you that often I feasted on milk and cookies in the farmer's house. Besides my memory of it I had a photograph of your grandmother's place to work from. It belongs to Father but I lugged it off to New York and — there we are! This noon — after leaving you and your stepmother — hope I didn't mess things up more — I confirmed the measurements. Like it? A man I know gave me pointers on a development scheme. See those marks? They indicate where more houses will stand if we make good on this. I'm out to make your real estate a going concern. We'll keep the cottages of the same type as the Leigh house. The severely straight lines cost less to build. Big central chimney in exact centre of roof, windows placed directly above each other, entrance door in centre.

No porches on old houses but I have added one. See the garage? Looks like a woodshed. Notice the pitch of the roof? Slightly less than a right angle. That, and no visible foundation give the squatty look."

"It is perfect. I hate to be little Miss Kill-joy, but won't remodelling cost more than four thousand dollars? There it is again. Money! Money!"

"It won't cost that. The model is made to scale of ¼ inch to the foot. If you okay it I will go on with specifications. We ought to get at it. You will have the time of your life selecting wall-papers. Got any furniture you are not using?"

"The attic is full of it."

"Bully! This will be the house of the month when we get through. Come in, Mother. What do you think of the development scheme? Houses going here and here and—"

"*After* we have rented the first cottage," Pamela interpolated gaily. She slipped her arm within Mrs. Carr's. "See the windows just like those at the Silver Moon, the black band on the chimney?"

"That band stood for loyalty to the King, in the old days. You have been wise to keep the lines simple," Mrs. Carr approved. "Sandy-the-carpenter can make those alterations and additions without supervision."

"I shan't leave it entirely to him. I mean to be here every week-end to boss the job, Mother."

"Really?" Her face was pathetic in its radiance.

The light of happiness waned. "Then you must be more diplomatic with your father. Try, *try* to agree with him at least one time in ten."

"I'll do my best for your sake, Mother, but nothing I say or think seems right to him. We are everlastingly arguing. He is so infernally suspicious of me. I'll bet that when he hears that I suggested moving the farmer's cottage he'll think I have a personal rake-off up my sleeve. Just because stuffy court rooms are the breath of life to him, he can't bear it that I prefer to work on houses and stagesets. I'm sorry, Pamela — don't mind if I scrap formality, do you — to rattle the family skeleton in your hearing."

Mrs. Carr defended, "There isn't a family skeleton, only — only Philip's father is so much older than he that he fails in sympathetic understanding. The moment a subject comes up they take opposite sides. They have many traits alike; oh, yes, you have, Philip, that is the trouble." She abruptly changed the subject. "Have you planned the inside of the cottage?"

Young Carr flung down his pencil. "Not yet. What say if we go nail Sandy-the-carpenter, Pamela? He won't mind talking business on the Sabbath day. When we get back to the Silver Moon I'll take another look at the cottage."

Pamela sensed his mother's wince at his curt answer to her query. It was as if he had slammed a door in her face. Did it pay to lavish love and care on a child? Even the best of them were brutal at times.

"Coming?" inquired Philip from the threshold. Pamela spoke to her hostess. "Thank you for a delightful evening. It has been perfect in this perfect house. May I say goodnight to Mr. Carr?"

What inexplicable urge had prompted the request, she asked herself, as she noticed the glance between mother and son. Why hadn't she let sleeping dogs lie? Mrs. Carr acquiesced smoothly:

"Of course. We will find him in the Ship Room."

The tall man rose as they entered. Courtly manner; no wonder Grandmother Leigh had liked and trusted him, Pamela thought, as she laid her hand in his. Again she felt the premonition that somewhere behind the curtain of the future he would cross her life-line and change the pattern. Uncanny feeling. She tried to shake it off as she said lightly:

"Sometime I will show you my one lone ship. It is bottled."

"I know that ship, Miss Pamela, it is a museum piece. I know every treasure in your grandmother's house. There is nothing finer in the country than the old maple she left you. I hear that you are talking of making over the farmer's cottage."

How had he heard? Pamela knew from the startled glances exchanged by mother and son that the information had not come from them. Milly! Had she overheard Phil at the telephone? She acknowledged quickly:

"It is more than talk. I shall do it. Philip has the model ready."

She was aware of the challenging earnestness of her voice, for all the world as if she were pleading a cause. Phineas Carr warned curtly:

"Don't rely too much on Philip. He is more artistic than practical."

Pamela refuted indignantly: "Not practical! I think him most pratical. Hasn't he figured out a way to increase our income, at least to take care of taxes and repairs? Turning the farmer's cottage from a liability to an asset is my idea of constructive planning."

"If — he sees it through," Phineas Carr amended drily.

"Believe me, I'll see this proposition through." Philip's voice was hoarse with anger. "Going to fool you this time. Come on, Miss Pamela Leigh."

Outside the air was cool and clear, scented with the fresh smell of wet earth. Pamela drew a long breath. What a night after the storm! Stars blinked through hazy patches of cloud; one low-hung, brilliant, was setting in the west. All day the world had been overcast. Now it was gleaming into beauty. Was life like that? While apparently it was befogged with problems, were happiness and good fortune just waiting their chance to break through the gloom?

Philip Carr yanked the roadster into gear. There was light enough for Pamela to see his angry eyes, his sneering lips. Evidently his father's words still rankled. His resentment boiled over.

"You heard him! Never gives me credit. Just because I hate law, he thinks I can't do anything. I'll show him a thing or two on this cottage."

"He didn't really mean it, Phil. Why don't you tell him about the stage settings, and the revue?"

"If he can't trust me he doesn't deserve to know. I'm his son and Mother's; that ought to count for something."

"Some day you'll make a grand crack at fame and then he will be so proud of you that he will bore his cronies to death talking about his wonderful boy. Meanwhile, cheer'o! Fair tomorrow!"

Not until the words were spoken did Pamela realize that she had adopted her grandmother's "sunshiny philosophy."

Chapter X

PAMELA leaned her head against the high back of
her chair in the Pullman and closed her eyes. Only
eight o'clock in the morning and she was dead tired.
It was the first time she had sat down since she had
risen before the crack of dawn that she might leave
everything arranged for Hitty Betts and Terrence
to carry on. Was a day off worth the exertion?
Yesterday had been hectic. Through her absorption,
at intervals, had pricked Phineas Carr's caustic
comment:

"Don't rely too much upon him. He is more
artistic than practical." Then his doubting, "If he
sees it through."

Had the indictment been merely an older person's
impatience with an obviously spoiled boy or was
there truth behind it? She liked Philip Carr.
Would he lose interest in the project he had started
once she was committed to it? Was life disappointment all along the line? Maybe everyone was
unstable inside, maybe everyone rebelled against
carrying through to the finish when a newer project
beckoned alluringly. Would she herself go on with

the Silver Moon Chowder House if old-man Necessity did not wriggle his automatic between her shoulders to keep her stepping forward? She would not. She would abandon it so quickly that a chance oyster left in stock would gape open in surprise.

Her eyes were on the confused blur flying past outside. The wheels ground an accompaniment, as her thoughts and time trooped on. Even if Philip Carr lost interest in the cottage she could carry it through. She had the money. Last night Sandy-the-carpenter had been eager to begin moving it. Scott would help. She would not tell him of Cecile's visit, of the Babe's attack on the second Mrs. Leigh, of her threat to hail her stepdaughter into court, of Philip Carr's acquaintance with her — most certainly not that. He was carrying enough of their perplexities now. Scott! The thought of him warmed her. That didn't get her anywhere. If numerous telephone calls were an indication he was still stepping out with Hilda Crane or her extravagant sister. Was Pamela Leigh a dog in the manger? That was what he could call a rhetorical question. She was.

The city! Already she could hear the main roar punctuated by crashes and bangs and an ear-splitting siren. She adjusted her hat, removed any possible speck of dust with her powder pad. Even before the train stopped, her mood was quickstepping to the stir and stimulation about her, so different from the unchanging sameness of the country. She smiled at the reflection in the mirror of her compact. That girl tired? Her eyes were brilliant, her color high. She was on the very top of the world. She could have done without that absurd dimple at one corner of her mouth which her smile routed from ambush. It was too childish for the business woman she had become. She would go directly to Scott Mallory's office, get the banking business behind her. Once her credit was established, she would cash the cheque she had brought to spend on electrical equipment for the Silver Moon.

The elevator shot to the fourteenth floor with a speed which gave her the sense of having somehow, somewhere lost connection with her breath.

"Far's we go," announced the boy. He cocked his head in its rakishly tipped, gorgeously braided hat toward a door down the corridor. "Mallory & Carter."

She gave her name to another boy at a switchboard. Her old tweed suit, garnished with the neckpiece she had had fashioned from Grandmother Leigh's Russian sables, had looked sufficiently smart in the mirror in her own room but one glance at the modish, obviously, girl-on-her-own, who opened a door marked "Mr. Mallory," made her hotly aware that fashion had broken into a forward run since she had retired to the country. Miss Cryder? She recognized her at once as the perfect office secretary of the talkies. Her head with its ruddy waves might recently have left the expert hands of a hairdresser;

her brown frock was smartly simple with collar and cuffs of incredible fineness; hosiery and shoes were the last word in shade and model; her hands were perfect with almond-shaped nails which gleamed like gems. Pamela was also aware that her arrival had interested the occupants of the outer office. It seemed to have paralyzed their fingers if one could accept the sudden cessation of the click of type-writers as a sign. Miss Cryder smiled.

"Mr. Mallory will see you at once, Miss Leigh."

As Pamela entered the book-lined office Scott Mallory stepped from behind a desk on which she noticed one perfect rose in a slender crystal vase. He seemed a curiously different person from the man with whom she had motored, upon whose shoulder — figuratively speaking — she had sobbed out — again figuratively — her troubles. He appeared as impersonal as the Chief Justice of the Supreme Court. Not that she ever had seen that dignitary while earning his daily bread, but as enthroned in authority as she imagined him to be. In short, he was a stranger. As Miss Cryder closed the door from the outside she had the sense of being abandoned on an unfriendly doorstep without the fictional locket of identification about her neck.

Mallory held out his hand. The sense of remoteness vanished. He picked up his hat.

"We will attend to the banking business first and then—" He answered the telephone in response to a buzz. As Pamela waited through a conversation

in which recurred the words "hearing"—"brief"
—"printer"—"away for the day," she looked out
over roofs alive with strutting, preening pigeons,
crossed with aerials like gigantic cobwebs, fluttering
with flags; looked down into innumerable sunless canyons where taxis scooted, busses lumbered like dino-
saurs. Haze dimmed the outlines of towering sky-
scrapers, of ships and tugs in the distant harbor. It
was like a huge Claude Monet canvas. The hum of
the city rose. From far away came the muffled beat
of a drum.

"Ready."

As beside Scott Mallory she crossed the outer
office under fire of a battery of eyes, she felt as child-
ishly self-conscious as she had her first day at school.
Down in the crowded elevator, along the street they
went, neither of them speaking. As they waited at
a corner for the traffice light to change to red and
yellow, Pamela looked up at her companion surreptitiously. He was looking down at her. He laughed
boyishly. Caught her elbow as she started to cross.

"Not yet! As a pedestrian's caution so shall her
days be. That is the first time you have seen me this
morning. You have looked through me before.
You froze me stiff back there in the office."

Pamela's voice reflected the lightening of her
spirit.

"Your obvious importance and the sartorial per-
fectness of your secretary struck me dumb."

"You look like a million yourself. Come on."

Nice of him to say it but she was increasingly conscious of the contrast between her costume and the last-minute frocks and suits — cheap though many of them were — worn by the women and girls hurrying past.

With the completion of their business in the marble and mahogany fastnesses of the bank the last tinge of Scott Mallory's professional absorption vanished.

"That's that! Now we'll celebrate! Let's plan before we leave here. You want to get that electrical stuff, don't you? Mind if I go with you? Luncheon, talkie — there's a super-production in town — dinner somewhere we can dance and then home."

His voice, his enthusiasm almost swept Pamela into the vortex of his plan. The sight of a woman with every accessory keyed to her chic costume, steadied her. Dinner and dance in her present clothes! Never! Then she would stay at home forever. When would she get money to buy new ones? Every cent she made for a year or two must go into equipment for the Silver Moon. A tide of rebellion swept her. Why should it? She had a purse full of money now. Why spend it for electrical gadgets? Why not on herself? Terry would say, "Sure, Pam! Go to it! You've earned it."

"Well? We have just this one day to spend together — at present. Where shall we begin?"

Heart-quickening impatience in Scott Mallory's voice, the least glint of the pursuing male in his gray eyes. A wave of recklessness left Pamela high and dry on a rock of determination. She would live this one day to the full — no matter if when the clock struck twelve she had to cut all thought of romance from her life for years. The Cinderella motif. Cinderella had had a godmother who changed her calico to satin and pearls. Pamela Leigh had a god-mother — of sorts — in her purse. She glanced at the marble and gilt clock on the marble and gilt wall.

"I will meet you at one-thirty."

"Not until one-thirty! It's a lifetime to wait."

"You are an eloquent advocate, aren't you? I have things to do — heaps and heaps of them. Tell me where to meet you for luncheon. After that my life is in your hands."

Sparks of laughter in his eyes flamed to fire. "Do you mean that?"

"With — reservations. Don't notice what I say. I'm a wild woman when I get to the city."

He hailed a taxi. Wheedled: "Sure I can't help? I left word at the office that I would not be back today."

"Very sure."

He stood on the curb, hat in hand, looking after her as the cab started. A taxi! The first step on her downward course in extravagance. Undoubtedly she would bring up with a smash — not literally, she hoped — but the going promised to be smooth and swift.

With mounting excitement she looked from the window. The city again! It was heady. Automobiles running the gamut of the scale from unbelievable shabbiness to amazing luxury, crawled up and down the broad street in response to a Cyclopian eye. Shop windows flaunted their riches. Garishness and charm. Elaboration and costly simplicity. Here a choice rug from the Orient; there a painting of tranquillity and beauty; a canvas blazing with color; a bronze depicting man and horse vital with primitive emotions. Jewels dazzled and tempted. Flowers lured by their color and fragrance. There were frocks in all the tints of the spectrum; there were florid hangings; there was furniture from palaces across the sea. A band! "Stars and Stripes Forever!" Marching men! The steady rhythm of feet on the sun-patched pavement. Flags! A bugle! The boom, boom, boom of drums. Pamela sat back with a little bounce of sheer exuberance. The city! The adorable city! She had been starved for it.

Mallory was waiting when she reached the green and gold foyer of the restaurant at thirty-five minutes after one a little breathless. He looked straight at her without a sign of recognition, before he turned to glare at a wall clock, to impatiently confirm its story by a glance at his watch. Why should he know her? Hadn't she spent the morning and most of the electrical equipment money in an attempt to look as little as possible like the girl who had entered his office? To save precious time she had confided to a shopping expert what she wanted, what she had to spend and the brief time in which she had to spend it. The capable about-forty woman, had appraised the Russian sable at a glance, had purred enthusiasm. The result was the hat of the week, with a sparkling clip the twin of one which glittered on her antelope bag, a chic short-sleeved black velvet frock with a coat for street and luncheon, cream chamois gloves, a string of synthetic pearls. Pamela—remembering the real gems she had sacrificed—flinched at those, but submitted—they were ravishingly becoming—and crowning extravagances, a pair of long gloves for evening and adorable shoes, smartly modern, fashionably impractical. She had spent the time while alterations were being made, in the beauty shop. She had emerged with a modish wave in her hair, a touch of perfume under one ear and a glaze on her nails like opaline glass.

"I'm here!"

Mallory wheeled. Regarded her incredulously. "What have you done to yourself? You look taller."

"High heels. Don't you like me taller?" She threw just the right amount of wistfulness into voice and eyes. Truly the decent to Avernus was as swift as it purported to be—and more heady.

Scott Mallory laughed. "Changed your line with your clothes, haven't you. Come."

To the accompaniment of the quick, stimulating syncopation of an orchestra, the major domo conducted them through a table-bordered lane with the air of one leading a legion into battle. Mallory responded to the greetings of a gay group. A smartly clad girl removed a cigarette from her lips with jeweled fingers. Hilda Crane! Pamela held her head a little higher. No chance of developing an inferiority complex in her present costume. This moment paid for all it had cost in money, all it would cost in labor.

"Scott!" Miss Crane cooed. Her eyes deep violet pools of amazement as she glanced at his companion. "Well, of all people! The cook!"

Mallory's eyes glowed like black coals as he took the seat opposite Pamela at a small table. A snowy Isle of the Blest. Not too wide for low voices to carry across nor hands to touch. Not too near the music. Not too deeply shaded by a synthetic palm. An old waiter, wise-eyed. Violets — a fragrant bunch with a gardenia heart. Candles, pink-shaded. Silver. Crystal. Roseate seclusion. A table in a thousand. A companion not inexperienced along the flowery paths of sentiment? Had he done all this for Hilda Crane, Pamela wondered as she lifted the lovely blossoms. She interrupted the order he was giving.

"Please! Not so much. Why spend our precious afternoon eating."

He revised the order. The major domo handed the slip to a minion. The minion scuttled away. Scott Mallory leaned forward.

"I'm sorry. You seem always to be the victim of the rotten manners of my one-time friend. Let's forget her." A laugh cleared his eyes and voice of annoyance. "Did you travel up from the Cape with a wardrobe trunk concealed about your person?"

"'The feel of Paris.' Like them?"

"The clothes? Mad about them."

She was conscious of a guilty accession of color. "These are not clothes. The frock and hat are a mammoth coffee tricolater. The electric ice-cream freezer — plus a few much needed kitchen utensils — completes the ensemble." His laugh brought her eyes to his.

"And it was only a short time ago you were wondering if you would forget how to spend money!"

"Ladies must dress. Then you are not shocked?"

"Shocked! My dear girl, I am inexpressibly relieved to find you so human. I had begun to fear that you were all saint and sacrifice."

"Me! There is something grammatically wrong with that exclamation, but we'll let it pass. All saint! That's funny. I was tempted and I fell. Crashed, is a better word. Besides what you see, I have a slinky frock the color of the gorgeous breast of an oriole for evening. I am sitting on the lid of my conscience at this very moment. Oh, I shall repent and pay and pay and pay — unfortunately Terry will too — when I struggle with inadequate equipment in the green and white kitchen. Let's forget my brainstorm."

"Just a minute. Breath-taking as you are now,

you will never look lovelier than in the white apron
and cap. You looked so young and troubled, yet
your eyes were so valiant that Thanksgiving day that
when I said good-bye, I felt as if I were heartlessly
abandoning an adorable child who was struggling
against fear."

"I remember that you called me, 'child.'"

"Not plain, 'child.'"

She leaned toward him. "Honestly now, how
could you call me 'plain child' ?"

His laugh was one of the nicest of the many nice
things about him, Pamela decided, his teeth were so
perfect.

"If a demure little Quaker had suddenly gone
tap-dancer I couldn't be more surprised. I didn't
know you had it in you."

"Dual personality. I told you that I shed my
work-day line with my linen frock. Hope you are
not disappointed."

"Disappointed? — Gorgeous!"

Her heart caught and plunged on. For a party
which was to be kept gaily impersonal that "Gorgeous" had been too deep, his eyes too ardent. Did
Cinderella suffer a warning ache at her heart, a,
"You know this can't keep on," reminder through
the gaiety and splendor of the royal ball and the
Prince's devotion? Silly to cloud the present when
she had recklessly mortgaged the future for this one
day. Did Scott suspect what she was thinking? His
eyes were tenderly amused as they met hers.

"Don't let a wraith from the past or the future

flit across our party, Pam. You won't be troubled by a word you don't want to hear from this minute till I leave you at the Silver Moon. Think I don't realize what I have to live down? That Thanksgiving dinner for one thing. Think I didn't know when you looked at the violets that you wondered if I had given violets to Hilda — never, she preferred orchids. I've got to prove to you that I am naturally a one-woman worshiper — when I find the right woman. Get the idea? I know better than to crowd my luck. It is luck to have you to myself for a few hours. How are things going at the Silver Moon?"

His casual question restored the equilibrium his impassioned voice had undermined.

"Wonderfully. Each week sees an increase in revenue. I had my staff up at daybreak this morning to help me off. Hitty wished to be remembered to Mr. Mallory, Terry sent his best, and the Babe his love."

"Thanks. Makes me feel as if I had a family which cared. I come of poor but honest parents — wonderful parents." His voice had deepened, the muscles of his mouth twitched as if he were mastering emotion. "I worked for my education, you know. I am quite alone now."

She hadn't known. Not until this moment had she realized how little he had told her about himself. She was forever referring to her family. She grew uncomfortably hot as she remembered Cecile's scathing:

"You and your family — I was bored to death by your talk of what your ancestors had done."

Live and learn. Did one keep on blundering all through life? It seemed as if one ought to be wiser than she was at twenty-five. She watched the super-prosperous appearing men, the chic and sophisticated women who chatted and smoked and tasted at the flower bedecked tables to the accompaniment of violin and harp. They appeared care free and gay. Were they preoccupied with problems, perplexities, perhaps tragedies, behind their smiling masks?

"Come back!" Scott Mallory's laughing reminder interrupted her reflections.

"I'm sorry."

"Don't be sorry about anything today. Glad the Babe remembered to send me his love. He and I were great pals when we shared bachelor quarters."

"You must miss him. Why did you send him to us?"

"With all sorts of patrons driving up to the Silver Moon, thought you needed a dog while Terrence was at school. Feel safer about you, with the Babe there. He wouldn't stand for nonsense."

He would not indeed if his attack on Cecile were a criterion. What would Scott say if he knew of it? He wasn't to know of it; that was that. He was to know nothing of what had happened during the second Mrs. Leigh's visitation. Pamela thrust the heckling memory of it into the background as Mallory continued:

"The city is no place for a dog. The Babe was born near the sea. I bought him of a fisherman who had raised him from a little pup. The man's weather-bleached eyes were full of tears when he parted with him. He had to let him go because his son, who also was a fisherman, had abused the Babe until the dog showed his teeth whenever he came near. It wasn't safe to have him around."

From luncheon to a super-talkie, on to a portrait show. Conversation, real conversation about things which mattered. They two seemed never to lack interesting subjects for discussion. Long silences. Laughter. She told him of the plan for the cottage, touched lightly on Philip Carr's interest. Dinner and dancing.

She never had danced with him before. She had a sense of security as his arm went about her with disturbing possessiveness. The music was throbby, muted. The leader sang softly:

"'Should I reveal exactly how I feel
Should I confess I love you—'"

Scott Mallory's arm tightened. Pamela fought an impulse to lay her cheek against his—other couples were doing it—and stiffened. Instantly he loosened his hold.

"Happy?" he whispered.

She lifted her face. "Top of the world!"

The musicians crooned, saxophones wailed, violins soared and sighed. The dancers swayed, making, breaking colorful patterns. Everyone caught the contagion of the music. Everyone hummed:

"'Should I reveal exactly how I feel
    Should I confess I love you.'"

In an intermission, above the babel of voices, a steeple clock ponderously told off the hour. Pamela smiled across the small candle-lighted table, sighed regretfully.

"We must go."

"So early? Is your fairy godmother lying in wait to snitch those swanky clothes at the stroke of midnight?"

Even as Scott Mallory protested, he held her coat, settled her sable scarf across her shoulders. His lingering touch sent a thrill feathering through her veins. Curious that the Cinderella motif should be in his mind as well.

"The Silver Moon is my fairy godmother. It watches out that I punch the time-clock when there is a full day ahead."

He signaled to the waiter. Pamela tried to appear sophisticatedly indifferent to the denomination of the greenback he laid on the tray and waved away. It seemed to her perturbed fancy that he had paid out a fortune since she had joined him for luncheon.

Money had Aladdin's Lamp beaten at its own game of magic, she reflected, as Mallory's shining roadster purred to the curb. Tucking in of rug. Touching of hat. Mumbled "Thank you, sir!" The slam of a door. They were off through streets twinkling with lights. A golden dome gleamed against an indigo sky for an instant and was gone. A beam from an air-beacon silvered roofs and leafless trees. In a pale tower a red eye flamed and faded. The river road. A line of lights hung like a glittering girdle where a bridge spanned water, kicked-up to white caps by a salty east wind. Buildings but vague outlines, their lighted windows — like the hundred eyes of Argus, fabled watch-dog of the gods — peered unwinkingly into the night. Moonlight glorified the unglorious, silvered factories and spires with lavish impartiality. The stars seemed nearer and brighter than the lights which gemmed the water-fronts and distant hills.

Glamorous night. Pamela drew a long sigh of content. Mallory bent to tuck the soft rug, which matched perfectly in color the morocco upholstery, more securely about her feet.

"Warm enough? Too much breeze?"

"It's heavenly."

"Happy?"

"Too contented to talk."

"Don't try. We have a long ride ahead. Better get a nap."

"Sleep! That last coffee was so strong it curled my eyelashes up tight. I shall be little bright-eyes for the rest of the night."

The road beckoned alluringly. A broad beautiful road, blanched by moonlight, jeweled with incandescents. Red lights warned. Green lights like cabochon emeralds beckoned. Spurts of conversation. Long, companion-conscious stretches of silence. Gay, amusing give and take of badinage. Far off the sound of a baying dog. Stars trembling on the obsidian surface of a lonely little pond. Houses with lighted windows. Scraps of gossamer mists in the hollows like fairy linen spread out to dry. A solitary horseman. Houses with no lights at all. Luminous shadows. Sooty shadows. A village like a toy town in the moonlight. Mallory slowed the roadster.

"See that white church and the dove-gray parsonage beside it: I helped put through a run-away marriage there before I went to South America, never have forgotten the place."

"Why the elopement? Cruel parents?"

"No. No one objected. The couple had planned a smash of a wedding. Both got nervous about it so slipped away by themselves. Have often wondered since if the wife ever regretted giving up the splurge."

"I doubt it. A large wedding is a terrific strain on a girl's disposition. The last time I was maid of honor, the bride — who really was sweet and lovely — had been lunched and dined, fitted and showered, till she was on edge. The emotional strain of the wedding was the last straw. She went to nervous pieces after the ceremony and snapped at her new husband. He was hurt to the soul. In a moment she was sobbing in his arms. He was dear, but — I've often wondered if the rapture with which he had looked at her at the altar ever again reached the same high peak."

"Would you be satisfied with a small wedding?"

Pamela remembered her father. "I shall be — satisfied not to have any — for some years — to come."

Mallory laughed. "You are half dead with sleep, aren't you. It is cruel to keep you talking."

The roadster picked up, and like a racer demonstrating speed, shot forward.

Plans, thoughts keen as rapiers, thrust their way into Pamela's content. Fluffs of haze dulled them as clouds scooting across the moon toned its brilliance to a dream-like quality. A song hummed over and over, "Should I reveal exactly how I feel." Fragments of stories she had written, characters she never had conceived, kept breaking in on her train of thought, just as when tired after a full day at the Silver Moon, she would lose her place in her prayers and begin over, lose it, and begin again. Perhaps if she closed her eyes — heavenly not to have to hold her head up. She was snuggled in the corner of the big couch at home. She could feel the copper-toned damask against her cheek. And she had thought that she was motoring. She hadn't been to Boston. Spending the equipment money was a nightmare. Queer things, dreams. One could laugh and cry in them. Happy things sometimes. She could smell violets.

Light. Morning so soon. "Pam, dear!" Terry calling her? Not Terry. He would shout "Hi there!" She lifted heavy lids. Gazed straight up into a man's eyes. Their expression shocked her wide awake. She looked about her. The roadster had stopped. The porch light of the Silver Moon had wakened her!

"Have I slept all the way from Boston?" she asked contritely.

There was a husky break in Mallory's laugh. Was he surreptitiously flexing an arm as he stepped from the car? Had she slept against his shoulder?

"Not all the way. For the last fifty miles, that's all. Come on. Watch your step!" He caught her as she stumbled. "Sleepy child. You are not awake yet."

"I am, wide awake. My heart is as light as a balloon, a gay balloon. I feel as if the tide of fortune had turned. I know that there's a grand and glorious bit of good luck about to round the corner. That's what a day off has done for me."

The door was flung open. Every red hair of Terrence's head seemed on end as he waved a paper.

"Thought you'd never come! Boy! I'm glad you're here, Mr. Scott!"

"What's the matter, Terry?" Pamela caught his arm.

"Go slow, Terrence. You are frightening your sister. What has happened?"

"Father?" The word caught in Pamela's throat. Terrence shook off her clutching fingers.

"Father! Nothing so simple. It's a summons! Cap'n Iry Crockett served it today! Cecile has attached this property for thirty thousand dollars!"

Chapter XI

————◆————

PAMELA raced to her room to answer the telephone. More privacy there. Scott had told her last night that he would call her as soon as he found out why Cecile had attached the property. The summons had merely stated the fact. That summons! Its content was burned into her brain forever. If she closed her eyes she saw in great letters:

COMMONWEALTH OF MASSACHUSETTS
To PAMELA LEIGH

WE Command you that you appear at our Superior Court —

She must put the thing out of her mind! Her heart pounded as she held the receiver to her ear. "The Silver Moon. Pamela Leigh speaking. . . . Scott! What was it? . . . For alienation of Father's affection! Good grief! What can she do? . . . She can? . . . Oh, no, I won't worry. What's a paltry thirty thousand dollar suit in my young life? . . . I'm not laughing, I'm not hysterical. . . . No! *No!* Don't leave your work again this week! . . . I know you will, but I won't let you. Good-bye!"

She hung up the receiver on his eager, "Pam, listen!" Hands clasped hard on her knees she stared at the sand dunes steeping in the sunshine. Scott had called the New York lawyer, who had brought the suit, on long distance. He had explained that Mrs. Harold Leigh, known on the stage as Cecile Mortimer, was suing her stepdaughter for alienation of her husband's affection. Of course Cecile had thought that up the day she had come to the Silver Moon. Hadn't she departed on the threat:

"I will start proceedings for an allowance, but —before that, I will drag you into court, Miss Leigh!"

Scott had said, "Don't worry. I will look after it for you." And she had refused passionately, "I won't let you."

She wouldn't. Even in the instant of his communication of the facts something within her had protested against his aid. He had done enough for them in attending to her father's tangled affairs. It had troubled him last night to leave her with the summons unexplained, but he had been due in court this morning. She would not be a ball and chain hitched to him. To whom could she turn? Scott must have anticipated some such mix-up. When she had accused:

"You are afraid Cecile will try to get that money,

aren't you?" he had answered: "If it occurred to her as a lucrative possibility, she might."

Cecile had tried it. Was she counting on an easy settlement? Settle! Pamela Leigh settle! She wouldn't if she could. She would make Cecile prove that she had come between husband and wife. She shrugged. Bombast. Commendable but inane. How could she make her prove it without a lawyer and how could she retain a lawyer without money? Her father's bell. He must be told. What would be his reaction?

Harold Leigh frowned as she entered his room. Sunshine patched his green lounging robe with gilt, lay warmly on the stamp strewn table by the side of his chair. He demanded petulantly:

"What has happened? Something going on, I know. Terrence was jumpy when he brought up my breakfast. There isn't a tinge of color in your face. I heard you at the telephone. What is it?" He rapped an irritating tattoo on the table. It set the tiny, colorful squares of paper a-twitter like autumn leaves doing a double-shuffle in a sudden breeze.

Pamela crossed to the window. Eyes on the placid sea and cloudless sky she flung over her shoulder:

"Cecile has attached this property for thirty thousand dollars."

"Good God! What for?"

"She is suing me for alienating your affection." She wheeled to face him. "It's a joke, isn't it?"

"What do you mean —' joke ' ?"

" This alienation suit. You don't want her here, do you? You are mighty glad to get rid of her, aren't you? You know that I never have said a word to influence you. You will have a chance to testify to that in court."

"In court! I am not able to appear in a court room."

" Not to help me? Thirty thousand dollars for Cecile if she wins the case. Perhaps, though, you don't care. Perhaps you have a few more antiques you can turn into money with which to pay the verdict."

" What do you mean? " His voice caught in his throat. He pulled at the collar of his soft shirt before he went on: " I have no money. Mallory will handle the matter for us, of course."

"He will not! He won't let us pay him for the time he has already given our affairs."

" That is nothing. I've told you before that lawyers, like doctors, expect to do a certain amount of work for which they are not paid. Look at Phineas Carr! He is one of the biggest men in his profession. Think he never helped anyone out? "

Phineas Carr! It was the first time her father had mentioned his name since Grandmother Leigh's estate had been settled. Would Mr. Carr help her? What effect would that daring thought-contact have on her life? Tangle it more or help unsnarl it? There she was again thinking in plot terms. Suppose he consented to appear for her? She couldn't pay him. Yes, she could. The old maple. He was a lover of antiques. He had said there was nothing finer than the furniture her grandmother had left her. Forgetful of her father she started for the door. His fretful voice halted her at the threshold.

"You needn't take it so hard asking Mallory to help. He butted in on my affairs. I didn't ask him."

Shame scorched Pamela like a flame. Why didn't the hot tears behind her eyeballs come out and relieve the smart? She opened her lips to protest. Where did a voice go when it left one's throat, she wondered frantically. With an inarticulate murmur she fled.

Her heart and mind were still stinging from her father's caustic comment when she poked her head into the kitchen.

"I am going to the village, Hitty. I won't be long. I will do the marketing." She stopped in the living room to snatch the summons from her desk. She ran to the barn and backed out the sedan. Lucky Grandmother Leigh had left something besides the old flivver. She didn't dare stop a moment for fear she would lose her courage.

"Don't wobble!" she admonished herself sternly as she rapped on the front door of the Carr house. The sight of the rare brass knocker halted her stampeding courage. Phineas Carr was mad about antiques. Hadn't he said there was nothing finer than her old maple? Wasn't she giving him a chance to earn it?

She caught a glimpse of her slim, vivid self as she passed the gilt-framed mirror in the hall. She had forgotten a hat. The breeze had ruffled her hair, little dark curls twisted about her ears. She had caught up a yellow cardigan as she ran through the hall. Color instinct. It matched her linen frock.

She followed Milly Pike, whose eyes were round with surprise, to the open door of a room, the walls of which were covered with a curious old sporting paper, all dull browns and reds, with queer little bob-tailed rabbits and beefy hunters with over-developed muscles and under-developed raiment and wicked guns. Was there a swift gleam of apprehension in Phineas Carr's keen glance as he dropped the rod he had been examining and rose to greet her, or was it her hectic imagination? Without a preliminary word she laid the summons on the broad table littered with a sportsman's paraphernalia.

"Please read that and tell me what I ought to do."

He glanced through its contents. This time she was sure of the relief in voice and eyes.

"Sit down, Miss Pamela, and tell me what has happened. You needn't wait, Milly," he spoke sharply to the maid who lingered at the door.

Swiftly, breathlessly, Pamela told of finding the summons when she returned from Boston the evening before, of Cecile's suit for alienation. Phineas Carr looked at the paper.

"You didn't see this until midnight. It does not state what the attachment is for. How did you find out?"

"Mr. Mallory got in touch with Cecile's New

York lawyer — he said his name is Horace Hale —
and phoned me this morning."

"Mallory of Mallory and Carter? The young
man who has had the vision to specialize in South
American law?"

"I don't know about the specialization but he is
the Mallory of that firm."

"I have been watching him. Fine old Cape family. His father died when he was a boy. His
mother, brought up in luxury, took in sewing to keep
the home going. The lad worked his way through
high school, through college — majoring in lan-
guages. The war came. He went to Plattsburg.
Was sent across as First Lieutenant, came home as
Captain. Probably saved most of his pay for he
pushed through law school." Pamela remembered
Scott's, "poor but honest parents — wonderful
parents."

She said eagerly: "He must be brilliant to interest you in his career."

Phineas Carr brought his hand down with a
thump. "Interested! I'm envious as the devil. I
have a son, younger to be sure, but with as good a
mind if he would use it. He fooled through college,
lost his crew letter because his marks were low, now
he wants to plan houses. I admire the man, who,
without foolishly sacrificing health, has ambition to
push ahead of the herd and stay there." He drew
his hand across his eyes as if trying to brush away
an annoying memory.

"You don't trust your son enough." Pamela caught her breath at her own daring. Phineas Carr's brows almost obscured his eyes.

"I don't? Perhaps you're right, perhaps you're right, Miss Pamela. I've been thinking over his plan for getting an income out of the farmer's cottage. That is constructive. Wouldn't believe he had it in him."

"That's the trouble. You don't believe in him. He would do much better if you did. The knowledge that someone believes in one keeps one trying to make good."

He smiled. "Philip has an earnest champion in you, Miss Pamela. That is to his credit. When you came in I thought you had come to report that he had let you down on the cottage."

"You didn't really think I would come to complain of your son, did you? I came for advice."

"Forgive me, my dear." He tapped the summons with a long finger. "If you already have a lawyer why come to me with this?"

Pamela denied breathlessly: "I haven't retained him — isn't that the legal term — on this case, really I haven't. Scott Mallory has spent hours and hours on our affairs — of course you have heard of Father's debts — he won't let us pay him. Now along comes this abominable accusation. I am aching with shame about it. He will think me a girl with a sheriff forever at her heels — The Girl and the Sheriff — there's a title! I won't let him do it!

I can't pay him. I know that Father was insulting to you, but—but Grandmother Leigh adored you and I thought that if you would take the case—you might accept the old maple in payment." Her voice sounded humiliatingly beseeching in her own ears.

Phineas Carr drummed lightly on his desk. A ghost of a smile haunted his stern lips. "Mm. The old maple is a temptation. Were you and your father's wife friends before she left him?"

"I rarely saw her. But even if we weren't, what an absurd move for her to make. I would think that the case would be thrown out of court. There is no sense, no reason in it," Pamela declared passionately.

"There is rarely sense or reason behind an alienation suit; it's generally hysteria, or greed, or jealousy. You have only to follow the newspapers, my dear, to find that there are litigants—and lawyers—so sure that in that bright lexicon which Fate has reserved for the daring contestant there's no such word as fail that they will try anything. From what you have told me I deduce that your stepmother has devised a plan by which she may possibly gain money—by which at least she may vent her jealousy and dislike of you."

"Would a respectable lawyer take a case like that?"

"The man who is bringing the suit has little to lose if he is defeated, much to gain if he wins. Several times he has been spectacularly successful. Don't underestimate the advertising value of this suit both to your stepmother — she's an actress, isn't she — and her counsel. It would cost them thousands of dollars to get the same amount of publicity in the usual way. The case has, at least, the element of beauty which comes from extreme simplicity. Jealousy is an old emotion. It goes back to the first domestic triangle, Adam and Eve and Lilith. I don't like Hale, I've run up against him before, but I hand it to him for being keen. You realize, of course, that I cannot appear for you if Mr. Mallory has the slightest claim. You must explain this to him before I can file our answer in court."

She was on her feet, her eyes starry. "'Our answer'! Then you will take it?"

"If it can be ethically arranged."

Ethically arranged. The phrase rotated through Pamela's mind as she did her errands in the village. Her exultation oozed. Had she been horribly unfair to Scott to turn to Mr. Carr? She glanced at her wrist watch. How had she dared take so much of a great man's time? She frowned at the bulbous-eyed storekeeper who left the sugar he was weighing for her, to rush to the street to watch a plane which was circling.

"It's coming down!" he called over his shoulder. The men who had been huddled round the stove shuffled out to see it. Pamela resisted the temptation to join them. She had not yet become accustomed to the marvel of the gigantic birds of the air.

She might as well have gone, she told herself, as she watched the clock tell off the minutes. Five. Ten. Fifteen, before business was resumed and she could depart with her purchases.

Had Hitty deserted to see the plane, she wondered indignantly as she stopped the sedan at the back door and no gaunt figure made an immediate appearance. She lifted a heavy package.

" Let me take that! "

" Scott! "

She dropped the bag. Twenty pounds of sugar spread in a white drift on the ground between them. Surprise, an oppressive sense of guilt, the expression of Scott Mallory's eyes, set fire to her temper which was not of the steadiest these days.

" Now see what you've done! Walking up behind me like that! "

Mallory caught her elbows, lifted her over the sugar, swung her to the threshold of the kitchen.

" Methinks the lady hath a guilty color. Did you suppose I would stay in Boston when you hung up on my half-finished sentence? You don't know me. I chartered a plane and here I am to fight it out with you."

" You flew! "

He followed closely as Pamela backed into the kitchen. "What did you mean, ' I won't let you ' ? "

She freed the hands he had caught tightly in his, clenched them behind her to steady their trembling.

" What I said, Scott. You have done enough for

us. I—I—have just re—retained Phineas Carr
to fight this case."

She shut her eyes for a moment to shut out his,
black, with little flames in them, in a white face.
Had she made him furiously angry? She couldn't
help it. This suit of Cecile's was only the last of a
long series of humiliations. She couldn't bear to
have him mixed up in it. This would end their
friendship . Wasn't that what she wanted? Hadn't
she an invalid father to support? Would she drag
him with his temperament into any man's life? Just
because her heart glowed whenever he smiled at her,
was no reason why others would forgive his moods.
Time she faced the fact that Scott Mallory had her
heart-fast, that her whole being responded passionately to his touch, to his voice.

"Carnation Carr! I am your legal adviser.
Carr won't take the case if he knows that. It
would be unprofessional."

She hadn't known that a human voice could be
so cold, that gray eyes could be so black, so inscrutable, that a fine hand could be so like iron on her
arm.

"I told him that I did not want you to appear
for me."

"What sent you to him? I thought he had given
up practising."

"He has, but Phil said—"

"Phil! Phil! So he's at the bottom of this! His
father is rotten with money. His mother has a

chain of power plants working for her. I have only what I earn. He is young and care-free. Already I have lived an ordinary lifetime of work. I am too old for you, of course. You think if his father takes the case you will see more of him!"

He dropped her arm. "You won't! I'll tell Carnation Carr to keep his hands off my business! I'll tell him now!"

Chapter XII

"MAKE the Babe stop wriggling, Terry, while I scrub his legs."

The sun brought out curious red-gold glints in Pamela's black hair, rouged the magnolia tints of her face and arms. A green rubber apron protected the front of her gay, sleeveless print frock as she vigorously applied a brush to the lavishly lathered dog who shivered violently in the galvanized iron tub set on a lawn, freshly, velvety, springily green. Terrence held the Babe's hindlegs down with one hand while with the other he grasped the leather strap about the black and tan neck. His red hair, ablaze in the sunlight, stood on end. His handsome face was crimson and moist from exertion.

"Easy enough to say. 'Make him stop wriggling.' Try it yourself." His indignation worked off in a chuckle. "Looks 's if he'd bust right out crying, doesn't he?"

A soft, salty breeze blew from the shore, picked up the scent of spring from the brown earth and danced on. Between house and barn a clump of white birches, with a vague misty aura of unborn leaves, murmured among themselves. Distant sand

dunes gleamed like nuggets of gold in a lapis lazuli
sea. Fluffs of feathery clouds, scattered haphazard
over a radiant sky, added the last perfect touch, the
dreamlike quality of a Daubigny pastoral. From
somewhere in infinite space drifted the faint far
drone of a plane. From the shore came the thud of
hammers on wood, the voices of men. A tipsy bee
lighted on the girl's bare arm. She cautiously
brushed it off before she tenderly removed the lather
from around the dejected Belgian's jaws.

"Cheer'o, Babe! The agony is almost over."

The dog shook himself violently. A monster
dab of suds landed in Terrence's eye.

"Boy! That smarts."

Stinging discomfort loosed his hold. The Babe
leaped to freedom. He dashed madly across the
lawn, shaking himself as he ran, showering suds like
foam from a water-wheel. He raced toward gaunt,
grey Mehitable Betts coming from the poultry house
with a basket.

"Go 'way, you pesky fella!"

Repulsed by her shrill squeak he ran toward
Harold Leigh in a wicker chair in a sunny corner
of the porch. Pamela scrambled to her feet.

"Why didn't you hold him, Terry? Hitty, who
boasts that she ' ain't afraid of any man livin',' is
frightened to death of a dog. Lucky she didn't drop
those eggs when he charged at her. If he spatters
Father there will be a riot."

The green and red parrot, sunning on his gilded
perch, mewed like a cat. Mocked stridently:

"Bad boy!"

The dog barked furiously at his tormentor. Harold Leigh put hands to ears. Called fretfully:

"Terrence, make him stop that infernal racket!"

"Come Babe! Come!"

The dog started toward Pamela in answer to her call, noted the galvanized tub. With soapy tail between his soapier legs he streaked for the long, white barn. The girl pulled off the green apron.

"That's that. We won't see him again for a while. His first fisherman master must have sent him into the sea for a swim. The Babe has been perfectly trained in every way except in the little matter of being tubbed."

Terrence furiously blinked a smarting eye. "And giving the glad-paw to stepmothers."

His sister dropped to the warm, fragrant lawn, clasped her hands about her knees. Her eyes were troubled. "And that day I stood as if turned to stone and let him fly at Cecile. When she appeared in Cap'n Iry Crockett's flivver in a fisherman's slicker and sou'wester, I thought for an instant that she was a villager come to sell tickets for something. Suppose — suppose he had bitten her!"

"What started him after her? He's never showed his teeth before nor since."

"Instinct. He knew what she had up her sleeve. Suing me for alienating her husband's affection! Perhaps had I been politic the day she came here I might have staved this off. Father told her brutally that he did not want her. Why sue me? She claims that he wrote her that I had advised him that he was happier without her. I never talked with him on the subject of his wife, but when her lawyer produces in court that red-hot letter I wrote months ago, and Cecile is on the stand with her beautiful face and her moanin'-low voice, adorning her tale with all the trappings which seem to her good theatre, do you think those twelve men will believe anything I say?"

Terrence patted his sister's shoulder. "Kick frog! Kick! Lucky we got the loan for the cottage before she attached the house and the rest of the land."

Pamela sprang to her feet. "Lady luck had nothing to do with that, it was Scott Mallory's foresight. I know now why he pushed through that loan, he anticipated this possibility." She waited for Terrence's return from emptying the tub in the drive before she exulted: "The cottage is finished — except for a few shelves the men are putting up today — and furnished. Philip Carr has attended to everything for me, even selecting papers and fixtures in New York. Never could have done it myself, the Silver Moon has kept me so busy. It is rented too. I'm all excited. Rented by correspondence. If stationery doth proclaim the woman, the widow, Mrs. Isabelle Stevens, is the last word in fashion."

"What brand of widow? Heaven, Hell, or Reno?"

"She referred to her late husband, not her former. It is a nice distinction. Phil Carr says she is top socially. A man he knows looked her up for me. She has plenty of money and is renting for a much longer season than we expected. I wonder though—"

"What's on the little mind?"

"The fact that she wouldn't sign a lease. She protested that her credit never had been questioned. Phil Carr said, 'Grab her. She's good for it. You won't pick another six-months' tenant in a blue moon.' I knew that, so I took her but — sometimes I wonder what Scott would say. He's such a demon about having everything signed on the dotted line."

"Knock us for a gool if she did walk out on us with that interest and the taxes to pay, wouldn't it?"

"Of course she won't walk out on us, Terry. Let's drop it. I'm sick of the thought of money. Since that clothes-orgy the day I went to Boston I squeeze every nickel till the Indian on one side whoops and the buffalo on the other bucks in protest. Such extravagance! I've never worn the costume since."

"You should worry. Got your money's worth out of it that one day, didn't you?"

As in a flash-back Pamela saw the flower-bedecked restaurant, saw Hilda Crane looking up at her with amazed, appraising eyes. A little smile of gratification twitched at her lips as she agreed fervently:

"I more than got my money out of it that one day, Terry. But, just the same, I held my breath when

I hired Hitty Betts by the week, and the two Academy boys to wait on table seemed the last word in extravagance. However, one can't get out of business more than one puts into it, any more than a writer can write any better than he or she is inside. Our clientele has doubled. That's the answer. With Hitty to cook I have more time to superintend the serving. Things are looking up. If only— ooch!"

"Why the groan?"

Pamela laughed unsteadily. "The suit. Every time I think of it I fight and die in spirit. The wicked injustice, the uselessness of it. But, Mr. Carr says that suing for alienation of affection is epidemic this year, that one case spectacularly head-lined, suggests to someone else a way to get satisfaction—perhaps—at least to vent spite. Besides that, the publicity is money in the bank for Cecile, even if she loses. He is confident that she can't win unless she bolsters up her case by perjury, that if her witnesses do lie the judge may hold them for conspiracy. A lot of good that would do me. Cap'n Iry Crockett gave Cecile the idea—when, innocently enough, he went lyric on the value of the land, when he told her that the Leighs never had occasioned a ripple of scandal. She thought we would settle rather than have her grievance aired in court —she had her plot. Know the best definition of plot? A problem and its solution."

"Cecile has furnished the problem and then some."

"And the solution is up to me. Philip Carr thought he was helping the day she was here, by championing me. He couldn't have picked a way to mix things more. Ossa on Pelion! That's flung in just so you and I won't forget our classics while digging at poultry-raising and housework, Terry. Of course I can't suggest that to him, he's such a dear. I see red with fizzy green pinwheels when I think of that suit. I, separate Cecile and Father! I wish she would kidnap him and take care of him for a while, she knows how to cook and do housework, although she wants to forget that as a girl she had it to do. There's a dutiful daughter for you."

The boy laid his hand on her shoulder. "You are dutiful enough. You are too sweet to him. You let him walk over you if he shows a vestige of appreciation. Forget it! Carnation Carr will win out."

"I hope so! He is pulling every wire possible to have the case set down for immediate trial. Wants to get it behind us. Cecile's lawyer has hinted—broadly hinted—at settlement. My attorney won't listen. She cheated about the operation and squeezed money out of Father—it was all right if he had it to give her—the money, not the cheating. Mr. Carr is determined that she shall get none out of me."

Terrence clasped his hands about one knee. "Found out yet where Father got the cash he paid the second Mrs. Leigh?"

"No. When he told me that he had sold the 'antique,' he seemed so appreciative of what you and I had done for him that I just couldn't ask questions."

"Of course you couldn't, I know you. You probably patted his hand and smoothed his hair. I've never tumbled to your reason for turning old Scott down on this court stuff. He's been such a swell guy to us."

Pamela dug viciously at a dandelion which had adventurously stuck its leaves above ground.

"That was the reason. He had done so much for us that I wouldn't let him do any more. We never can pay him."

"How are you going to pay Mr. Carr? They say in the village that one of his fees makes the income tax of a successful business man look like an atom."

"With the old maple."

"Will he take it?"

"He thinks it the finest in the country."

"I'll hand it to you for having nerve to suggest it. If you were going to dispose of the stuff, why not sell it and pay Scott Mallory?"

"You don't understand, Terry! I just couldn't bear to have him know any more about our sordid, debt-logged lives."

Terrence dug his heels into the turf. "Perhaps you're right. I guess he was pretty well fed-up with the Leighs' hard-luck problems. Hasn't been here since the day you spent in Boston, come to think of it, has he?"

What would Terry say if he knew of that stormy interview the day Scott had flown from the city? Pamela corrected hastily:

"I have seen him once. He has been in California and in Mexico. He is the traveling member of the firm, I judge."

"I miss him. He's a great boy." Terrence jumped to his feet. "I'm parking here as if this were a henless world. Gee, I wish it were! If there is any creature on God's earth dumber than a hen, lead me to it!"

"Nothing dumb about that fierce rooster you've dubbed the White Hope. He flew at me as I passed the gate of his yard this morning. I was thankful that there was a wire netting between us."

Terrence grinned. "A dozen like him would repel an advancing army. They'd make good shock troops. He's some bird." He lifted the tub to his shoulder. "Phil Carr showing up today?"

"Tonight. To check up on the cottage, wants to make sure everything is according to contract."

"Check up is good, but not good enough. He hasn't been chasing to the wilds of Cape Cod every week-end because he's all excited about making over the cottage, nor because you've given his father a job, believe it or not. Woman, unless you like him a lot, watch your step." He scowled at her darkly as he quoted the temperamental Mrs. Micawber.

"'All I say is, remember what I say now, and when I say I said so, don't say I didn't.'"

"Terry, you are a hang-over from the nineteenth century! What young person reads Dickens now?"

"I'd rather spend an hour with him than with many of the people I know." He grinned tormentingly. "Think over my tip about Philip Carr. He's a good sport. I like him even if he can't see anything approaching in skirts — young or old, fat or lean — without settling his tie and squaring his shoulders." He shifted the weight of the tub before he asked awkwardly, "You don't suppose he is the reason old Scott has stopped coming, do you?"

"Of course not and I wish you would stop calling Scott Mallory 'Old Scott.' He is only thirty-five."

"Didn't know you were so touchy about his desertion. I'm sorry."

"I'm not touchy, Terry Leigh. I would rather he didn't come. I have no time to spend with him. Doubtless he is running round evenings with Hilda Crane. She is light-weight enough to be mental relaxation for the tiredest attorney at law."

"Meow!"

"It was catty. And I was hateful to you too. You have been such a dear, Terry, about my having spent all that equipment money on myself. Grandmother Leigh used to say, 'I am a jelly fish in paradise with money in my pocket among the shops.' I'm just like her. No sales resistance."

"There you go again, re-morse. Why shouldn't

you spend it? You earned the most of it. You need a change of scene more than anyone I know."

"I won't leave the Silver Moon again. So long as I keep plodding I am all right. Life seems to be just the bursting of one iridescent soap-bubble after another. Nothing but dampish spots left."

Terrence shouted with laughter. "Orphan Annie! You're low, aren't you?"

Pamela flushed. "I'm a poor sport, that's what I am. If the trial of this fiendish case doesn't come along soon I shall begin to scratch and bite. I feel as if we were walking on the thin crust above a volcano which might blow-up at any moment. Cecile is capable of springing anything. Run along and forget your disagreeable sister." She turned to wave and smile at him before she entered the kitchen.

"At this hour watch-out for storms!" she warned herself as she noted the clamped lips of Mehitable Betts who was forcefully wielding the rolling-pin at the porcelain-topped table. The gaunt woman's mouth was an unfailing barometer of the state of her temper. Better to ignore the storm-signal.

Pamela observed chattily as she tied on an apron: "The rhubarb plants are showing pink above ground. Won't be long before we can add your marvelous tarts to our menu. They will make our patrons sit up and take notice."

"Hmp! I guess somebody else'll be making those tarts."

Apparently deaf to the prophecy Pamela hummed as she washed lettuce.

" ' Should I reveal exactly how I feel
    Should I confess I love you — ' "

With the words came the memory of the gaily
lighted restaurant, the feel of Scott's arms about
her. Her heart ached intolerably. She had not
seen him since the day he had stormily announced
that he would warn Phineas Carr to keep his hands
off his business. Mr. Carr had told her casually
that he had talked with Mr. Mallory, that after
some discussion it had been agreed that it would be
better if he — who was so near — were to handle
the suit. Inconsistently she had been fiercely hurt
that Scott had dropped her case so easily.

"Guess you didn't hear me say I might not be
here to make rhubarb tarts."

The sharp voice cut into Pamela's absorption.
The proprietor of the Silver Moon Chowder House
had little time for sentimental regrets — fortunately. What line would she better take? She
would like to tell Hitty Betts to pack up and remove
herself and her temperament from the kitchen. She
couldn't do that. She needed her. She must be
diplomatic. Diplomacy! She was tired of being
tactful with her father, with Hitty, with fussy patrons.

"What is the matter? I thought you liked working at the Silver Moon."

"I like it well enough and I like being with you,
Pamela, but, there can't be but one skipper on a
ship and you're my boss. I won't take orders from

Harold Leigh and he'd better up and learn that or I walk out."

"Orders from Father! What has he been telling you to do?"

The surprise in Pamela's voice was oil upon a troubled sea. Miss Betts calmed down. "I thought you wouldn't approve. While you and Terry were washing the dog he wanted me to leave my work an' walk to the post-office in the village to mail an important letter. Postmaster Highty was sayin' that he has a powerful lot of correspondence for a sick man. Sick! He's well and he don't know it!"

Another surreptitious letter? Was her father in correspondence with Cecile? Was he taking sides with her against his own daughter? He wouldn't do it. She must not harbor that suspicion for an instant. Then what was going on? She felt as if she were living in a dream with a nightmarish mystery drifting wraith-like just beyond reach. She thrust the question into the back of her mind. Her first task was to placate her dour but invaluable handmaiden.

"You were right, Hitty. It takes not-seriously sick persons to make cracker-jack executives, doesn't it? They can't move about themselves but how they can plan activities for others. Every manufacturing plant ought to have its efficiency invalid — with a bell to tinkle. Forget it. You know that I don't want you to do a thing beyond your strength."

Mehitable sniffed. "I know you don't, Pamela.

You're real thoughtful. And you've got a hard row to hoe. Folks is sayin' that when your case comes to trial the verdict's likely to go against you, spite of the fact that you have one of the smartest lawyers in the country trying for you. Don't see how you ever got him. 'Course everyone knows that Phil Carr's your beau, but everyone knows too that Phineas and your Pa quarreled something terrible. Well's I was sayin', your Pa has been so snifty with friends he knew as a boy that they won't have much pity for him if they get on the jury."

" Why should the jury decide against me because some members of it do not like Father? He isn't being sued. I am."

" I know, but, they think he's hiding behind you, that he got tired of the stage woman and left her in the lurch as soon as he lost his money." She cleared her throat. A sure sign that she was about to hurl a gossip bomb. Pamela unconsciously braced. " Who do you think's arrived at the Inn with a maid, and a trunk full of clothes and a car an' all?"

" Who? "

" That Crane girl. Came last night. Milly Pike saw her and then the whole village knew it. It's her sister that's taken your cottage and she's come ahead to get things started."

" Her sister! Mrs. Isabelle Stevens Hilda Crane's sister!" Through Pamela's memory swept Scott Mallory's comment: " A rich woman who spends her income before she gets it and is everlastingly being sued by creditors." She had rented the cottage to a woman like that without a lease! Hilda Crane in a cottage at their very door. Oh, what a snarl, what a confounded snarl!

Pamela carefully examined each crisp green leaf before she dropped it into the cheesecloth bag. If only she could talk the situation over with Scott. That was the one thing she couldn't do. His eyes had had the most curious effect the few times she had been with him before their clash over the handling of the alienation suit. It was as if they held her, while she struggled, powerless to escape. Why look at her like that if he didn't care enough about her to come to see her? Was he that type? Afraid of being caught in the snare of matrimony? Quite ready to philander where the going was safe? Her sense of justice pinched her sharply. Suppose Scott were to tell her he loved her? She would refuse to listen. She would not permit him to come again. Keeping a home for her father was a full-time contract. She should be glad that he had stopped coming. She must put him out of her life sometime, the sooner the better.

" If you haven't anything to do but stare out of the window, Pamela, you might get the butter balls made. I haven't but one pair of hands. Getting to be an awful lot of work round here."

" I know it, and we really need a waitress, Hitty. The Academy boys do well but they can't come every day." Pamela hated herself for the placating tone. Fear of losing Hitty was undermining her boasted independence. "I will try for a girl in the village. I wish I might find one as perfectly trained as Milly Pike."

"M's Carr taught her, but how she stands her round beats me. Curious! Why you can see that girl's ears stand right out when she's listening. She tells everything she hears, that's the worst of it. Have you heard that M's Carr's sister's sick and she's gone to be with her? Folks is sayin' they don't see how she dared go and leave Phil and his father without being there to step between. They get on about as well as that green and red parrot an' that pesky dog would if they were shut up in a room together. She's been a sort of buffer ever since the boy grew up."

"Perhaps Mr. Carr is too stern." Pamela tilted a lance in Philip's defense as she deftly manipulated unsalted butter.

"Stern! He's a disappointed man." Miss Betts held a pie plate on the palm of one hand while she expertly pared pastry dough with the other. "Thinks a lot of handing on the name. He is a big lawyer, even foreign countries tried to get him to represent them. His health broke from overwork and he restored the old Carr place and settled down a few years ago, that is if you can call being in Europe most of the time settlin' down. He must be a lot better to take your case. Phil came along when he was about forty. He had all sorts of plans and dreams, sure the boy was goin' to be a lawyer. I guess he visioned him Chief Justice of the U.S."

"If Philip's taste was for architecture it would have been a crime to have forced him into law."

"He wasn't forced. Folks is sayin' that—Land's sake! Is Judgment Day a-com—"

Her voice was drowned in the frenzied clatter of an engine, the lugubrious bellow of a horn. She and Pamela crashed as they met in the doorway. A coughing, spitting flivver wheezed into the drive, whirled in a crazy circle and charged at the back porch like an infuriated, if consumptive, bull. It sliced off one side of the trellis before it whipped around and lunged at the woodshed. Eddie Pike gripped the wheel, his sister clung to his arm. His vacuous blue eyes bulged like glassies as he shouted:

"Whoa! Back up! Let go, Milly! You're twisting the steerer!" The chalky-faced girl shrieked as the car described a circle on two wheels and with demoniac intent rushed uproariously for the porch again. Pamela emerged from a trance of amazement.

"Shut off the engine, Eddie! Shut off your engine!"

"Now, whoever let that half-baked idiot get a license!" rasped Mehitable Betts as the flivver veered, gouged up the gravel in an about-face turn and with a backfire which would have been no mean accomplishment for a baby Big Bertha, bucked convulsively and shed its forward wheels. Man and girl catapulted through space where once had been a windshield. "There, he's stopped it."

"Stopped it! I'll say he has." Pamela's voice

was choked with laughter as she ran toward the car. "You are not hurt are you, Milly?" she asked, as the girl, with hat smashed over one eye, crawled from the wreck. Miss Pike cast a murderous glare at her brother as she restored her headgear to its usual coquettish angle.

"'Tisn't Eddie's fault that I'm not. He paid ten dollars for that flivver —"

"And got cheated at that," interrupted Mehitable Betts grimly as she tried to restore the splintered trellis to place. "What you doing riding round in racing cars this time a-day, Milly Pike?"

Milly wrinkled her nose at gaunt Miss Betts' sarcasm before she turned to Pamela.

"I came for the eggs, Miss Leigh. Eddie offered to bring me to save time. It isn't his fault I'm not doing time in a hospital. Is Terrence anywhere around?"

"Terrence!"

With Pamela's echo of the name came the memory of her distrust of the girl, so pretty, so vital, so — cheap.

"I will get the eggs for you, Milly. My brother is at school."

Eddie Pike looked up from the wreck he had been studying to scowl at his sister.

"Don't you go chasing after Terry, Milly. Terry's a fine boy. Shan't stand for you hangin' round him like you've been hangin' round Phil Carr lately."

Chapter XIII

AFTER all, this morning Eddie Pike had not accused Phil Carr of "hanging round" Milly, it was just the reverse, Pamela comforted herself as she curled up in a corner of the couch in the living room. Light from the floor lamp brought out the splashy pattern in the pale green Chinese damask of her frock, illumined the pile of magazines on the stand beside her. She was through work early tonight. She would have three whole hours in which to read.

The fire snapped companionably. The Babe, stretched at length on the hearth-rug, cocked one ear as a vine brushed against the window-pane, like tapping fingers begging for entrance. From the radio upstairs thundered the music of one of the stormier symphonies. Its sweep, its strength, its passion, set Pamela's pulses throbbing like muted drums; made her feel like a small and lonely soul battling a tempest of emotion. She tried to shake off the effect as she absentmindedly turned the pages of a magazine, her eyes on the copper and blue flames. Of course what Philip Carr did was nothing to her, but she liked him. It would be unbearable if he were to mess up his life for a silly girl like Milly Pike. His mother was away. Would he be furious were she to speak to him about it? What business was it of hers what he did? He was a man grown. He had been wonderfully helpful about the cottage, sympathetically understanding of her turmoil of mind in regard to the lawsuit. His father had been right; he was more artistic than practical. She had made a mistake when she took his advice about the tenant. Commonsense should have told her that a woman who refused to sign a lease would be irresponsible. What would Scott say? Song sparrows, robins, redwing blackbirds, meadow larks and purple linnets had appeared since he had been at the Silver Moon. Last night she had heard a hermit thrush. The arrival of the birds would have recorded the passing of the weeks even had she forgotten. Was he still furiously angry? She had had a few clean-cut business letters from him, that was all. She had not answered them; they had not called for a reply.

A car sweeping up the drive? Scott? Of course not. It would be Phil in his creamy yellow roadster. He was coming to report on his check-up of the cottage.

She heard a step on the porch, ran to the front door and opened it. "How is our talented boy archi — Scott!"

Mallory stepped by her into the hall. He dropped coat and hat on the settle. As he waited for her to precede him into the living-room his face was curiously colorless, his eyes inscrutable. He said lightly:

"Sorry to disappoint you. I take it you expected Carr."

Pamela returned to the couch corner. A safe and sane refuge in time of trouble. The symphony above crashed in a stupendous finale; the music was like fingers pressing hard at her throat. Mallory backed up to the fire. His height and sternness caught at her breath. The deep lines between his nose and the corners of his mouth had not been there before. She struggled for nonchalance as she asked:

"When did you return from your coast to coast trip?"

"Just back."

"Was it successful?" She felt as if she were editing a question and answer column.

"Yes."

Silence, unbridgeable silence, rising, rising like a Chinese wall between them. What did one say, what could one say to a man who had left one furiously angry?

"Did you — you find people stirred up over the political situation?"

"Not especially. The country is still fundamentally sound," Mallory assured curtly.

She had reached the end of that line. What next? Stupid of her to be so dumb. Had he lost interest in her or was his attitude merely a carefully thought-out defense mechanism? Pamela crashed blindly through the wall of reserve.

"Don't be so wooden! Why did you come if you have nothing to say?"

He became absorbed in lighting a cigarette. "I have been asking myself why I came ever since you greeted me at the door, thinking I was Carr."

She caught her lips between her teeth to steady them as memory seared like lightning. Hilda Crane had arrived at the Inn today. Scott was here for the first time in weeks! A coincidence? Not likely. She forced her voice to lightness.

"Phil was to check up on the cottage and report that everything was as per contract before I made the last payment. Our Tenant — Terry and I speak of her with a capital T — moves in tomorrow."

"Really!"

Nothing wooden about him now, his eyes were alight with interest, his smile was heart-warming. Pamela felt as if she had been transported into a patch of sunlight.

"That's great. Who is it?"

"Mrs. Isabelle Stevens."

The muscles of his face hardened, his eyes narrowed. Did Mallory of Mallory & Carter look like that when cross-examining a witness? No wonder he won cases.

"Not Mrs. Isabelle Stevens of New York? Hilda Crane's sister?"

She nodded. His change of expression had done things to her voice.

"Where did you get hold of *her?*"

"She wrote to me. Why do you ask so many questions? Philip Carr had her looked up. She is impeccable socially. Has heaps of money and — a charming sister."

He regarded her steadily. "I suppose young Carr drew your lease or did his father — your present legal adviser — attend to it?"

It had come! She might have known that it would. "I — I — haven't any lease." That break in her voice was equivalent to an admission of guilt, Pamela realized furiously.

"What!"

Mallory caught her by the shoulders, drew her to her feet. He administered a shake, too slight to be actionable, but unmistakably a shake.

"Don't tell me, Pam, that you have let your cottage to that woman without any legal hold on her."

She met his blazing eyes defiantly. "Why do you call her 'that woman'? She has money, she has social standing. You don't for a moment believe that she will back out at the eleventh hour and leave me financially in the lurch, do you?"

"That's just what I believe! Don't get me wrong. She isn't planning to do it now. She is a woman who spends her income a year, sometimes two, ahead; she is always in arrears. She gets by because she is so wealthy that dealers lift the price to pay them for waiting for their money. There are worse but also less exasperating women. You can't afford to let your house to a person like that. You've got to meet your interest."

"Phil said—"

"I don't care what Carr said. We've got to get that woman out of the cottage before the renting season is over or make her pay in advance."

"We!" He was still interested. Pamela caught the lapel of his coat.

"Scott, I'm terribly sorry to have been so unbusinesslike. Way down deep, I knew that I ought to have a lease, but, I was so eager to rent the cottage. The prospect of six months' tenancy went straight to my head — we had figured on three, four at the most — I planned to make a payment on the mortgage."

His eyes smiled warmly into the troubled depths of hers. With gentle fingers he brushed back a strand of her hair which had escaped from the smooth wave to stray over her forehead. He reassured:

"Don't worry. I'll straighten it out."

"Phil said—"

Mallory's eyes hardened. He moved abruptly to the fireplace. "If you mention Carr's name again I'll beat him up for letting you in for this mess. He ought to have known better. Why didn't you consult his father?"

"He is doing enough for me."

"Terribly afraid that someone will help you, aren't you? I—"

Voices on the porch. Whom had Phil brought with him, Pamela had time only to wonder, before the front door swung open.

"Oh, Pam! Here's the sister of the Tenant! Wants to ask you some questions about the cottage.

She is here to get things started. How are you, Mallory? When did you get back?"

"Scott!" Hilda Crane paused effectively on the threshold. Her blonde hair was exquisitely dressed; her reddened lips were parted in an ecstatic smile; her eyes were deeply, darkly purple; a wrap of ivory satin only partially covered an azure frock.

"Scott!" In a little rush she was across the room, both hands clasped about his arm, the sophisticate gone ingenue. "It is wonderful to see you. You were marvelous to come the moment I arrived. Did Miss Cryder give you my message that Belle had taken the Leigh cottage?"

A steel hand closed ruthlessly over Pamela's heart. Had he known when he came tonight that Hilda Crane's sister was her tenant? He was an excellent actor. How she hated men.

"I have not been to the office since my return. Drove straight here from New York. What lured Belle to this Sleepy Hollow? She won't find many card players here."

Miss Crane smoothed his sleeve. He freed his arm and poked the fire. She pouted:

"You don't seem a bit thrilled at my coup, Scott. Belle is planning to have you with us every moment you can spare. In spite of the fact that you have ground the money for some long due bills out of her, she adores you. She will have her cronies coming and going. The doctor recommended a quiet summer and I thought of this place."

"When does she come?"

"Tomorrow. She is motoring from New York. You look worn to the bone. Have you been working terribly hard?"

He put his hand to his face. "I've driven over three hundred and sixty miles today. I'm dusty. I want to see Belle the moment she arrives." He turned to Pamela. "Is your father still up? I would like to talk with him."

"I think so. I will find out."

Pamela was thankful for an excuse to escape from the charged atmosphere. Philip Carr had been patently seething with resentment at Scott Mallory's curt greeting. She herself had been unbearably hurt at Hilda Crane's monopoly of Scott.

Her father, who was reading, frowned at the interruption as she entered the room. "Now, what is it?"

"Mr. Mallory wants to talk with you."

"What is he after?"

"He didn't say. Perhaps to persuade you to produce more antiques."

It was an aimless answer, a shot in the dark, one of those things one flings out when one is in a mental turmoil, for the sake of something to say. Pamela was totally unprepared for its effect. Her father's face turned livid.

"What do you mean, 'more antiques'?"

She shrugged. "Nothing, absolutely nothing. It was a fool remark. Will you see Mr. Mallory?"

"Tell him to come up."

Had Scott heard his loud voice? He was half way up the stairs when she met him. He caught her hand.

"What was he saying to you?"

Before she could answer, Philip Carr appeared at the newel post in the hall below.

"Come on, Pam. The younger set is going to the speakies in the village. We'll leave the old duffers to talk business."

With a muttered imprecation Mallory dropped her hand. He took the stairs two at a time. Pamela lingered.

"You look a hundred per cent better, Mr. Leigh," she heard him say before he closed the door.

"That was a bad start. Father will be furious that anyone considers him physically improved," she thought before she joined Philip Carr. Hilda Crane was standing beside him. She said playfully:

"Go on, you two children. I will wait for Scott to take me home."

Had she waited, Pamela wondered the next morning. When she had returned from the village the house had been quiet, no sound except the weird stirring of an old board or two. There was a scrap of pale blue chiffon on the living room couch. The handkerchief gave out a faint scent of *Nuit de Noel* as she picked it up.

As she prepared grapefruit for breakfast she tried to shut out the picture of the man in front of the fire with the blonde girl clinging to his arm. She would much better consider what she should do about her unreliable tenant. It seemed incredible that a woman of wealth would be unable to pay the comparatively small rent of that cottage. If she didn't —

"What are you exclaiming 'ooch' for at this time in the morning," demanded Terrence from the foot of the stairs. "What's gone wrong now in this vale of tears?"

Should she tell him what Scott had said about the Tenant? Why worry him?

"Did I groan? Must have bubbled up from my subconscious where I park that maddening old alienation suit. Take the grapefruit into the dining room, Terry. I will bring the coffee and muffins."

The green and red parrot executed a clog on his gilded perch as she entered.

"Look who's here!"

Pamela laughed. "Not so much to look at, Mephisto. Who do you think called last night, Terry?"

The youth's eyes met in a sharp frown. "Not Milly Pike?"

"Milly Pike! Of course not. Why did you think of her?"

Terrence's ears were unbecomingly red. "She's been racing up for eggs about every other day. Who came?"

"Miss Crane with Philip Carr. I wonder where they met — somewhere socially of course, he knows

people in all the large cities.   Ostensibly she came
to inquire about details of the cottage — she forgot
her questions when she saw Scott Mallory."

" Did he come?   When did he get back? "

"Yesterday.   Terry, I didn't intend to tell you,
but, I've got to talk with some — I — "

" Hold on a minute before you confide the mistakes of your young life.   Car coming up the drive."
He dashed to the window.   " I'm getting so rural
I just have to see the pass.   It's old Scott in that
black and red roadster.   Gee, how it shines! "

Why had Scott come this morning, Pamela wondered, as she saw him step from his car.   He had the
best taste in clothes of any man she knew.   His gray
suit, with a blue shirt and tie were immensely becoming.   Last night he had seemed travel-fagged and
worn.   This morning his face was unlined, his skin
was as fresh as a boy's.   His eyes and mouth flashed
into a smile as he saw Terrence at the window.   The
youth had the door open before he reached it.

" Come in, Mr. Scott.   We're at breakfast.   Join
us?   It's great to have you back."

Mallory flung his arm about Terrence's shoulder
as they entered the room together.   His eyes as they
met Pamela's had the no-surrender glint she had
come to know and dread.   " Unflinching," was the
word her father had used.

" I have breakfasted, thanks.   Pam, I have some
documents for you to sign."

" Documents! "

Terrence looked from one to the other. "Like me to do a fade-out, Mr. Scott?"

"No. I will give you a real estate lesson." He took two papers from his pocket. "These are the leases for the cottage, Pam. Read them. Are they correct as to time and price?"

Pamela blinked several times before she came to the place for the signature. He still was interested enough in her to care. She looked up.

"Quite right. Don't think I'm so stupid as not to have tried for a lease, Scott. She just wouldn't agree to one, that's all."

He held out his pen. "Sign. Witness her signature, Terry." He waited for the ink to dry. Folded the papers and slipped them into his breast pocket.

"Mrs. Isabelle Stevens will sign these, hand over a cheque to cover advance payment, or she won't get into the house. She will find me parked on the front steps when she arrives. I have had dealings with her before." He caught Pamela's hands close in his. "For a hard-boiled business woman you need someone to look after you more than anyone I know."

Terrence coughed. Mallory laughed. "Sorry, Terry! It shan't happen again — at present. Good morning. I'm off to hold-up the Tenant on her porch." He paused on the threshold.

"When I come back I will have a cheque for you, or a cottage for you to rent. Guess which, Miss Pamela Leigh."

Chapter XIV

———◆———

SUNSET in Fairyland, the Silver Moon in the lap of May, apple trees like gigantic pinky pom-pons. Lilacs: yellowy whites, purples, dusty maroons and rosy orchids bordering the picket fence; yellow-throated vireos, flitting through them, twittering as they flew; somewhere in the orchard a thrush singing his heart away.

Seated on the step of the porch Pamela clasped her hands softly in her lap. Heavenly music. She might not hear it again this year; it was time for the singer to fly north. She drew a deep breath of air freighted with the perfume of lilacs. She looked from the riot of blossoms to her frock, shaded yellow, orange and flame like the breast of an oriole, to the sparks in the synthetic topaz in her bracelet. Her heart spread plumy wings. That streak of blue through the orchard, the mellow green of the lawn, the lemon and rose of the afterglow, the lights like misty opals in the village, the heathery tinge of distant cranberry bogs, the gold of the star just above the horizon, the ultramarine sea, the silver of the dunes, set her pulses thrumming, set her very soul afire. Curious how deeply color moved her.

She gently stroked the Babe's head as he snuggled his nose against her knee. His eyes closed spasmodically; his body sagged as he succumbed to sleep; he braced, relaxed, braced again. The girl's dreamy gaze was on the purplish column of smoke which spiraled from the cottage chimney. A fire-worshipper with no need to economize on wood, was the Tenant. Was Mrs. Belle Stevens paying her bills in the village? Over a month now since the day Scott Mallory had returned from the cottage to the Silver Moon with a signed lease and a cheque for advance payment on the rent. His eyes and voice had been grim as he advised:

"The next time you rent property consult a lawyer, not an architect."

He had left her staring unseeingly down at the slip of paper vainly trying to think of a reply which would be sufficiently appreciative without sounding as if she were a penitent, prostrate at his feet.

She had not seen him since. From Hilda Crane and her sister, who had discovered a contract affinity in Harold Leigh, she heard that he had been frequently at the Inn in the village, that business had taken him often to New York City.

Had she known that it was Hilda Crane's sister who was hiring the cottage, that she would have the girl whom she thoroughly disliked and distrusted, for a neighbor all summer, would she have leased it to her? Silly question. Of course she would. One didn't permit one's emotions to nuzzle opportunity aside when one had interest and taxes to meet. Besides, the Tenant was a lavish patron of the Silver Moon. Forewarned by Scott, she had firmly, if smilingly, refused credit at Mrs. Stevens' first visit, had explained that she had to conduct her business on a cash basis. The wealthy, but financially skiddy, widow had graciously complied with her terms and had come again and again. Now that Scott had stopped coming, what difference did it make where he went? Each morning when she awoke her first thought was:

"Was I right or have I needlessly sacrificed a friend?"

Right or wrong, Phineas Carr would appear in court for her. The trust and confidence she had had in him when he was her grandmother's adviser, had returned, strengthened twofold during the interviews in which he had instructed her as to her part in the trial. Counsel for the prosecution would present the plaintiff's case first, it was up to the defense to shoot holes through it, he had explained. Leigh vs. Leigh was marked for next week, he had told her this morning. Occasionally, like an echoing step a long way off, would come the remembrance of her impression that somehow, in some way he would change the pattern of her life.

A soft light stole over the apple trees — those beautiful trees on which blossomed the promise of next year's taxes — a light all pink, yellow, amethyst and silver, delicate as malines, colorful as a fairy rainbow, a radiant wash of gold on the tops, flickering, unearthly shadows below.

The letter crushed in her free hand recaptured Pamela's attention. If Scott had not come he had written. The contents pertained to her father's finances to be sure, but he had not forgotten the troublesome Leighs. She spread out the sheets. As she read she could hear the vibrant tones of his voice, see his amused eyes, feel his hand settling the fur about her shoulders. Heart-warming to be near him even in spirit.

No word about the suit — perhaps already he approved the wisdom of her decision — no word except about business until the end. He wrote:

Your father may be interested to know that I attended a stamp auction in New York week before last. Not to buy for myself, in the interest of a client. The place would have provided you with material for an article. Atmosphere to burn. Seats arranged like those in a small theatre, a few prospective bidders scattered about absorbed in catalogues. A black velvet stand illumined by a skillful arrangement of lights. The auctioneer in the shadow, his face a ghostly blur. He seemed indifferent, but he caught every signal almost before it was given. Was it uncanny intuition or years of practice? The room filled for the great smash in the lot. It was an English, 10 shilling, King Edward stamp overprinted I.R. Official.

Sold for two thousand dollars! Tell your father about it. Probably he knows all the royalties in the stamp world and won't be surprised. I'll confess that the value of that small square of paper rocked my mind. Suppose I had dedicated my career to collecting instead of to law? I might have been a millionaire by this time.

Sincerely yours,
SCOTT MALLORY.

"Sincerely yours." The stereotyped phrase hurt Pamela even as she assured herself that she had deliberately cut off any chance of a warmer ending. He thought Philip Carr's money would be a lure for her. Better for him to think so. She tucked the letter inside her frock as she gazed across a strip of darkening water to purple blurs which were the sand dunes crouching beneath scooting clouds. Did living up to one's convictions always take the joy out of life?

The auction room would have provided her with material, he had written. Would she ever, ever write again? She bit her lips till she flinched. Quitter! Hadn't she figured that making good as a writer wasn't such a different proposition from making good in matrimony? Both professions were a matter of sportsmanship, of keeping on keeping on in the face of discouragement, of continually giving one's best, and trying, everlastingly trying, to make it better.

A night-hawk shrilled overhead. Eerie sound. From the poultry house came the creak of closing doors. A cloud of swallows fluttered above the barn, darting and soaring like a troop of miniature black witches astride their broomsticks. Terrence's voice rose in the words of Holman Day's verse which he had set to music.

> "'Now when the milkman got to town
> And opened the can, there lay
> The fool frog drowned; but hale and sound,
> The kicker he hopped away.'"

Did he keep the legend of the kicking frog always in mind to bolster up his morale? The dog lost his balance as Pamela sprang to her feet; he regarded her with reproachful eyes. She patted his head.

"I'm sorry, Babe. The thought that Cecile might be the 'kicker' who hopped away, upset my repose of manner and incidentally yours."

Was that a streak of pink in the orchard? Milly Pike again? She was making daily appearances on the place, ostensibly for eggs; perhaps she really was curious to see the patrons of the Silver Moon, they would supply her with talking-points for some time. Was Terrence the attraction? Pamela's heart stopped. He would be, he must be immune to anyone so blatantly cheap. Would he? Must he? Who would have thought that fastidious Harold Leigh would have fallen for a woman like Cecile Mortimer?

"Hi Pam!"

She waved in answer to her brother's shout. Her eyes were tender as she crossed the lawn to meet him, the dog close at her heels. How good looking he was! He radiated a sort of mischievous gusto, as if life were an amusing show in which he was cast for the part of comedian. The open collar of his madras shirt set off the fair perfection of his throat which would not tan. Out of school hours he should be enjoying the carefree life to which a seventeen year old boy was entitled; instead he worked on the place early and late, occasionally squeezing in a set of tennis. He no longer waited on table except in a rush. The Academy boys were thrilled to take his place and tips.

Terrence grinned at his sister. "Did you see Milly Pike beating it for the orchard?"

"Then it was Milly?"

"Unless it was her astral personality. If so, it is as pink as those gingham dresses she wears."

"Did she speak to you?"

"Sure. Said she came for eggs."

"Did you give them to her?"

"I did." His lips twisted in his adorable one-sided smile. "The Carrs will have jaundice eating so many eggs, if they don't watch out. Want to know what I think? She's a spy."

"A spy! For whom?"

"That's what I'm trying to find out."

Pamela teased, "You have been over-indulging in talkies, Terry."

"Perhaps I have — but — that case Leigh vs.

Leigh is coming on, isn't it? The second Mrs.
Leigh may want to know how many people come
here, may want to get a line on what we are making.
Lately Milly has been sidling up to Father, talking
to him when he has been on the porch."

"To Father! Do you mean that she may have
been asking questions about the case? Terry, he
wouldn't be so simple as to tell that girl anything,
he would snap her head off for impertinence first —
but, Mr. Carr warned me not to let him talk with
anyone. What a muddle. Weren't there enough
complications without having Milly Pike cross our
life-lines? She only comes when you are here. I
thought — I was afraid — "

"That she hung round here to see me!" Terrence's face crimsoned with amazed resentment.
"The female mind sure moves in a mysterious way
its wonders to perform! Thought you had more
sense, Pam, even if you have an imagination which
works overtime. Whatever she comes for, the next
time will be the last." He chuckled. Pamela caught
his arm.

"Terry! You won't hurt her?"

"I won't hurt her." He grinned as at an amusing
thought before he demanded, obviously to switch
her train of thought, "Why the evening get-up?
Special company?"

"Have you forgotten that the Tenant and Miss
Crane are coming to play cards with Father? For
the third time in the last ten days he has discarded

his lounging robe and is attired like a man and a gentleman in blue serge. He doesn't look in the least like an invalid. Play with them, will you? They don't really want me. Card playing is not my métier. I have no card sense."

"You have but you don't want to play, do you?"

"No, I don't. In New York I never had time, there were so many thrilling things to do and see when I wasn't at work."

"Picking up the little plot germs, I suppose." Terrence's voice dripped mystery as he added, "You don't have to go to the city to get them. This place is squirming with 'em."

Pamela's eyes sparkled with laughter. "Folks is sayin'! You are excited over that spy hunch, aren't you? Hurry and change. Father doesn't like to be kept waiting for his game. I am going to the orchard for one spray of blossoms for the bronze jar in the hall. Japanese effect. I will be back before the guests arrive."

Terrence sighed resignation. "If I've got to play, I've got to, I suppose, though I have plenty of studying to do. I'll change as soon as I've shut the Babe into the barn. I'll leave the door open a crack so he'll see and hear but can't break out."

"See and hear *what*, Terry?"

"Go on, giggle; you think that's another hunch, don't you, Miss Pamela Leigh? It isn't. Someone or ones tried to break into the poultry houses last night."

Concern shadowed Pamela's eyes. "Really! You would better tie the Babe if you mean only to frighten the would-be raiders. Remember his rush at Cecile. He would tear a trespasser to pieces if he caught him."

Terrence grinned. "Chicken thieves would sure be his meat. Come on, Babe."

Pamela's mind was on the card players as she opened a gate in the picket fence. She had a little more card sense than she had acknowledged to Terry, but her playing set her father's always quivering nerves on edge. He had rallied to the stimulus of his contract-avid neighbors. She had doubted her ears the first time he had asked her to put studs and links into a shirt to wear with his blue clothes. He must be better, much better physically, though he never admitted it. Was the day approaching when she would be free, when she would look back upon the Silver Moon experiment with a tolerant smile, when her present feverish determination to keep out of the quagmire of debt would seem fantastically exaggerated?

Petals dropped as softly as snow-flakes as she entered a fragrant lane between gnarled tree trunks. Shadows wrapped her round. They seemed to fill the world, as they lengthened, darkened in the windless hush. Milly had disappeared among the trees. She looked down the blossom-bordered grass path. Her heart stood still. Was it — it was, Philip Carr standing with Milly Pike under an arch of pink and white branches. Was he arguing with her? No, his attitude was more that of a suppliant. Phil and cheap Milly! Unbearable! They looked up. Had she broadcast her concern? The girl slipped away, wove like a pink ribbon through the distant orchard, and vanished. After an instant of hesitation, Philip Carr approached slowly. What should she say? Nothing, unless, he referred to his meeting with Milly Pike.

Even in the dim light she could see him redden to his ears as he looked at her. But, his eyes met hers steadily, honestly. He, stoop to clandestine meetings with his mother's maid? Where had the odious suspicion come from? Eddie Pike's suggestion and her plot-complex, of course. If ever again she had time to harness the last to her typewriter it ought to make her fortune. How could she have been so unjust to a man she liked so much? Yet— he had seemed to be pleading fervently.

"Greetings, Miss Pamela Leigh." The jauntiness of Philip Carr's voice was somewhat strained; beneath the lightness she sensed an undercurrent of excitement. "Came up tonight to talk over a plan for a second cottage. Now that we have one leased and bringing home the bacon, we'd better get another started. You're a knockout in that gown, you flitted into the orchard like an oriole."

It was evident that he intended to ignore the tableau he and Milly had presented in the blossom-scented lane. In that case she must not refer to it,

Pamela decided. Her insouciance matched his as she approved:

"Nice of you to come, Phil, but I can't talk cottage tonight. We have guests. Want to do something for me?"

The arm he slipped under hers twitched as if his nerves were jangling. Was Milly responsible for the turbulence of his body and spirit? It showed in his voice, in his eyes. Was Philip Carr shaken by conflicting passions; was he struggling to prove himself more than the mere puppet of physical attraction? She sensed an implication she didn't understand as he repeated:

"Do something for you! That's why I'm here. If you don't know how I feel about you—" He cleared his voice, steadied it to ask, "What do you want me to do?"

"Take a hand at contract and let Terrence get to his studies." Pamela intended to clear the air of sentiment by her practical tone. She succeeded as thoroughly as a brisk wind clears the atmosphere of fog. His grip on her arm relaxed. She explained lightly:

"I am a total loss at cards. Miss Crane will have a much better evening if you are her partner; she is politely bored with Terry though he plays a fine game."

"What is she doing in this tidepool, Pam? After Scott Mallory? The man who introduced me to her a couple of months ago at a dance, said that Mallory was her shadow when he first came back from South America, then apparently the affair was off. Now that he is in the public eye — the politicians are after him hot-foot — she wants him back, I'll bet. Understand he did some week-ending here for a while. Don't have to tell you that though, do I? Perhaps she got her sister to hire your cottage that she might spy — "

"Spy! Good grief! Have you picked up the spy germ too?"

"What do you mean, 'too'?"

His face reddened, his usually lazy brown eyes glowed. He was startled, undoubtedly startled. Why? If she told him of Terrence's suspicion of Milly Pike he might think that she was doing it because she had seen him with the girl in the orchard; it might complicate the plot more. Whatever Power was mixing life-lines was getting on extremely well without help from her.

"Did I say 'too'? My mistake. Miss Crane is wasting her time if she is expecting to meet Scott Mallory here. He never comes to the Silver Moon now that Father's affairs are straightening out. Be a dear and devote yourself to the snappy Hilda, will you?"

"Take me for a sheik?"

The protest was denatured; his voice held a hint of cocksureness; his lips widened in a pleased smile.

The all-conquering male! As they stepped into the open from the dim, weird beauty of the orchard, Pamela encouraged gaily:

"Not a sheik but the very king-ripple on the wave of romance, Phil. You — "

Her voice trailed to a thin whisper as a man stepped from the purple shadow of a lilac bush. Scott Mallory! Why had he come? He was unpredictable. If he had to come, why appear as she was patting Philip Carr's hand? Silly habit she had of patting the hand of anyone whom she happened to like at the moment. As she met Mallory's turbulent eyes a typhoon of emotion caught her, swirled her along while mentally she clutched frantically for a hold on something. Into her confusion broke Philip Carr's voice.

"See who's here! And you said he never came. Mallory will take Terry's place at the card table, Pam. You and I will go joy-riding."

"Sorry!" Scott's curt regret slid down Pamela's spine like a cube of ice. "I can't take anyone's place. I want to talk with Miss Leigh — alone, Carr. Business, important business of — her father's."

Chapter XV

ONE impish eye of the half-moon glimmered through a fluff of cloud as if gloating over the holes it was making, over the strange light it was casting on the faces of the girl and the two men. Philip Carr's mouth was set in a stubborn line, his hands were thrust hard into his pockets.

"What's the big idea high-hatting me, Mallory?"

Pamela could appreciate his mother's sensations when spiritually she stepped between father and son. A "buffer" Hitty had called her. She placated hastily:

"No one is high-hatting you, Phil. You told me that you would take a hand at contract. Please go."

"Oh, all right. I'm going because *you* ask it, Pam, understand?"

He strolled away, as if at any moment he might change his mind and return. Pamela's eyes followed till the front door slammed behind him. The hurt, the sense of loss, the disappointment of the days which had passed since she had last seen Scott Mallory, smoldered as she looked up at him defiantly.

"All the dictators are not in Europe."

His amused eyes tore at her heart. "Was I dictatorial? What's the difference so long as I carried my point? He's gone. Come over to the seat. I have something to ask you."

He laid his hand on her arm. She shook it off even as her whole being responded passionately to his touch. "Are you that kind of a person?" she asked herself. "Lucky, you have found it out in time. Just an aching, spineless jellyfish when he touched you, weren't you?" She was conscious of a nervous break in her flippant protest.

"Sit on that damp, rustic seat in the only evening gown I own?"

In answer, he pulled off his coat and spread it over the rough wood. Before she realized what had happened he was seated beside her. Behind them the drowsy quiet of the orchard was stirred by a plaintive "Whip-poo'-will! Whip-poo'-will!" The moon had withdrawn its watchful eye to sulk behind a silver fleece. Had it not been for his white shirt sleeves she could hardly have made out Scott Mallory's figure in the scented dusk. She could feel his presence. Did little currents of suspense and passionate emotion pass between them? Apparently he was unconscious of the tension. Perhaps it was she who was at once broadcaster and receiver.

"Why didn't you tell me about the Babe's attack on your stepmother?"

Surprise tripped Pamela's breath. How had he known?

"Why should I tell you?" The desire to hurt him as he had hurt her — if that were possible, which it probably wasn't — sent her plunging on. "Expect me to keep a line-a-day book for your perusal? I don't tell you everything that happens in my life, you know."

"I know, all right. I know that a lot is happening you don't tell me. But, he is my dog and I am responsible if he makes trouble."

His anger was masked quickly in well-bred calm. Poise with a capital P. One couldn't imagine Scott Mallory, with his background of good breeding, his cool smile, blowing-up unless under extreme provocation. Even as she acknowledged that, Pamela remembered his passionate fury when she had told him that Phineas Carr was to be her counsel. Nothing calm about him then.

"Did you tell your father about the stamp sale?"

An intuitive flash told her that that question was the real reason for his coming. The give and take about the dog had been but a preliminary. Was that all he had to ask her? Had he no explanation to make of his reason for staying away? No regret to express that he was not to handle her case? Were she submitting her own story for criticism would her instructor point out:

"You have employed a complication here, Miss Leigh, which could easily be unsnarled by a question, a word of explanation. It won't get by as a story."?

Lot that instructor would know about it! As a general theory his criticism was justifiable. As a practice in this case it would not work. Could she say to Scott, "Why haven't you been to see me?" She couldn't, not with Hilda Crane in the offing. She answered his question with another.

"Were you skulking in the shadow like a super-detective in a mystery story to ask me that? I thought you had some dark, dour bit of evidence to contribute to my case. I forgot. You know nothing about it."

He caught her arm as she rose. "Why do I know nothing about it? Why?"

Lordly impatience. Sparks falling on dry grass. Words setting flares in her imagination like little incendiaries out to start a conflagration. Her voice answering flippantly:

"Because, I couldn't afford to retain the rising light of the Massachusetts Bar — my mistake — I should have said, 'risen.'"

He slipped into his coat as he explained irrelevantly, "Thought I heard a mosquito's faint, far song. They are bloodthirsty devils at this time of day."

So easily did he put out the fire, blow away the smoke of battle. He walked beside her toward the house. She stopped at the steps.

"Won't you come in? Miss Crane and her sister are playing contract with Father and — "

"Carr?" He supplied the name quickly, asked

as he had asked weeks before, "Do you like this Carr boy?"

She answered as she had answered then, "Quite mad about him."

Defiantly unmindful of the fact that her flame-color slenderness was visible from the living-room window, he caught her by the shoulders.

"Did he give you that topaz bracelet?"

The touch of savagery in his voice set Pamela's heart soaring like a little balloon which had flung over crippling ballast. Had she her friend back again? Her voice was tormentingly gay.

"Topaz! Don't you recognize one of Mr. Kresge's choicest products? I bought it that epoch-making day in Boston when I lost every shred of sales resistance."

His hands tightened on her shoulders. "Was it epoch-making?" His grip hurt. "We will have another like it. I am only temporarily out of the ring. Temporarily — get that — Pam?"

The front door of the house opened. Mallory stepped back into the shadow of the shrubs. Pamela ran up the steps, slightly breathless. Hilda Crane stood on the threshold, her blonde hair like a halo against the light.

"I came out for air. I'm dummy. Thought I heard voices. Wouldn't for the world barge in on a twosome."

Evidently Scott had seen her and had side-stepped recognition. Why? Didn't he want Hilda to know that he had come to the Silver Moon! Why should she herself care what he did? Why *should* she care? How life tore at one's heart. Was it ever simple? For her there seemed always some crippling complication. Would she go on for years fighting herself? Fighting in a circle? As she entered the house she answered Miss Crane's implication.

"You need not have been so sensitive. A man came — with a message for Father. How is the game going?" She approached the card-table where Mrs. Belle Stevens, the Tenant, was dealing.

She was an ample woman with the back of her plump white neck unmistakably going dowager. Her violet eyes were on her reflection in the gilt-framed mirror as she studied the effect of her long fingers manipulating the brilliant-backed cards. Her small mouth puckered fretfully at the corners — a horrible warning to a person who habitually let her temper get the better of her. Her nose was curiously flat with spreading nostrils. She never looked at one directly but had a way of staring into space as if listening to celestial voices. Harold Leigh was watching her with an annoyed frown. His daughter knew from his expression that he had been losing. He took his contract seriously. He rebuked peevishly:

"We have been waiting for you, Miss Crane."

Philip Carr rose, pulled forward a chair. "Come and be my mascot, Pam."

Mrs. Stevens laid down the cards to direct her whole battery of charm at Pamela.

"Your father tells me that you write, Miss Leigh."

Pamela laughed. "A fact except for the tense. I haven't touched my typewriter for months. Looking back from the 1950s I may sparkle on the pages of Who's Who, but at present my name is not one to be used on a magazine cover to lure subscribers."

Hilda Crane picked up her cards. "Belle has a flair for lions: literary, artistic, musical. Some whom she traps are big ones entitled to roar their way through society, some are little more than tame cats. Look out that she doesn't annex you, Miss Leigh. Three spades!"

Had Miss Crane intended to imply that she was little more than a tame cat, Pamela wondered. Nothing subtle about the suave blonde's methods.

"You never want a thing till you suspect that someone else wants it, do you Hilda? Five hearts!" snapped the Tenant.

As Pamela left the room to prepare a cold drink, voices in a heated game-post-mortem followed her. Philip Carr's whole attention had not been on the cards. She had realized that. He had laughed, then gone suddenly serious as if a shadow had passed over his mood. What had he on his mind? Mephisto removed his head from under his wing as she passed him in the dining room.

"Look who's here!" he croaked, blinked lidless eyes and shivered.

"You are a great little stabilizer, Mephisto. You always get a laugh out of me."

Thoughtlessly she allowed the swing door to strike her heels. The bang wrenched an explosive "Gosh" from the parrot. With the sound came the memory of Thanksgiving Day when, for the first time, Scott Mallory had come to the Silver Moon. A, the advertiser, she and Terry had called him. Sometimes her life seemed like one of her own plot diagrams, criss-crossed with an invisible web, with every contact marked with an ineradicable dot.

She removed a pan of ice-cubes from the electric refrigerator. Lucky Grandmother Leigh had installed it. Her heir might, doubtless would — if that day in Boston was an example of recklessness — have squandered its price on clothes.

What a day! It had left a technicolor memory with sound effects of saxophones whining, piccolos whistling, violins sighing, drums throbbing, voices crooning to voices which crooned in turn:

"'Should I reveal exactly how I feel
 Should I confess I love you?'"

She and Scott had been the best of friends then. If only — The Babe! Barking furiously. Chicken thieves? She ran to the foot of the back stairs, called in a voice she hoped was not audible in the living room:

"Terry! Terry!"

Her brother was already half way down. He took the last three steps in a jump. Pamela caught his hand in which something bright glistened.

"Terry Leigh! You're not going out with a revolver!"

"Boy! Don't you know a flashlight when you see one?"

"You mustn't go out, Terry! They might s-shoot!"

"Let me go! The Babe's stopped barking! I'll bet I've lost 'em."

He dashed from the house, his sister at his heels. The world was white with moonlight. At the barn they collided with Hilda Crane and Philip Carr. The Babe was frantically wriggling his head which he had thrust through the opening between the big door and the casing. His eyes were ruby red, he snuffled and whined.

Hilda Crane's blonde head shone like silver in the moonlight, her bare neck and arms were alabaster fair. Carr's voice was curiously shaken as he demanded:

"What started the dog on the warpath? We were in the midst of a rubber when he let loose."

"Chicken thieves, we think," Pamela answered. Her anxious eyes were on Terrence who was making a round of the few poultry houses in use. Suppose it hadn't been chicken thieves? Suppose it were someone spying? "Anything wrong?" she called as he tested the lock on the nearest door.

He joined them, a troubled frown wrinkling his brow. "Everything okay so far as I can see. What was it, young fella?" he coaxed soothingly as he approached the door. The others followed close.

"Perhaps Mallory came back and he heard him," suggested Philip Carr.

"Mallory! Mallory came back!" Miss Crane's repetition was faintly contemptuous. "What do you mean, Phil? Scott left in his roadster — for Boston, I presume — directly after dining with Belle and me. He had planned to spend the evening but he answered the phone and immediately after said he had been called away on important business."

Carr's eyes met Pamela's. He lifted one brow slightly before he acknowledged:

"My mistake."

He spoke in a low voice to Terrence, who nodded before he pushed open the great door, switched on the lights. The dog leaped on him, dashed out to sniff the ground.

Four pairs of eyes traveled over the shadowy barn as their owners remained near the door. The place was fragrantly musty from the hay which fringed the lofts. The old horse scrambled clumsily to his feet, thrust his head over the door of his box stall and whinnied; the cow contributed a soft "Moo!", and went on chewing her cud; the Babe dashed in to snuffle vociferously around a mouse hole.

Terrence whistled to the dog as he flashed the

light along the mows. He tweaked the Babe's ears as the Belgian thrust a cold nose into his hand.

"You're a false alarm, young fella. You—" the words trailed off in a faint whisper. All eyes followed his. In the spot of light focussed on the hay dangled the sleeve of a yellow slicker.

Chapter XVI

Terrence tipped back his chair, clasped his hands behind his head as he frowned at his sister across the breakfast table. Sunshine streamed in at the window. It dappled with gold the gem-like colors in the rare hooked rug, lingered lovingly on the Lowestoft punchbowl which lent superdistinction to the maple lowboy, shot a vagrant ray through the diamond-shaped panes of the corner cupboard to set the Sandwich glass agleam, gently touched the white hair of John Leigh on the wall as he looked down upon his descendant with speculative blue eyes under bushy gray brows. With many shivers, much rolling of eyes, Mephisto on his perch was practising the rising, falling notes of a motor horn. The aroma of coffee, the smell of golden, crisp curls of bacon were in the air.

"How the dickens do you suppose that slicker got on the hay-mow?"

Pamela thoughtfully creamed her coffee. "Perhaps Eddie Pike threw it there, Terry. He was here yesterday dressing chickens."

"Eddie Pike! You couldn't pry him out of that

old army coat if you gave him a dozen slickers. I'll bet there's nothing under it but skin. No sirree! Someone was sneaking round the poultry house and made his get-away when the Babe barked."

"Then I suppose the wearer of the slicker crawled through the loft window, deposited his garment on the hay to give local color and departed via airplane."

"Think you're comic, don't you? Just naturally helpful, aren't you, Miss Pamela Leigh? Oh, shut up that confounded tooting, Mephisto!"

The parrot dodged the muffin the boy flung at him. Head coyly on one side, snickered.

"Bad boy!"

Terrence scowled at his sister's ripple of laughter. "I suppose you think that's funny."

"I do. You shouldn't spend hours teaching Mephisto to talk if you don't care for repartee." She rose and began to clear the table. "Onward Christian Soldiers! I have heaps to do."

Still in the tipped-back chair, Terrence ran his long, capable fingers through his red hair.

"What did Philip Carr mean about old Scott? Did he show up last night."

Pamela paused in the process of placing glasses on a tray. "He did. Just before I went into the house."

"What did he want?"

"To know if I had showed Father a letter he had sent me. He only stayed a few moments."

"That's kind of funny. Miss Crane said he left the cottage after a telephone call to go to Boston. I'll bet he was using business as an excuse to break away from her."

Pamela sternly disciplined an impulse to hug him. "Then you don't think Hilda attractive, Terry?"

"Who me! Nothing doing! I hate a girl who paws. She — I'll answer."

Pamela followed him into the kitchen, set down the tray as he picked up the receiver.

"Silver Moon. . . . She's here. Hi, Pam — "

Pamela answered the call.

"Right here. . . Judge Carr! . . . I know you are not a judge, but I have caught the habit from the villagers. . . . Today! Ten o'clock! I thought it was set down for next week. . . . I'll be there. . . . Yes, I remember. No — I will be glad to have it over. Good-bye!"

She hung up the receiver. Sat back for a moment in the little chair. Terry caught her shoulder.

"What is it, Pam? You're chalky!"

"The trial begins today."

"Thought it was set down for next week."

"It was, but Mr. Carr — he corrected me when I called him Judge — said that the cases ahead of us had gone off the list — if you know what that means — and ours would go on today. He knew it yesterday afternoon but didn't tell me for fear I would lie awake all night thinking about it. Terry, I'm panicky. Suppose Cecile wins the fight?"

Terrence patted his sister's shoulder. "Brace

up! It will be great to have the darn thing behind us. Pull yourself together and don't let the lawyer on the other side get you on the run. His name is Hale, isn't it? I'll bet he's the big-hearted-Otis type. Hale by name and hearty by nature. Watch your step. He'll get you all messed up if he can."

"How can he, if I am telling the truth?"

"What does that guy care about the truth?"

"Mr. Carr said that he had little to lose if defeated, much to gain if he wins; that several times he has been spectacularly successful. Suppose this is another victory?"

"Don't get excited. I don't know anything about him except that he is attorney for the second Mrs. Leigh. That's enough for me. I'll bet 'He's tough ma'am, tough is J.B. Tough and devilish sly.'"

A smile lightened the gravity of Pamela's eyes. "Been reading *Dombey and Son* again, haven't you? I wonder if Cecile will stay at the Inn."

"In our village? Why should she? The county-seat is in the next town. She'd be likely to put up as near the court-house as possible. Wish I could drive you over, Pam, but there'll be the dickens to pay and then some if I don't report at the Academy. The powers that be don't like it much that, with exams in the offing, I have to appear as witness."

"I'm sorry, Terry. Isn't it maddening that our lives can be upset like this by a lie? Put up the 'Closed' sign as you go down the drive, will you? Hitty must call off all reservations by phone. Disappointing people may permanently disable our business, but, Mr. Carr warned me that because Cecile had been in the talkies and he was appearing in court again — he looked as embarrassed as if he'd been caught beating the tom-tom outside his own show, when he added that — the case would be front page news and the curious would flock to the Silver Moon if it were open."

"We've got to lose money, pay out money, hand the second Mrs. Leigh publicity which will be meat for her, because she has accused you of something you didn't do. Ain't law humorous! Wish old Scott were on the job."

"I don't, Terry. I am thankful that he won't be in court to hear the bones of our family skeleton rattled."

"Will Father be called to testify?"

"Only if our side needs him. Phineas Carr wants to keep him out of it if possible, though he admitted acidly to me that nothing would please him more than to force his ancient enemy to the witness stand and put him through the third degree. He has warned me time and again not to let him talk with anyone about the case. Think I'd better tell Father that it goes on today?"

"Sure, Pam. It will give him time to mull over his testimony. Maybe the defense will be reached tomorrow. You'd better get going."

Pamela glanced at the clock. "I didn't realize it was so late. Good luck to you, Terry."

She hastily changed from her morning frock to her last year's slim little tailored outfit of navy blue crêpe printed with white for jacket and skirt, with a smart sash of green, and a blouse of finely tucked net. She pulled on a hat of knitted straw which matched the sash in color, caught up a green bag. She critically regarded the ensemble in the long mirror. Her navy shoes and stockings might not be the last word in fashion but they were effective.

She was too colorless. Her anxious eyes were like black glassies in her white face. It wouldn't do for the jury to get the impression that the defendant was frightened at the start. She deftly deepened the red of her lips, added a touch of rouge to her cheeks. Better, much better.

She caught up Scott Mallory's letter. Her father was adjusting a stamp in a book as she entered his room. She laid the envelope on the table.

"Here's a letter from Mr. Mallory. He has sold some of your securities for a better price than he hoped. I believe he is getting stamp-minded. He thought you would be interested in an auction he attended where a ten shilling, King Edward stamp — I think it was — sold for two thousand dollars!"

"What!" Harold Leigh's eyes blazed at her from a livid face. What a fanatic he was about stamps! "What did you say it was?"

"Look at the letter. I can't stop to read it to you. I am due at the court-house in fifteen minutes."

"The court-house! Does the trial start today?"

"Yes. I hope, Father, that you will feel able to testify if we need you."

He looked down at the sheet of paper in his shaking hand. There was a sardonic glint in his eyes as they met his daughter's.

"I'll be there, if I never do anything else in my life."

Pamela ran down the backstairs, dashed through the kitchen explaining as she went.

"The case is called for this morning, Hitty. Cancel all reservations for today and tomorrow and don't make any more. Business as usual after the trial. Keep an eye on Father. Don't forget you will be called to testify."

Mehitable Betts wiped her bony hands on a towel as she followed to the drive.

"Forget! I guess Phineas Carr hasn't drilled me in what I'm to say for nothing! If 'twan't goin' to be trouble for you I'd be tickled — "

The engine of the sedan drowned her voice. Pamela waved to her as the car coasted down the drive. She glanced at her watch. What did the law do to a person who was late when summoned to court?

She flashed past charming old houses, glimpsed fragments of gardens: some weeded and ordered, patched with stately tulips, starred with narcissus, bordered with purple, orchid and white lilacs; some as devil-may-care as a village ne'er-do-well, yet with a rakish charm. She passed orchards like great drifts of pinkish snow. A southerly wind sprang up. Petals fell like flakes, platoons of little clouds quickstepped across the blue infinity of sky. When the breeze was not blossom-scented it was laden with the tang of the sea.

She parked her car in a crooked lane which had strayed from the highway arched with fine old trees. Her breath quickened as she approached the gray stone court-house. What was that across the street? In an interstice between automobiles she made out the letters NEWS. A sound wagon! Phineas Carr had been right. His return to the arena was not only of front-page importance, it was news-reel material. How had she dared ask a man, whose appearance in court started a horde of reporters on his trail, to take what must seem to him a trivial case? What a break for Cecile! She was being handed publicity worth its weight in gold.

"Stts!" A hand jerked Pamela behind a tree.

"Phil! Oh, Phil, I'm so glad you are here."

"Are you, Pam? Then that makes it worth while."

Made what worth while, Pamela wondered, even as she approved the Panama in his hand; it had exactly the right slant to its brim. His gray suit was a masterpiece of tailoring; his shirt, tie, socks, the boutonnière of bachelor buttons achieved a harmony in blue; his brown eyes glowed with a curious light. As she met them, Pamela felt as if she were being swirled along on a tidal wave of excitement, much as she had felt last night when she was with him, only to a lesser degree. What did it mean? Milly Pike couldn't be responsible for this mood.

He caught her arm. "This way, hurry. I'm rescuing you from the cameras. We'll beat it to the rear door."

"I feel like a conspirator sneaking in like this," Pamela protested as they entered an ante-room. "Have they taken any pictures?"

"They snapped Carnation Carr and the plaintiff. Not together, of course. She was keen for it. She would be."

"This trial will be a grand advertisement for her just before she appears in your revue."

"It isn't my revue and she isn't appearing."

"Phil! Did you really turn her down?"

"I didn't, but I made it plain to the producer that he would have to choose between her and me. He cocked his ear to the siren clink of gold, took my backing and my stage sets." His voice broke on the last word.

"Phil! What has happened? Beneath your concern for me you are all twinkle, twinkle. I feel as if I had been dropped into a fireworks demonstration with sparks flying in all directions."

"You won't wonder that I twinkle when you hear. Didn't mean to intrude my affairs while you are so anxious about this infernal case, but I've got to tell you, Pam, I've got to tell you." His breath caught in a gulp. "My work for the revue has gone over big."

"Really! Phil, how marvelous! When did you hear?"

"Phone an hour ago. Show opened out of town last night. Didn't tell you it was imminent, didn't want you to know if it was a flop."

"Last night!" He had known that his work was being tried out. No wonder his nerves had been jumpy. And she had suspected him of being emotionally upset by vapid Milly Pike. Her spirit was on its knees in apology as she demanded, "Why weren't you at the premiere?"

He avoided her reproachful eyes. "Well, you see, I knew this case might be called any minute and I thought — I didn't know but what in some way I might help. Mouse and lion stuff, with Carnation Carr as your counsel, but you never can tell. Mother was there."

"Phil, what a dear you are! Tell me quickly what you heard about your work in the revue."

"One dramatic critic of parts wrote: 'The settings by Philip Carr furnished a sure-fire combination of economy and illusion. That young man will go far.'"

"Isn't it wonderful! Now you will tell your father, won't you?"

"Not until he is through trying your case. He will be too absorbed to take it in."

Her case! Apprehension swept Pamela in a suffocating tide. Phil didn't realize that by his ultimatum to the producer he had strengthened Cecile in her determination to humiliate her stepdaughter.

Oil on smoldering coals! Cecile! She pulled Philip Carr nearer by the lapel of his pocket to prophesy shakily:

"The second Mrs. Leigh will make every man on that jury believe her a martyr. Getting emotional effects is her profession."

"Beat her at her own game. Pack a little IT into your voice and eyes when you face the twelve good men and true."

"When I do that, you may expect to see our sand dunes shed their tin-can fringed petticoats and dive into the bay in a swimming contest. It isn't my line."

The lightness of her tone belied the turmoil within her. Suppose — suppose Cecile won a verdict for thirty thousand dollars? She looked at the gilt lettering on the frosted glass in front of her as she laid her hand on the knob below it.

SUPERIOR COURT
Jury Sessions

Her throat tightened, she moistened suddenly dry lips. Was success or was defeat waiting for her on the other side of that door.

Chapter XVII

As Pamela entered the court-room, Phineas Carr, with a white carnation in the lapel of his perfectly tailored morning coat, a lustrous black pearl in his gray four-in-hand, beckoned to her. His dark eyes were reassuring, the clasp of his hand was steadying as he met her at the opening in the railing and led her within the bar.

She was conscious of the stir, the hum of interest as he pulled out a chair for her behind the table at which he had been sitting. She swallowed hard, attempted an imitation of complete indifference to the human element in her surroundings. Her feature work had taken her into court but never before had the Stars and Stripes on the wall above the judge's bench assumed such dramatic significance. Her eyes traveled from the flag, past shelves of books, to the patch of blue sky visible through the tall window, on to her stepmother, Cecile Mortimer Leigh, seated at a table, the twin of the one over which Carnation Carr was bending. With a nice sense of values the morning sun shot a shaft of light straight at the plaintiff's face. Her black suit was lissome, very French and very costly; though the jury, being men, would think it simple because it was black. Her white turban, gloves, bag, were the latest word in fashion. Her lips were delicately accented, her green eyes set in brilliantined lashes held an appealing hint of wistfulness. They sharpened as they met Pamela's but only for an instant; they softened so quickly that the girl wondered if the flash had been the product of her own tricky imagination. Whether it had been or not, the second Mrs. Leigh was a shrewd and dangerous woman.

Terrence's quotation from *Dombey & Son* recurred to her as she studied the man beside Cecile. He might be forty, he might be fifty; no youth left in his face.

"He's tough ma'am, tough is J.B. Tough and devilish sly."

He shook his mane of black hair as he talked to his client, gesticulated with a plump hand on which his glistening nails gave the large diamond on his finger a hard run in the matter of brilliance. His teeth flashed whitely between heavy lips; his eyes were too small, his nose too large. He might have stepped from the Well Dressed Man page, so immaculately and smartly was he apparelled. Cap'n Iry Crockett's word, "natty," fitted him as perfectly as did his spats.

A brass-buttoned, blue-coated sheriff rapped with his striped wand of office, announced in a stentorian voice:

"Court!"

Attorneys, clients, jurymen, spectators who filled
every available seat, rose. The black robed, white
haired, fresh skinned judge entered. Pamela regarded him curiously, wondering what a judge thinks
when he first steps into the court-room into which
virtue and viciousness, crime and expiation, right
and wrong, beauty and ugliness, have been pitched
for trial.

"Hear ye! Hear ye! Hear ye!" intoned the
sheriff and court was open. The jury was impaneled.
Pamela thoughtfully observed the men as they took
their seats. Strangers to her, all of them. One of
the two smoothly, sleekly, conspicuously urban jurors
wore an elk's tooth on his chain. They must be city
men who paid taxes and kept their residence in the
county. She knew by their appearance that they
were preordained champions for Cecile. The others
were farmers, small storekeepers. Phineas Carr's
gray brows almost obliterated his dark eyes as he
scrutinized each man as he took his place. The
business of impaneling the jury finished, counsel for
the prosecution opened his case.

"May it please the Court, Mr. Foreman and
gentlemen of the jury." Hale made a few suave
comments and explanations before he called the
plaintiff.

Cecile approached the witness-stand with the
rhythm and dignity fashionable at the moment.
Pamela stole a glance at the jury. To a man they

were impressed by her pink and white femininity, by the wistful sweetness of her long green eyes. The minor note in her voice was bound to rouse the protective instincts of the male — if he had any. The judge sat with elbows on the arms of his chair, the tips of his long, nervous fingers pressed together. The blue-coated, brass-buttoned sheriffs slumped in their seats on platforms on either side of the room, their red and white striped wands of office resembling nothing so much as lean and hungry barber poles. In their time they had seen too many pink and white plaintiffs and defendants with wistful eyes come and go, to have their spines unkinked by the specimen now before the court.

Under the skillful questioning of her attorney, Cecile told a story of neglect and hardship and shaken nerves — the result of her stepdaughter's machinations — of the effect of a heartless letter on her already bruised heart. Adroit questioning by her attorney brought out the story of the vicious attack of the dog, deliberately set on her by the defendant. Spectators reacted. A murmur of indignation swept the court-room like the preliminary mutter of an oncoming storm. Phineas Carr looked at a sheriff from under bushy gray brows. That dignitary rapped smartly on his desk.

"Order! Order! Order!"

Pamela bit her lips till she tasted the sickish sweetness of blood. Cecile's story would bring an acceptance by wire, were it submitted to a confessional magazine, she appraised bitterly. Cheapness unbelievable. How could the woman — if it were true, which it wasn't — bear to advertise her unhappiness, send the details shrieking across the country by wire, by radio, by the printed page? — Bear it! Wasn't the desire for publicity one of her reasons for bringing the suit?

Hale, counsel for the plaintiff, waved his large smooth hand dramatically in the direction of counsel for the defendant, smiled his flashy smile, patronized in his large smooth voice:

"Your witness, Mr. Carr."

Phineas Carr rose. He touched the carnation in his coat lapel as if to make sure it was there before he looked down at a slip of paper in his right hand. At the first sound of his rich resonant voice, the jury, which had been noticeably lolling, straightened to a man. With counsel-trained expertness the plaintiff answered his questions. Then he seemed to draw himself together like a panther about to spring.

"Mrs. Leigh — you have entered complaint in this court in that name, though outside it you have resumed your maiden name, I understand — you are an actress, are you not?"

"Yes, I have acted." Plaintiff's voice and eyes were wary.

"I understand that you are a most convincing actress."

Pamela choked back an appreciative "Marvelous!" Clever of him to set the jury to wondering how much of Cecile's testimony was real, how much histrionics. Hale fidgeted in his chair. Phineas Carr went on serenely.

"You testified under oath that since you left your husband on June first of last year you have made a bare living, that you had received no money from him."

"I said, except what he sent me a short time ago for an operation."

"And that amount was?"

"I said eight hundred dollars."

Counsel for the defense toyed with the carnation, apparently refreshed his memory from the paper in his hand before he asked suavely:

"Mrs. Leigh, you testified that because of the strain on your nerves occasioned by your husband's neglect you had been unable to earn money for some months. My brother Hale will correct me if I am wrong."

As his "brother" merely answered with a glare, Phineas Carr continued:

"Yet, two weeks ago, you bought stock and gave a check for seventeen hundred and fifty dollars in payment, did you not?"

The plaintiff gave an excellent imitation of a victim contemplating a yawning trap. Her counsel blinked as if from a knock-out blow. Was he surprised? Through Pamela's mind echoed Scott Mallory's words:

"That client is a menace who, before trial, wil-

fully or in ignorance, withholds facts from his lawyer which are brought out in cross-examination."
It was quite evident that Hale had not known of the
seventeen hundred and fifty dollar payment. The
effect was but momentary. He was on his feet with
a catlike pounce.

"Your Honor, I object. The fact that my client
bought stock has no place in this evidence."

"Your Honor, considering that the plaintiff has
testified that she has been almost in a state of destitution because defendant wilfully and maliciously
diverted the flow of money from husband to wife, I
insist that the fact that Cecile Mortimer Leigh had
seventeen hundred and fifty dollars to invest, has a
place in this evidence."

"The question stands."

"Your Honor—"

"Sit down, Mr. Hale."

Hale sat down. Phineas Carr patiently repeated:

"Mrs. Leigh, two weeks ago, you bought stock
and gave a check for seventeen hundred and fifty
dollars, did you not?"

The green eyes wistfully sought the jury as if im-
ploring them to observe one poor little woman being
heckled by a big strong man.

"I think I—"

"I don't want to know what you think. I want
to know what you did."

The judge reminded patiently:

"Answer yes or no, Mrs. Leigh."

"Yes."

"That will be all."

Phineas Carr sat down. Pamela's thoughts sifted and resifted like the golden dust in the shaft of sunlight as she looked at him in consternation. Did he intend to ignore Cecile's accusation that her step-daughter had — with malice aforethought — set a dog on her? Would he ask no questions about the letter which counsel for plaintiff had read with such devastating effect?

Hale, who had gripped the edge of the table as if ready for a spring, stared at counsel for the defense; his lower jaw sagged. The jury registered disappointment, for all the world like small boys who had gathered for a fight only to see the champion walk out on them. Pamela caught a twinkle in the judge's eyes, a twitch at the corner of his lips. Had he seen Carnation Carr in action before?

Hale summoned witness after witness to testify to the state of destitution and nerves to which the plaintiff had been reduced through the machinations of her stepdaughter. He was prodigal with his smile, suave to the women, impassioned at strategic points. He pulled out the *simpatico* stop in his voice organ at the dramatic moment and set his listeners sniffing. A high-voltage advocate, indubitably.

Only once he seemed perturbed. After the noon recess, pink-frocked Milly Pike slipped into a seat left vacant by a witness. He scowled at her inquiringly for an instant before he returned to the matter

at hand. Pamela looked quickly at Philip Carr
where he sat on the front bench reserved for spectators. His eyes were on Milly, his lips were tightly
compressed.

Phineas Carr's cross-examinations were superficial, quite as if having established the two facts,
first, that Cecile Mortimer Leigh was an actress,
second, that she had paid out seventeen hundred and
fifty dollars for stocks, nothing else really mattered
to him. Nevertheless, by questions and pleas for
exceptions, he managed to keep the plaintiff's witnesses on the stand, Hale jumping up with objections, until the afternoon session closed. Why,
Pamela wondered impatiently, why didn't he push
along and get it over with? Was he stalling, waiting
for certain evidence? The case had come to trial a
week before he had expected.

"Hear ye! Hear ye! Hear ye! All persons
having anything further to do before the Honorable
the Justices of this Court, at present depart and give
your attendance at this place tomorrow morning at
ten o'clock, to which time and place the sitting of this
court is now adjourned.

"God save the Commonwealth of Massachusetts."

The judge left the room. The jury filed out
their special door. Spectators whispered, looked
back curiously as they straggled to the street.

"Be on hand promptly tomorrow morning, Miss
Leigh. Hale says he has one more witness to present. After that—we'll mop 'em up," with which

prophecy Phineas Carr picked up his papers and departed.

Pamela's courage trailed its wings as she left the court-house. It seemed as if Cecile and her attorney had stolen the show. As she hurried toward the lane where she had parked the sedan, a sarcastic voice drifted back to her.

"Thought you said Carnation Carr was a fire-eater? A spell-binder?"

The second voice was distinctly apologetic. "He is usually. Don't know what cramped his style to-day. Perhaps he's got notional."

"Perhaps 'twas the plaintiff. She's a honey. Like to see her on the screen. The jury just lapped her up."

"The defendant was more my style. She's got class. She was as white as a dead girl but she sat with her hands quiet. Notice how the other one was twisting her beads, or jingling her bracelets, or straightening her hat, or arching her neck like a bird looking for a worm? Every minute on the move. If I'd been her lawyer I'd have knocked her one over the head — as you do a drowning person when they struggle, so you can save them. That plaintiff needs to be rescued from herself."

Philip Carr was waiting for Pamela beside the sedan. His eyes were brilliant; he pulled at his slight mustache. He was taking this case hard. From time to time she had glanced at him in the court-room. His expression had been tense. Had he doubted his father's skill?

"What was Carnation Carr saying to you just before you left, Pam?"

"That the plaintiff's counsel had but one more witness to put on in the morning, then it would be our turn. Don't worry, Phil. I have absolute faith in my attorney."

She knew that he watched her as she drove away. Something was on his mind. Doubt of his father? Doubt clutched at her own heart. Carnation Carr had seemed so — so casual.

As she drove up to the Silver Moon, Mehitable Betts, gray hair streaming like the witch of Endor's, rushed out before she could stop the car.

"Pamela! Pamela! Your Pa's gone!"

"Gone!"

The girl slid out of the seat. Caught the woman's bony shoulder.

"Gone where?"

"I don't know. He flew off in a plane!"

Chapter XVIII

———◆———

PAMELA stared at Mehitable Betts with the incredulity she would have felt had the gaunt woman announced Harold Leigh's departure for the moon.

"How did he get to the field?"

"Now don't take it so hard, Pam, he'll come back all right — if he don't, I don't know as 'twould matter. Eddie Pike was here working over the chickens. I nearly lost my mind when your Pa walked into the kitchen — though I know he'd been talking excited over the phone; the minute you left he put in a long distance call — he pushed me aside when I would have stopped him, just as though he was lord of the universe and I a laborin' ant in his way, and announced he was going out. He was dressed fine. 'Course Eddie hasn't any mind to lose, but, I thought his lower jaw had come permanently unhinged when your father stood over him and ordered him to take him to the field in that old flivver of his — somehow Eddie's got the front wheels on again — he kept looking over his shoulder as if he thought a goblin'd got him."

"Do you suppose Father ran away to avoid testifying in the case? The defense begins tomorrow."

"Land's sakes, does it? Glad I know so I can put my hair up in curlers tonight. How did it go? Did Phineas Carr lay 'em all out flat?"

"No, he didn't. He was as mild as cream cheese." Pamela's eyes were troubled as she remembered the comment of the stranger. "Don't know what cramped his style today." And yet the way in which her counsel had seared into the jurors' minds the fact that Cecile was an actress, that it was her business to get her effects across, had been masterly.

"Any telephone calls, Hitty?"

"Six for reservations. I turned 'em all down. You'd thought I was talking a lollipop away from a baby, they were so resentful. Seems restful, doesn't it, not to have a lot of cars tooting up the drive, and folks walking all over the house as if they owned it, and wantin' to buy the furniture? Later, Terrence is going to have supper with one of the Academy teachers. When it's time I'll bring you something to eat in the living room on a tray."

"Will you really, Hitty? It would be marvelous." Pamela's voice was unsteady. "I am tired. Not physically, but tired of turning things over and over in my mind, wondering what is the best thing to do in the extraordinary complications of my life. Things were in a mess before, but with this queer get-away of Father's I don't know what to expect —but," she added loyally, "of one thing I am sure, had he thought he could help me he would not have gone."

With an angular, work-worn hand Mehitable Betts awkwardly patted the girl's shoulder.

"Keep on keeping on, Pam. Things will straighten out. Things have a cur'ous, unbelievable way of straightening out. When they get so 's it seems as though you just couldn't bear 'em another minute, something breaks to clear them up. I've seen it happen over and over again. 'Fair tomorrow!' your Grandma used to say. Stop worrying about your Pa. He'll land on his feet like a cat. You go change your clothes — 'twill rest you."

In her own room Pamela thoughtfully regarded the telephone. Any chance of reaching Scott Mallory at his office? Even if he were not interested in her, he would advise her what to do about her father. She glanced at the clock. Not too late to try.

She put in the call, drew a bath, recklessly emptied into it the perfumed crystals she had been hoarding, laid out fresh lingerie as she waited for the telephone to ring. She eagerly answered the bell.

"Mr. Mallory's office? . . . Gone! . . . Out of town! For two weeks! . . . No. No message. Good-bye!" That was that.

She was about to slip her frock over her head — the georgette frock the color of orangey-red zinnias which always buoyed her spirit — when she heard a commotion. She dropped the filmy thing as she ran to the window. Milly Pike was at the gate of the

White Hope's yard! Her head was superciliously tilted as if challenging doubt of her courage. Coral comb and wattles twitching, the great rooster was preparing to charge. Didn't the silly girl know better than to go near that fighter?

Pamela bolted down the back stairs, dashed through the kitchen to the accompaniment of Hitty Betts' shrill protest.

"For the land's sake! Where you goin'—"

As she sprinted from the door, Milly was shrieking toward the drive with the infuriated rooster on the hop, skip and jump after her. Pamela ran after them calling as she went:

"Terry! Terry! Terry!"

Milly looked over her shoulder. Strategic error. She stubbed her toe, fell. With a victorious squawk the rooster pounced. Pamela grabbed for the bird's legs. He pecked at her as she caught them. She held the heavy, flapping creature at arm's length.

"Get up, Milly. Quick! Run. I can't hold him."

The girl scrambled to her feet. She sobbed, panted, gurgled. "Terry said he bet I wouldn't dare go into the rooster's yard. I'm not afraid of anything but—he flew at me and—"

"Run, Milly, run! I can't hold him much longer if he flaps like th-this."

The girl shot down the drive.

"Hi, Pam!"

Breathless, crimson-faced, Terrence erupted from

nowhere. He was in the throes of mirth as he grabbed the rooster. Indignation crowded at the heels of Pamela's relief.

"Terrence Leigh! What did you mean by daring Milly to open that gate? The rooster might have injured her seriously. Want another law-suit on our hands?"

"I was watching." The youth's jaw tightened. "She's been sneaking round here long enough. Either she's spying for the second Mrs. Leigh or she's in league with chicken thieves. Haven't decided which. She pretends that she likes me. Hooey!" He grinned. "I told her that the White Hope after this would be on the loose, he needed more exercise. She——"

"Pamela, what you doing prancing round here in your underclothes?" Hitty Betts' shrill protest drowned Terrence's explanation.

"In my what?" Pamela looked down at her slim body simply and revealingly attired in a pink crêpe step-in. Terrence checked an hilarious shout, to tilt a lance in his amazed sister's defense.

"Don't get excited, Hitty. Pam's bundled up compared to most of the girls when they go swimming." He chuckled infectiously. "Just the same, you'd better beat it, woman. There's a car shooting up the drive. One of the Academy teachers coming to take me off to supper."

Pamela shot for the house with Mehitable Betts breathing hard at her heels. Safely in the kitchen, she explained:

"I saw Milly fooling with that gate. Forgot I hadn't my gown on, forgot everything but that she was in danger of being spurred."

"Serve her right if she had been. She comes hanging round here every day — hmp, she wouldn't have so much time if M's Carr was at home. She comes poking her nose into what I'm doing, asking questions about the folks who come. Yesterday, she sat on the porch rail for almost ten minutes talking to your Pa. I told Terrence about it. Says she comes for eggs. Eggs! It's Terry she's after. She's boy and clothes crazy. You better go put something on or you'll catch cold."

Had she done everything she could do to locate her father, Pamela asked herself, as after supper she curled up in a corner of the swing couch on the porch. She missed him, missed the feeling that he was in his room, missed the murmur, the music, even the static of the radio which so often had exasperated her. Heavenly night. Not too cool for a thin frock, not too warm. A spatter of pale stars, a gay old-blade of a moon, if the come-hither glint in the one eye visible, the quirk of the corner of a mouth, were a token. A pink glow in the west, sleepy chirps from the orchard, a mint-scented breeze, satin-fingered, on her lids when she closed them.

She kept the seat gently in motion with one foot. In the excitement of the rooster's attack on Milly she had forgotten to ask Terrence if he knew of his father's mysterious departure. She would not worry about him. He had been gaining steadily in health and strength. The fact that he was able to dress and walk through the kitchen "as if he was lord of the universe," proved that he was infinitely better. She should be grateful for his desire to get away, not alarmed by it. Perhaps she had needed this anxiety to make her realize how much, deep in her heart, she loved him. Flying! Where? He still kept his box in a Trust Company's vault in New York. She knew because she had typed an order for certain securities to be sent to Scott Mallory. Brown of Boston! The name boiled up from her subconscious. Had her father gone to confer with the man with whom he had been in correspondence? If so, Brown would undoubtedly notify his family if he showed signs of dementia. Dementia! That hectic suggestion helped. She would not worry about him. She would drop responsibility on the broad shoulders of Brown; somehow she was sure they were broad.

Several times she had assured herself of the absurdity of worry about a man of the world like her father before a light swept up the drive. An engine purred softly as a car disappeared behind the house. Only two persons she knew drove a high-powered roadster. Philip Carr and Scott Mallory. Could it be Scott? His secretary had said that he was out of town. Gone for two weeks. Had he purposely planned to be away during the trial? She waited on the steps. Two coming. Terry's whistle. A laugh, Philip Carr's—not Scott's. She had the sensation as of a non-stop drop from the top floor of a skyscraper. She heard Terrence say in a high, excited voice:

"Hitty reported that yesterday she cornered Father again. I tell you, Phil—we've got to—"

"Sssh, not so loud, boy—oh, there you are, Miss Pamela Leigh." The change in Philip Carr's voice from mystery to simulated casualness would have been funny at any other time than at this, Pamela reflected.

"How'd you make out today, Pam?" Terrence chuckled reminiscently. "Your appearance at the ringside at the White Hope's little bout, in your pink undies, knocked the trial clean out of my head."

Pamela smiled at young Carr. "Greetings, Phil! Counsel for the prosecution got his testimony in except for one witness, Terry. He will put him or her on first thing tomorrow, then we present our side. You were there all through it, Phil. Who else can that man Hale produce? It seems tragically possible that he already has put in an unbeatable lot of evidence. Of course, it wasn't true, but, what have you?"

Carr dropped to the steps beside her. "I think I know whom he's got up his sleeve—if he can catch her—him. Cap'n Iry Crockett's testimony that, 'It looked as if Pam-ee-lia had set the dog on her stepmother,' was a bomb. I thought you and he were great pals."

"We are. He was under oath. He had to tell the truth. He said the same thing to me here."

"Did Carnation Carr know that?"

"Yes. After our first interview I felt as if I had told your father everything I had thought, done, or emoted since I left the cradle."

"He knew also about the letter you had written your stepmother?"

"Boy! Did the second Mrs. Leigh's lawyer lug that in?"

"He not only lugged it in, he read it to the jury, Terry. Such passion. Such fervor. It certainly was good. As a piece of creative literature I was proud of it. It would have taken a prize in a hew-to-the-line contest."

"I'll bet it would. You can sling a mean type-writer when you get started."

Philip Carr observed thoughtfully: "I followed the testimony as close as a trailer hitched to a fliv. That man Hale handed out some body blows which seemed as if they must knock the stuffing out of the defense. I thought Father would start out on high and smash through their evidence till the plaintiff's counsel would be put to it to scoop up the splinters. He didn't. He just sat there and took them. As a parent I may not be crazy about your attorney; but, as a lawyer I've thought there was nothing bigger, better, bull-dogisher in the world. This time he's got me guessing."

His voice was troubled. Pamela took up cudgels in defense of Carnation Carr. There was more assurance in her voice than she felt.

"He is doubtless saving his ammunition — including a few poison-gas bombs — for tomorrow. You must be on hand, Terry. Get excused from the Academy."

"That'll hurt. Will our invalid be able to testify?"

For the first time since their arrival Pamela's thoughts reverted to her father.

"He's gone!"

"Gone! What d'you mean, gone? Passed out?" The boy's face was pale with surprise.

"No, Terry, no." Swiftly she repeated Mehitable Betts' story of the departure. "At first I was stiff with anxiety; then I got hold of myself, tried to get hold of myself — I'm still panicky inside — argued that if he were able to carry-on like that, he was able to see the project through."

"Perhaps he shot for the promised land to side-step testifying."

"Meaning New York City, Phil?"

"What else could I mean? If I'd been caught in this tidepool for months and a nice big wave of energy washed me out, I'd keep going till I reached the white lights."

"Where do you suppose he went, Pam?"

"I am as stumped as you are, Terry. It costs heaps of money to fly. I don't believe he had enough to go far. He might think we were treating him like a child and be furious if we try to find him."

"Might phone old Scott and set him detecting."

Pamela felt her color deepen. She was glad that the gay old-blade of a moon had hidden its light as well as its come-hither eye behind a cloud.

"I—I thought of that. Called his office. He is out of town for a few days."

"Then I guess you have done all that is possible. Father has played us a low-down trick, after the months we've been waiting on him hand and foot, to step out without an explanation. I hope he does get lost. I hope he spends the night in the hoose-gow."

"You don't mean that. You are as anxious as I am in your heart, Terry."

"Perhaps I am, but he might have had the decency to let you know after the way you've coddled him." Terrence unfolded his long self like an extension ladder from the chair in which he had been slumped. He stretched his arms and yawned. "Don't you worry, Pam, he will come home when he is hungry and his money gives out. His get-away shows that he's a lot better, doesn't it? And so to study. First, though, I'll go out and tuck in the hens and kiss the cow and horse good-night. Do you know the first thing I'd do if I came into the money —I'd go the rounds and thumb my nose at every item of live-stock on our ancestral estate; then with an incubator full of eggs to draw on for balls, I'd practise my curve on the barn windows. That's how crazy I am about the poultry business. Where's the Babe?"

"Hitty shut him in the barn and left the door partly open."

"I thought the old girl was frightened to death of him?"

"She is. That act was a triumph of affection over fear. I must have seemed a little low when I came from the court-house. She did everything she could to help." Pamela was indignantly aware of the unsteadiness of her voice. Terrence awkwardly patted her shoulder.

"Looks as if you had managed to chip her granite heart. Don't worry, Pam. Everything's going to be all right. Nightie-night."

The light of Philip Carr's cigarette glowed and faded as his eyes followed Terrence on his way to the barn. Came the sound of the great door being pushed open, the joyous yelping of a dog, the fragrance of hay, the warm, sickish scent of animals."

"That boy is pretty well fed up on farming, if you ask me. Don't blame him," he sympathized.

Pamela bit her lips furiously to steady them. What had happened to her tonight? She was all shaky inside. Was it the shock of her father's sudden departure? She should be happy that he was well enough to go. Had she lost grip on her courage because she had stopped work for twenty-four hours? Had she lost faith in her attorney? He had seemed horribly casual. She tried to speak lightly.

"Terry is a dear. He is the sweetest, bravest boy. I—" Her voice broke. Philip Carr flung his arm about her and pulled her head to his shoulder. She tried to draw away, relaxed against him.

"I—I—don't know what is the m-matter with me. Things are in s-such a m-m-mess." The last word was a sob. He laid his head against her soft hair.

"Cry it out, dear. You've had this coming to you. You know I love you, don't you? I've been waiting to hear from the settings before I told you. I wanted to have something of my own to offer you. You know—"

A light swept the steps. Pamela jerked her head from the comforting shoulder. A roadster. A soundless roadster! A high-powered roadster! Scott's? Had he seen the tableau on the front steps? Of course, unless he was blind. Served her right for being such a weak sister.

Voices in the house. To whom was he talking? She ran into the hall. Scott Mallory, his face colorless, and her father were at the foot of the stairs. Harold Leigh, pale, but defiant, forestalled his daughter's protest.

"Now, don't make a scene, Pamela. I had business in New York. I flew there and back to Boston. Had a conference with Mallory and he drove me down. That's all." He gripped the rail. "Hang these confounded stairs, must have been designed for a chamois."

Scott Mallory caught Pamela's hands as she took a quick step toward the door.

"Wait. Was Carr kissing you?"

Her temper flamed in one of its periodic reactions to his authority. "And if he were? Would you have me go to my grave unsung and unkissed? How dare you come into this house and ask questions? You haven't been here for weeks and now you — you—" her voice broke. Try as she would she couldn't piece it together.

Mallory looked up at the man who was just disappearing in the hall above, before he caught her in his arms, held her so close she could hear the heavy pounding of his heart.

"Go unkissed? Not so long as I'm on earth." He crushed her closer. "You've got to listen, Pam—"

"Sitting alone in the dark, Phil?" Hilda Crane's voice on the porch outside. "I thought I heard Scott's car. I phoned his office and Miss Cryder told me that he was on his way down. I—"

With extraordinary agility Mallory kicked the door shut. From the floor above drifted the sound of strings, deep and full, high and shining, in forward marching rhythms. Tightly as she was held, Pamela managed a shrug of disdain.

"Philanderer!"

His laugh was reckless. "Am I? Well, if that's what you think of me I'll take some of the perqs that go with the title." He crushed her mouth under his, lingeringly released her only to snatch her close again, his eager, ardent lips on hers.

He let her go as the knob of the door turned. Pamela caught at the newel post to steady herself. She was half way up the stairs, Scott was lighting a cigarette when Hilda Crane entered the hall. In spite of her thrumming pulses she managed her voice creditably.

"I will give your message to Father, Mr. Mallory, it will not be necessary for you to wait."

His eyes met hers. How dared he smile? Hilda Crane linked her arm in his.

"Scott, take me home, will you? I came up to make a reservation for tomorrow, Belle wanted to entertain a party at luncheon, but Phil Carr tells me that the Silver Moon won't be open for business. Is that true, Miss Leigh?" Her voice was aggrieved.

Pamela resented her tone. "It will be closed until after the trial."

Miss Crane clasped a hand over the one already on Mallory's arm. "I spent the day in court. I was thrilled. Of course, I don't know anything about it, but it seems to me that Mr. Hale's argument was unanswerable."

"He hasn't argued yet, Hilda." Mallory's interruption was curt. "Though I haven't a doubt he attempted it."

"How do you know, Scott? You weren't there."

"Didn't have to be there to know that counsel do not argue until both sides have put in their evidence."

"Why, oh why didn't they go? Was each one waiting for the other, Pamela protested mentally. She couldn't bear looking at them another instant. With an attempt at gaiety, she suggested:

"Would you mind finishing the discussion of the case on the way home? Phil asked me to go for a drive — and — "

Face darkly red, eyes black with anger, Mallory opened the door wide.

"Our mistake. Profuse regrets for having detained you."

Philip Carr entered, blinking at the light.

"Just came in to say good-night, Pam. Got to call a man I know on long distance. May I take you home, Miss Crane?"

There was a note in Scott Mallory's laugh which tightened Pamela's throat unbearably.

"Too late, Carr. I am already elected for the honor."

Chapter XIX

OBVIOUSLY Phineas Carr was uneasy. He kept glancing at the clock on the court-room wall as he sat behind the table with his client beside him. He was as immaculately apparelled as yesterday except that there was no flower in his coat lapel. Five minutes before ten. The spectator benches were packed, the jurors were in their seats. Cecile and Hale were conferring. Pamela's courage mounted as she watched them. The plaintiff was maddeningly complacent but her counsel was unmistakably disturbed. Had he discovered a weak link in the evidence for the prosecution?

In spite of her effort to keep her attention on her surroundings, Pamela's thoughts persisted in slipping back to the scene in the hall last night. Scott's face had been colorless, his voice icy when he had bade her a formal good-night. Of course, he had known that she had had no date for a drive. Why had she thrust Phil Carr between them? Because she had been unbearably hurt that Scott's secretary had told Hilda Crane where he was — under instruction doubtless—and had put her off with, "Away for two weeks." That was the answer.

If he cared so little for her that he kept away from the Silver Moon, why had he kissed her? What was one kiss in this age of promiscuous kissing? She closed her eyes, every pulse in her body quivered, her lips still burned from the pressure of his. Of course he had seen her head on Phil's shoulder as the car lamps had spotted them; equally of course, being a man, it wouldn't occur to him that she might be so low in her mind after a day in court, that any masculine shoulder—it didn't matter much whose, so long as it was a sympathetic one—would be a comfort. She had been too fiercely hurt to explain.

Phil had stood beside her on the porch as Scott Mallory's roadster coasted down the drive; moonlight had turned the hair of the girl beside him on the seat to silver-gilt. Carr had whistled.

"Something tells me I made a break somewhere? What set Mallory on his ear? Did he think I was trying to cut in on him when I offered to take Hilda Crane home? He needn't worry, I don't want her. You asked me to be nice to her and I was doing my darndest."

"Let's forget them. Will you be at court tomorrow morning for the opening, Phil?"

He had deliberated before answering. "Can't tell yet. I may—be called away on business."

She must stop looking back, hadn't she enough in the present to think about? She glanced around the crowded court-room. Philip Carr had not come. She missed him.

A chauffeur in navy blue uniform with brass buttons — such as the old-time coachman used to wear — his face red, his breath short, hurried into the court-room. He spoke to a sheriff who nodded affirmatively. The man entered the bar and laid a small package on the table behind which sat Phineas Carr.

"Sorry to keep you waiting, sir, but the mail was late."

He opened the package, removed a perfect white carnation. Phineas Carr fastened it in the lapel of his coat. The chauffeur picked up the box.

"All right now, sir?"

Carr's face relaxed in a whimsical smile. "Quite. Now the trial may go on. Take care of those flowers."

"Yes sir."

The chauffeur departed. Pamela looked after him, then at the man beside her. He had stopped fidgeting. Was it possible that a flower in his buttonhole could work that change?

"Court!"

The occupants of the room rose as one. The sheriff intoned. The judge took his seat. Hale put his witness on the stand, a witness who merely corroborated what those before had testified. Phineas Carr waved away cross-examination. He spoke to the girl beside him.

"It is your turn now, Miss Pamela. Nothing to

be afraid of. When you go on that stand say to yourself, 'I am right! I am right!' You'll get that across to the jury. Tell the truth and stick to it, no matter what Hale asks you. Answer my questions as I have coached you. Answer his with 'yes' or 'no' when you can get away with it."

The room whirled before the girl's eyes as she stepped to the witness stand, steadied at the first word of her counsel. She felt as if he had gripped her hand tight in his. By question after kindly question, he led her on till she had told the story of her father's financial and physical crash, of his wife's desertion, of her utter bewilderment at the sudden turn in their fortunes, of the decision of Terrence and herself to take the invalid to the Cape. She touched on the necessity of selling her jewels to pay nurses and doctors. Counsel for plaintiff sprang to his feet, roared objection. The judge ordered the evidence stricken from the records, Hale resumed his seat obviously exultant.

The defense attorney smiled. The bit of testimony had been indelibly recorded in the minds of the jury. He touched on the dog episode, emphasized his client's statement that the animal never before nor since had shown antipathy to a visitor on the place. Wasn't that a slip, didn't that play into Cecile's hands, Pamela wondered nervously, in the instant before he passed on to the next question, quite as if the little matter of the dog were unworthy of his valuable time.

"Your witness, Mr. Hale."

He sat down. Counsel for the prosecution rose. Pamela's heart threatened to choke her with its clamor, she gripped the rail in front of her. Hale smiled suavely. His smug satisfaction at her evident perturbation steadied her as nothing else could have done. She slipped the betraying hand into the pocket of her jacket and returned his smile. He was plainly disconcerted. He pushed the papers about on his table, as if undecided, before he asked his first question. Strategic blunder. It reminded Pamela of Phineas Carr's command:

"Say to yourself, 'I am right! I am right!' You'll get that across to the jury."

Hale, counsel for the plaintiff, shook out his whole bag of tricks; he smiled, he insinuated, he accused, he roared. He assumed a ponderous solemnity, he set traps. He featured the letter she had written to her stepmother, in which she had refused to give her sanctuary in time of need. He went dramatic over the attack of the dog. Phineas Carr interrupted in the midst of a heart-shaking peroration.

"Your honor, may I remind my brother that this is not the time to argue his case to the jury?"

"Keep to the cross-examination of the witness, Mr. Hale," rebuked the judge dryly.

Pamela found herself anticipating Hale's questions. "I'll wager he has taken the same plot-construction course I took," she reflected with half her mind, while she fixed the other on the prosecuting attorney. She returned to her seat as limp as if she had been put through a wringing machine. Phineas Carr approved:

"Well done, my dear. Horace Hale didn't advance plaintiff's case by so much as the fraction of an inch."

One after another Phineas Carr examined his witnesses. Pamela listened tensely. She forgot that she was being sued for the alienation of a husband's affection, forgot that a verdict against her might mean the loss of the home Grandmother Leigh left her. Her attorney was superb. He experimented with his witnesses as a master-scientist might with potent, inflammable chemicals. So much of this, so much of that, a suave reminder here, a flick on the raw there, never enough to precipitate an explosion nor cause collapse into a dud.

Terrence's tenure of the witness-stand was brief. Pamela's heart thumped with pride as she looked at him. He was so loyal, so clean, so boyishly honest, the jury could not help but be impressed by his testimony for the defense.

Intermission followed. Brother and sister drove in the sedan to the shore. In the shadow of a bathhouse Pamela spread out the tempting luncheon Mehitable Betts had provided.

"Better take it," she had insisted. "You may not want to go to the Inn today, you an' Terry can picnic somewhere. 'Twill do you good to get away from people."

"Wise Hitty," the girl thought as her spirit quickened to the beauty, the mystery beneath the rippling cobalt sea. She shook her head as Terrence offered sandwiches, temptingly thin ones, suggestive of crisp lettuce, and olives and cream cheese. She sifted white, shining sand through her fingers.

"Couldn't swallow. I — I — have a horrible premonition that something will break this afternoon."

Terrence filled a cup with steaming coffee rich with cream from the thermos, added sugar with a lavish hand.

"Something will break, all right, if you don't eat. What can happen to us — unexpected, I mean. Counsel for the prosecution has put his case in, hasn't he?"

"Yes — but I can't explain the curious feeling. Perhaps it is the effect of the strain. I missed Phil Carr in the court-room. He said he might be away on business."

Terrence threw a pebble with practised skill at a gull soaring and dipping overhead.

"Phil's a good scout. Was Hale broken up when his witness wasn't on hand at the opening of court this morning?"

"Wasn't on hand? What do you mean? She was there. Just another sob-sister for Cecile."

Terrence's eyes, big and velvety and black with surprise, were in striking contrast to the snowy hunk of angel cake in which he had set his teeth. He swallowed convulsively.

"She was *there?* Sure, Pam?"

"Sure? Of course, I am sure. What are you talking about?"

He rolled over in a paroxysm of mirth. "Now what do you know about that?" He shouted again.

"Terrence, if there is anything funny in this awful case, sit up and tell me about it. I'd like to see a joke, if there is one."

His hand shook as he refilled his cup. "Can't tell — now!" He choked over the coffee, dropped his head on his arms folded on his knees and shook with laughter.

His sister maintained an ominous silence. He raised his head, wiped his eyes. With a too evident attempt to divert her attention, he pointed excitedly toward a husky, smartly designed cruiser driving at full throttle, churning snowy fountains of spray as it hit the high spots.

"Watch her bank as she turns at full speed! Turning in her own length! Cutting through the water at a sixty-mile clip — if it's an inch! What a boat!"

"She is a beauty. Her nickel bright work glitters in the sunlight like diamonds."

"The glitter would catch your eye. You're a North American Indian, Pam, when it comes to color and sparkle."

"I'll be as bronzed as an Indian if I sit here in the sun and wind much longer." She drew a deep breath of the soft, briny air. "I feel made over. The breeze has blown the cobwebs from my mind."

"Sure you won't eat anything? All right, let's go." Terrence collected the remains of the luncheon. Pamela glanced at her wrist watch.

"There is still half an hour before court opens."

"I know, but I must go for Hitty," he gurgled irrepressibly, "*et als.*"

"You're all gales and giggles inside, aren't you, Terry? What others?"

"Did I say 'others'? Just a figure of speech, woman." He chuckled again: "Come on, let's get going."

Mehitable Betts was the first witness called at the afternoon session. Lucky Terrence had started when he did. What had sent him into such paroxysms of laughter, his sister wondered. She would make him tell when she reached home.

An iron-gray frizz fringed the brim of Miss Betts' pansy-laden hat — a hat unquestionably of the vintage of the merging 'twenties. Her slinky drab dress accentuated her height and angularity. She was primed for combat, as spiked with aggressiveness as a hedgehog with quills.

Phineas Carr had her confirm two of Pamela's statements before he turned her over for cross-examination. Without rising, Horace Hale waved a plump hand.

"No questions."

Mehitable's jaw dropped. She blinked incredulously. She stared truculently at counsel for the prosecution before she turned to the judge. His lips twitched.

"That will be all, Miss Betts. Step down."

His Honor had a nice sense of humor, Pamela told herself, in the midst of her own suppressed, nervous laughter. Hitty was a pricked balloon if ever there was one. Minutes on end, while at work in the sunny kitchen, she had rehearsed the incontrovertible evidence she would present under oath, which would leave the "actress woman" and her lawyer "without a leg to stand on between them." Poor, disappointed Hitty, the great moment of her life gone flat.

"Scott Mallory."

The name crashed into Pamela's sympathetic reflections. It unseated her heart. Scott a witness in this case! Why? To what could he testify? Not once in their conferences had Phineas Carr mentioned the possibility of his appearance. What had her counsel up his sleeve? How good looking Scott was! How clean-cut! Was his fine, lean face less colorful than usual or was her imagination playing tricks? She especially liked that blue serge suit. He was the only man of her acquaintance whose taste in ties she approved. How could she sit here appraising him when her whole financial future was at stake? Without looking, she sensed the consternation of plaintiff and her counsel, a tightening of the spinal vertebrae of the jurymen, concentration on the part of the judge.

Phineas Carr settled the white carnation in his coat lapel before he began the examination of this witness. For the rest of her life the spicy scent of a pink would project this court scene on the screen of her memory, Pamela predicted.

"Mr. Mallory, you own the dog known in this case as the Babe, do you not?"

"Yes sir."

"Will you tell the jury where and why you bought him?"

Mallory's voice produced an instant emotional effect. No wonder he was a successful advocate, he had fire and personality plus. No editor would blue-pencil that story, Pamela thought as he answered the question. His evidence was boiled down to essentials. He told of buying the dog of a fisherman who sold him because his son, a fisherman, hated and abused the animal. Counsel for plaintiff, eyes wary, waived cross-examination.

Phineas Carr rose. "I present my next witness, your Honor. The Babe."

A chill of excitement cavorted up and down Pamela's spine as the Belgian police dog dashed through the jurors' entrance dragging Eddie Pike at the end of his leash. Was it Eddie Pike? Gone was the rope-belted army coat. The man's clothing screamed. Checks. Stripes. Dots. A blinding rhinestone horseshoe in his tie. A huge ring shot passionate purple lights. There was a hint of frightened vacancy in his eyes, on his sagging lips. The jury grinned to a man, the spectators tittered, the sheriff rapped for order.

Noble tawny, proudly conscious of his swankish

new breast-strap, the Babe stood with forepaws on the rail of the witness-stand. Head cocked, ears pricked, he regarded the faces bent eagerly toward him. Without warning he yelped joyously. With a leap he jerked the leash from the lax hand of his keeper and cleared the shoulders of the clerk of the court by an attenuated inch. With forepaws in Pamela's lap he snuggled his cold nose into her neck. She smothered her laughter against his shoulder as she encircled him with her arms.

With a cry of well simulated terror Cecile clung to her counsel's arm. Pandemonium. Laughter. Shouts. Raps! Raps! Raps! The sheriff's stentorian command.

"Order! Order! Order!"

Phineas Carr caught the dog's leash, dragged him to the stand.

"Take him in there again, Pike, and *hold on to him*. Understand me? *Hold on!*"

Eddie gasped like a codfish out of water as he gripped the leash. With forepaws on the rail, mouth open as if in hilarious appreciation of the riot he had staged, tawny eyes snapping, red tongue dripping, the Babe surveyed the court-room. His Honor covered the betraying twitch of his lips with a transparent hand. Counsel for the plaintiff seemed in a daze. One of the jurors indulged in a nervous chuckle. Phineas Carr addressed the judge.

"May it please the Court, I have put this witness on the stand to account for his attack on Cecile

Mortimer Leigh, alleged to have been promoted by the defendant in this case."

"Ready!"

At the quick command a sheriff opened the jurors' door. Someone in a yellow slicker backed into the court-room. The dog turned. He stiffened. The hair on his neck ruffed. He glared at the oilskin clad figure with eyes gone red. Ears laid back, ivory tusks gleaming, he strained at the leash. Eddie Pike turned as purple as his ring from the strain of holding him. The dog snarled, growled, barked, bristled; his jaws dripped. Phineas Carr snapped his fingers. The figure turned, peeled off the slicker. Terrence! Pamela went limp as her brother laughed, inquired soothingly:

"What's it all about, young fella?"

Except for the growl rumbling in his throat the dog might have been turned to stone. Then with an apologetic "Whoof!" he extended a placating paw. Terrence accepted it with grave ceremony. At a word from Phineas Carr, youth, man and dog departed.

Hale shook his black mane and shot up.

"I object to this melodrama, your Honor. It is irrelevant to this case. I move that it be struck off the record."

Counsel for the defense suavely addressed the Court.

"Your Honor, you heard Mr. Mallory's testimony to the effect that he bought this dog from a fisherman, whose son, also a fisherman, abused the animal. Fishermen spend much of their lives in oilskins. Would that not account for the Babe's yellow-slicker complex? You saw what happened when his young master — whom, it must be evident to the least intuitive person in this room, he loves — appeared in a yellow slicker. Does that not explain to any intelligent person the attack on Mrs. Leigh when she appeared at her stepdaughter's residence attired in Iry Crockett's oilskins which she had borrowed? After this demonstration, is it not rank nonsense to claim that the dog's attack was instigated by this defendant?"

The judge scrutinized a paper on his desk. Peered over the rims of his horn spectacles at Hale.

"On the testimony in this action so far presented, I rule this evidence admissible. Motion denied. Proceed, Mr. Carr."

"I have but two more witnesses, your Honor. I may need but one." He cleared his throat. Was the pause due to nervousness or his appreciation of the dramatic value of suspense?

"Brown of Boston."

Chapter XX

WHAT possible connection could the man on the witness stand with a large loose-leaf book in his hand, have with this case, Pamela wondered. Brown of Boston. She had imagined him broad of shoulder, ruddy, a balloon-tire sort, who would ride lightly over the ruts and bumps of life. On the contrary, he was tall, hawk-faced, with large eyes magnified by the strong lenses of horn-rimmed spectacles; he suggested a wire-spring quality of mind. His well-tailored clothing needed pressing.

She glanced at the plaintiff and her attorney. Unless their expressions belied them they were as much at a loss as she to account for this witness.

Phineas Carr tenderly fingered the petals of the carnation in his coat lapel. The room was uncannily still, the atmosphere pulsed with suspense. Motes of golden dust coasted down a sunbeam. Outside, the trip-hammer tap of heels in the corridor; somebody whistling "Kiss Me Again" from Victor Herbert's *Mlle. Modiste;* the bang of a door. Inside, the montonous tick-tock of the wall clock.

"Mr. Brown, you are a collector and dealer in stamps, are you not?"

There was a sharp jingle of bracelets. Pamela looked swiftly at Cecile. She was colorless. Her counsel's expression remained faintly puzzled. One of the two urban jurymen leaned forward eagerly. The witness attested:

"I am a philatelist, sir."

Phineas Carr smiled, explained suavely: "I used the simpler term for the benefit of my brother advocate. Of course his Honor and the gentlemen of the jury understand the more technical name."

His brother advocate audibly snorted but let the gibe pass while he watched warily for a chance to jump into the ring.

"Mr. Brown, a short time ago, you purchased at auction a rare stamp, an English, 10 shilling, King Edward stamp overprinted I.R. Official, for the sum of two thousand dollars."

A murmur of incredulity rippled through the court-room.

"Order!" rapped the sheriff.

"Will you show that stamp to the jury?"

Brown of Boston removed a leaf from his book. Counsel for the defense waved away the Clerk of the Court when he would have taken it, himself held it before the twelve men. The urban juror with the elk's tooth on his watch chain lost his balance in his eagerness to see. Counsel for the plaintiff appealed to the judge.

"Your Honor, I protest against the holding up of this case for irrelevant testimony."

"Your Honor, the testimony is not irrelevant."

Phineas Carr's contradiction lashed. "I propose to show that this plaintiff, who claims that the defendant did wilfully and maliciously poison her husband's mind against her until her nerves were so shaken that she was unable to fill her theatrical engagement, sold this rare stamp for two thousand dollars, less commission."

Counsel for the prosecution sprang to his feet, shook his mane, bowed formally to the judge.

"I move that that statement be stricken from the records. The sale of that stamp has no bearing on the question before this jury, which is, did the defendant or did she not influence the plaintiff's husband against her? The introduction of this stamp act is a ruse to rouse the sympathy of the jury."

"This is not the first time a Stamp Act has roused the sympathy of citizens of this Commonwealth, your Honor," Phineas Carr reminded dryly.

The gentlemen of the jury smiled broadly, the spectators tittered, the sheriff rapped. The judge fitted finger-tips together and deliberated.

"I agree with counsel for the defense. The sale of the rare stamp has a bearing on this case. Motion denied. Proceed with your witness, Mr. Carr."

Counsel for the defendant stood tall and straight. The fingers of one hand gripped the carnation-decked lapel of his morning coat, the other held a slip of paper. Color burned in his high cheek bones, his dark eyes were smoldering coals.

"Mr. Brown, how did you know that this rare stamp was to be sold?"

"Collectors and dealers are usually notified of sales, sir; besides, there's a sort of wireless over which news spreads when a rarity is about to change owners."

"Were you surprised when this specimen was offered for sale?"

"Yes sir. Right off the reel I had a hunch—"

"Just a moment. Aren't rare stamps constantly coming into the market?"

"Yes sir."

"The collecting of stamps is a costly fad, is it not?"

"I would rather call it an investment, Mr. Carr. I have several clients who spend between twenty-five and thirty thousand dollars a year for contemporary and rare stamps. Of course, during the late depression, values shrunk—except in outstanding rarities—as in everything else."

Was Carnation Carr dragging this out to create suspense, Pamela wondered. If he were he was succeeding. She was on the edge of her chair, there wasn't a person in the room who wasn't listening avidly—except counsel for the plaintiff who was whispering to his client. Thirty thousand dollars a year for postage stamps! Unbelievable.

Counsel for the defense continued: "You spoke of a hunch, Mr. Brown. You mean, I suppose, that you were suspicious that something was wrong about this sale. Explain to the jury what you mean by hunch."

The plaintiff's attorney sprang to his feet. "I object to that question, your Honor."

"Objection overruled. Proceed, Mr. Brown."

Hale had the temerity to glare at the judge before he sat down. The lips of his Honor set in a straight line. Brown looked at counsel for the plaintiff over the horn rims of his spectacles before he explained:

"I had a hunch there was something irregular, because when the owner of a stamp like that had bought it of me he said, 'It has been one of the ambitions of my life to own this. I'll starve before I part with it.' He is a philatelic fanatic. I felt sure that if he were to sell it, he would offer it through me."

"Any other reasons for suspicion, Mr. Brown?"

"Yes sir. From time to time, previous to this, to be exact since last July, several rare stamps were sold which I knew to be from this same collection. I began to suspect they had been stolen."

The judge bent forward. "How did you know they were from that collection, Mr. Brown?"

His voice was drenched with interest. Had he also collected stamps as a boy? Pamela glanced about the court-room. If his Honor's expression was a test, every person present had at one time or another been bitten by the stamp-bug. Absorption unbelievable. The witness smiled indulgently.

"Just as a collector of works of art knows where

to locate a Rembrandt, a Corot, a Daubigny, or any one of the great masterpieces."

Hale rose. "If these stamps were such rare treasures, how could they be so easily stolen, may I ask?" His amused skepticism was well done.

"You may not ask." Phineas Carr's protest was a roar. "Your questions are in order when this witness is turned over to you for cross-examination, not before." Counsel for the plaintiff dropped to his chair somewhat heavily.

"Did it occur to you to query the owner of these stamps as to the reason for their sale, Mr. Brown?"

"It did. Then I heard that he had lost his fortune and was up against it. Thought it might hurt his pride if I seemed curious. He had been doing a little exchanging of stamps with me to keep him amused, he wrote."

"But you did finally question him? Why?"

"In a registered letter he sent a mint block, which I had bought for him, with instructions to sell it."

Pamela remembered her father's wail: "My mint block! My mint block!" And she had thought it might be a rare print!

"Please explain to the jury what a mint block is, Mr. Brown," Phineas Carr requested.

"The term is borrowed from the numismatists — coin collectors. It means a block of six or more unused stamps with the original gum." Witness opened his book, extracted a leaf. "You will notice on this example of twelve stamps that the perforation between the two rows is missing."

The judge leaned far forward, there were red spots on his cheek bones, his eyes shone boyishly eager. Brown indicated a place on the page.

"Here is the lot I bought. A mint block of twelve stamps of the partly perforated six-cent 1894 issue. It is one of the largest blocks of its kind known. Notice the sheet-number in the margin. I ordered it put up at auction. Bid it in for $1000."

The concerted "Oh!" of the spectators passed without rebuke from the sheriff. He was pop-eyed with amazement. Phineas Carr returned the precious leaf to its owner and inquired:

"It was after that sale that this English stamp came on the market?"

"Yes sir. I bought it. I was so keen to get it — stamp collecting is just as exciting as horse-racing at times — that I didn't think where it came from. It isn't the only example of its kind. When I came to I began to wonder. Yesterday morning, the man whom I had thought might be the owner, phoned me. He had just heard of the sale of a stamp like his. I told him of my suspicions, with the result that I picked him up in a plane. We flew to New York, checked up on his stamps and found that several were missing from one of the most famous collections of English stamps in the country — in the world."

"Did you inquire of the bank officials if anyone but the owner had had access to that box?"

"We did."

"And the answer?"

The ticking of the clock boomed through the silence. A bee buzzed in at the open window, realized its intrusion and buzzed out. Someone caught his breath in a nervous gasp. Phineas Carr fingered the petals of his carnation. His face was quite white as he repeated:

"And the answer?"

"Mrs. Harold Leigh."

Counsel for the prosecution pulled his client back to her chair when she would have risen. His face was patched with purple, his voice was shaken as he demanded:

"Your Honor! Do you realize that witness has intimated that an innocent woman stole and sold those stamps?"

"Sit down, Mr. Hale."

The plaintiff's attorney swayed for an instant as if debating the wisdom of obeying the judge's command, before he resumed his seat. Phineas Carr addressed the Court.

"Your Honor, before I turn this witness over for cross-examination, I wish the jury to understand our claim, which is: that the plaintiff has not been without funds; that she sold rare stamps to the amount of ten thousand dollars, which she took from the safety-box of her husband without his knowledge or consent."

Cecile Mortimer Leigh sprang to her feet. "Suppose I did?" Her voice was shaken, her green eyes were wistful. She was attempting to charm, less obviously than on her appearance on the witness-stand, but with deadlier purpose. "Hadn't I a right to support from the man I married? His daughter had turned him against me —"

"If counsel for the prosecution does not restrain the plaintiff I will fine her for contempt of court!" Thus the judge. The spectators showed symptoms of applause.

"Order! Order!" The sheriff was crimson from the volume of his roar. Horace Hale caught his client's arm. His face was expressionless as he talked with her in a low tone. A playful breeze danced in at the window, cut antics with the pages of the stamp book of Brown of Boston on the witness-stand, before it danced on.

Phineas Carr addressed the Court. "Your Honor, the plaintiff has by that last admission substantiated our claim that she has been far from destitute during this last year." He waved a transferring hand. "The witness is yours, Mr. Hale."

The face of counsel for the prosecution was livid as he rose. His contemptuous eyes rested for an instant on the plaintiff before he spoke.

"May it please the Court, Mr. Foreman and gentlemen of the jury, I find that this case has been falsely represented to me by my client. I withdraw."

He swept up his books. With elaborate formality he bowed to the judge, to the jury, to opposing counsel. Head high, with catlike tread, he left the bar.

Phineas Carr fingered his white carnation.

"*'Te morituri salutamus!'*" He delivered the gladiatorial salute in a voice, which, though low, must have been audible in the most remote corner of the weirdly still court-room.

Chapter XXI

HER father owner of one of the most famous collections of stamps in the world! Pamela's mind steadied from the shock of Brown's statement. It must be worth thousands if that King Edward specimen was a sample. He had owned them when his daughter had sold her jewels to pay his bills and those of his wife, when she had given up the chance to make good in the profession she loved, Terrence the school in which he was happy, to carry on the Silver Moon that he might have proper food and care. She tried to excuse him. He had been ill then, prostrated, hadn't realized conditions. But the months since? Had Scott Mallory suspected that he had concealed assets? Of course. Hadn't he asked her for the address of the stamp firm? Brown of Boston!

Phineas Carr returned from a conference with the judge. Pamela sensed the tense concentration of jury and spectators. What would happen now that counsel for the plaintiff had withdrawn from the case? His client had been close on his heels as he left the court-room. Carr swept up his papers. Smiled his whimsical smile as he said in a low voice:

"That will be all for the present, Miss Pamela.
Went off with a bang, didn't it? Hale justified my
belief in his flair for theatric values. Pretended
that his client had not told him all the facts — probably she hadn't — and walked out of the court-room
with the sympathy and admiration of every spectator in it. This case will bring him business. Unless
I am mightily mistaken — and I'm sure I am not —
that is the end of the suit for alienation of affection."

The kindly words with their tinge of humor
smashed Pamela's self-control. Her body shook,
her voice caught in a sob when she tried to speak,
her breath came in gasps. Phineas Carr laid his
hand on her shoulder.

"Take your time, take your time. Stand up, my
dear. His Honor is leaving the court-room."

He waited for the echo of the sheriff's proclamation to die down. "You are coming home with me.
I shan't allow you to go back to the Silver Moon till
you get your grip. Your father might be — well he
can be very unpleasant. Mrs. Carr has returned.
She told me to bring you for tea no matter which
way the verdict went, said she had some wonderful
news to tell you. We will slip out the rear door and
dodge reporters. I told your brother not to wait,
that I should run away with you."

He nodded to a sheriff. The brass-buttoned one
cleared the way to the door by which the judge had
departed. A chauffeur in a white linen duster with

cuffs and collar of the deep blue of the shining town car, at the door of which he stood, touched his cap as they approached. Phineas Carr seated himself beside her on the broadcloth cushioned seat. He folded his hands on top of the curved handle of his cane. Apparently unmindful of the curious crowd which had collected or the fact that she was shivering from reaction, he observed as the car shot forward:

"Of course, Miss Pamela, that stamp testimony had no legitimate right in this trial." He chuckled. He was boyishly exultant, not so unlike his son when he was pleased with an achievement. "But we took a chance on it. I happened to know that the presiding judge was a stamp addict. I recognized the Elk juror, when he took his seat, as a plutocrat and a philatelist. We got by."

We! It was the "we" of a crowned head or an editor, Pamela thought, as she tried to control her shaking body.

Mrs. Carr met them on the threshold of the Ship Room. Even in her turmoil of mind Pamela paid tribute to the lustre of her pearls, the exquisite amethyst frock, the sparkle of excitement in her lovely eyes. Her husband tenderly patted her shoulder.

"We licked them, my dear. Let this child cry it out for a few minutes, then bring her in for tea."

So he had observed her reaction. Pamela pulled off her hat in the charming yellow and lavender room in which Mrs. Carr had left her. Cry it out! Not she. She sopped her face and throat with cold water until they glowed. Dusted her skin with powder. Her pulses steadied, her heart quieted, gay courage got the upper hand of taut nerves. Her eyes shone like dusky brilliants as she pulled her green hat over her dark hair before the mirror. She nodded to her reflection.

"Ashamed of you for going to pieces over good fortune. What would have happened had you lost the case? If you knew the relief I feel —"

"Should I reveal exactly how I feel —"

The song rose in her heart. The tightening lips of the looking-glass girl warned her. With a stifled exclamation she turned away.

On the threshold of the Ship Room she paraphrased gaily:

"See the conquering heroine comes! Sound the —" The sentence thinned into a mumble as Scott Mallory looked up from contemplation of the fire which, even on this spring day, flickered and faded on the hearth. Where had he come from? Why was he here? Was that her father talking with Carnation Carr over by the window? Her father?

The stiffening went out of her knees. She sank into a chair beside the tea-table. Mrs. Carr smiled at her as she sugared the rare cups as richly, darkly red as the carnations in a tall slender vase on the table. The fat Georgian tea-kettle snorted a white puff of steam, rattled its silver cover.

"I thought we would wait tea for Phil, Phin. He—he has something wonderful to tell you." Mrs. Carr's voice shook with eagerness.

Her husband's face darkened. "He doubtless is still engrossed by the business which kept him away from court when I was trying a case. I had hoped he would be sufficiently interested to hear it through. Wait if you like. Mr. Mallory has something of importance to tell us." His eyes cleared of annoyance, his voice was almost boyish as he amended:

"But, before he begins, I want you to know that the sudden termination of the alienation suit—don't interrupt the Court, Mallory—was due to him. He worked up the defendant's case; I merely presented it. Day before yesterday when I found that it would come up for trial the next morning, I phoned him. At the risk of being chewed to pulp he experimented with the yellow slicker and the dog."

The mysterious appearance of the oilskin sleeve on the hay-mow was accounted for. Pamela's first reaction was relief; she hadn't cared for the possibility of skulking chicken thieves in this era when automatics were as easily acquired as a daily paper. Terrence was so careless of his own safety. So had Scott been when he had angered the Babe. The evening she and Philip Carr had met him in the orchard, he must have been lingering about for a chance to get to the barn unobserved. Why couldn't Phineas Carr be friendly with his son as he was with others? Was he jealous of his wife's affection for the boy? He was too big a man to be so small. It was abundantly evident that he had been hurt that Philip had not been in court to witness his victory. What would he say when he heard Phil's grand news? Father and son were playing at cross-purposes.

"Miss Pamela! Miss Pamela, you are not listening," Phineas Carr reproached. "The stamp business was all Mallory's idea. I stalled yesterday at the trial to give Brown of Boston and your father time for their investigation. The case was sprung on us a week earlier than we had expected, we were not quite prepared. Brown spent last night in this house, Mallory and I the evening working up his testimony. I waive my claim to the old maple, Miss Pamela. Settle the question of fees with my associate. I merely served as senior counsel. Now, Mallory, it is your turn."

Then she was still head over ears in debt to Scott? Pamela's heart stopped and raced on. What next!

Scott Mallory stood back to the mantel, hands thrust hard in his pockets. He shook his head. "Not my turn. Mr. Leigh's."

Harold Leigh left the window. The skin over his knuckles was strained shiny as he gripped a chairback. He seemed years younger than before his air trip. There was about him a trace of the gay and gallant man who had won the adoration of his small daughter. Pamela steeled herself against him, kept her eyes on the fantastic pinkish shadows the firelight cast on her crêpe jacket and skirt, as he explained:

"Of course, when the right time came I intended

to make up all you had spent for me, Pamela, but this last year of depression has been a bad time to sell stamps. I have traded under an assumed name always. Saves publicity. Cecile had a duplicate key to my box — it had not occurred to me that she would use it after she left me. They knew her at the bank. When we were first married she went there with me several times — I was fool enough to take the box in both our names and more of a fool to leave some of my valuable stamps there in a sealed package." His eyes were as anguished as might be those of a parent parting with an adored child. "Brown sold the mint block for me and sent the cheque directly to Cecile. I told you that I wouldn't let you mortage your property for her; besides, I was afraid she would come after the money. I didn't want her poking into my affairs." The slow color rose under his waxen skin. "She has an infernal way of getting what she wants."

His daughter looked at him steadily. "What is the value of one of the most famous collections of English stamps in the country — the world perhaps?"

He cleared his throat nervously. "That is no one's business but mine, now." He drew two cheques from his pocket. "Mallory has advised me that as Cecile will undoubtedly win in her proceedings for an allowance, I would better give you and Terrence what I owe on the legacies your mother left. I had intended to make good when prices went up. I may be a stamp fanatic but I am not a thief. When the crash came and my wife deserted me, I was too numb mentally to realize what my collapse was doing to your life and Terry's, Pamela. Then, then somehow I didn't care. I never would have lost that money nor my own had I stuck to the business I know, but Cecile was all for speculation. I am not afraid to stack thousands on my knowledge of philatelics. These are Brown's cheques for a portion of my holdings. He was only too eager to buy what it was like tearing my arm off to part with."

Irritated resentment in his voice, the furtive gleam Pamela had seen before in his eyes. She felt as if she were looking on at a play with the lead acted by a stranger. Even as she told her father that she was happy that he was well again; that she was glad for Terrence, more than for herself, that he was able to make good on the legacies; she was hurt, intolerably hurt, that he had hoarded when he might have helped. Her voice sounded in her ears like that of an automaton. To Harold Leigh it must have seemed as usual for he approved:

"Glad that you are facing the facts without a fuss, Pamela. Mr. Carr has agreed to act as guardian for Terrence, it is the arrangement your grandmother wanted. The income from fifty thousand dollars, augmented by some of the principal if necessary, will see the boy through college."

He dropped a cheque into his daughter's lap. "Here is the same amount for you. Mallory has fought tooth and nail to get it for you. I would have preferred to wait until prices went up before I turned some of my holdings into cash, but he is so — so unflinching. I hope he will show as much fight for me when Cecile comes after that allowance. May I commandeer your limousine, Carr, to take me home? I notice it is at the door." He coughed hollowly. "I am beginning to feel the nervous strain of the last forty-eight hours."

Pamela sat stiffly erect listening to the departing purr of the motor. Had that touch of exhaustion in her father's voice meant that he was returning to his role of invalid? She looked at the slip of pink paper. Fifty thousand dollars! Scott had practically forced that money from her father. He had been working for her all the time she had thought him indifferent. He and Phineas Carr were conferring. Would he give her a chance to thank him, to explain that she liked him more, infinitely more than she liked Philip Carr? A voice crashed into her repentance.

"I don't care if they've got the judge of the court in there! I'm goin' to see his folks. I'll tell 'em!"

Eddie Pike! Eddie in his variegated court costume on the threshold! What had happened now? His ready-to-wear bow tie was under an ear, his china-blue eyes bulged, the rise and fall of his lurid plaid waistcoat registered turmoil, his slack mouth gaped.

"Say, Judge, I want to know about my sister."

Phineas Carr scowled at him, growled, "Inquire of my wife. She hires Milly."

Mrs. Carr smiled at the belligerent intruder, said soothingly:

"We don't know where Milly is, Eddie. Cook says that at about nine o'clock she saw her meet someone — a man, she thought — outside the back gate. She hasn't come home."

Pike took a step into the room, his face worked horribly. With an unconscious sense of dramatic values he paused long enough for suspense to get in its nerve-tickling work.

"Course she hasn't come home. She's run off with your Phil in his slick roadster!"

Mrs. Carr swayed, steadied. "Have you lost your mind, Eddie?" Her fixed smile never wavered as her eyes met her husband's. Face ashen, he looked back at her.

How ready he was to doubt his son, and how it hurt him, Pamela thought as she met his tormented eyes. Phil and Milly! Memory projected a picture of the two under an arch of apple blossoms, the man apparently pleading. Hateful suspicion. She wouldn't believe it.

"Where did you pick up that crazy idea, Pike?" Scott Mallory's coolly amused question snapped the tension.

Eddie blinked vacant blue eyes. "You're the lawyer fella that got Terry and me to take the dog to court, ain't you? My idea ain't crazy. I've watched 'em. I've follered 'em. This mornin' I see 'em start off. Milly and a suitcase."

"A suitcase!" Mrs. Carr's repetition quavered.

"Yes sir — ma'am. An' if Phil Carr's run off with my sister —"

Scott Mallory caught his shoulder. "Go slow, Eddie!"

Pike waved a wild arm. "You can't softsoap me. I say he's got to marry —"

"Who's got to marry who? What's all the shouting about?" demanded Philip Carr from the threshold.

Chapter XXII

——◆——

YOUNG CARR grinned engagingly as he asked the question, but the lighter he held to his cigarette was not quite steady. In his effort to produce a voice Pike gasped like a goldfish snapping at food in the water of a crystal bowl.

"What did you think of my coup, Judge? Masterly, what?"

His son's question brought a faint color to Phineas Carr's cameo-like face. Was it generated by relief or anger?

"Not knowing to what you refer I can't express an opinion."

"Phin! Don't be so hard!" pleaded his wife. She smiled at her son through a mist of tears. "What was the coup? Tell your mother, Philip."

That "mother" contracted Pamela's throat. She had not known that a word could sound so like shaken music. Pike recovered his voice to demand, with that brand of truculence which only the drunk and the mentally retarded achieve:

"You tell me what you done with my sister! Ran away with her, didn't you?"

Philip Carr deliberately turned his back on his father to smile boyishly at his mother. Her eyes responded with a lovely light.

"Sure, I ran away with her — in a sense. Didn't Terry tell you of our scheme, Mallory?"

"No."

Scott was as unsympathetic as Phineas Carr, Pamela thought indignantly. There were little flames in the dark grayness of his eyes, a tenseness of jaw which she had come to recognize as steel against which it would be futile to batter.

"Tell me what you done with my sister, you—"

Philip Carr roughly interrupted. "Shut up, Pike. Cut out the whine. Your sister is in the kitchen. I promised her that if she would tell me something I wanted to know I would take her to a city shopping and pay the bills — the girl is clothes mad. She was canny enough to withhold the information I was after until we drove into the yard here a few minutes ago. Now you know the truth, fade-out. You smell horsey."

"He is on the level. Go, Eddie." Scott Mallory answered the question in the troubled china-blue eyes interrogating him.

Pike loped to the threshold, stopped to wag a threatening head. "I'm goin'. But if it ain't true, if Milly ain't in the kitchen, I'll be back. I'll be back!"

His mutter thinned into the distance. A girl's shrill exclamation was shut off by the slam of a door.

Philip Carr drew a long breath. "That's that!"

His father crossed the room to stand beside Scott Mallory before the fire. Two powerful, forceful men. The same fairness of spirit — except in the elder man's attitude toward his son — the same sincerity and competence in their profession. Would they have been sympathetic as father and son, Pamela wondered, or were they too much alike?

"What's this about a coup?" The elder Carr's voice was as implacable as when he had a witness writhing under cross-examination, his fingers tightened on the lapel of his coat under the white carnation.

His son chuckled boyishly. Phil was *sweet*, Pamela told herself; most men would have furiously resented that tone.

"It was this way, Judge. Terrence and I got a hunch that Milly Pike was in the pay of plaintiff's counsel. No family the size of ours could possibly consume the number of eggs she personally conducted from the Silver Moon — you will find them all charged on your bill, Mother. We didn't know what she was snooping for but we were convinced that she was spying. Remember the time you caught me talking to her in the orchard, Pam? I was trying to make her tell me what she was up to."

"Why didn't you tell me your suspicions?"

"Don't bite, Mallory. Who knew that you were interested in the case? Each time I met you in this tidepool you were zealously preferring a blonde. Thought that was why you came to the village."

From under her lashes Pamela observed the

tightening of Scott's lips. Why didn't he deny that implication about Hilda Crane? Only one answer to that,—he couldn't, and tell the truth.

"Why didn't you tell me? You knew I was counsel for the defense."

Philip Carr abandoned boyishness as he might an outgrown garment. His face was colorless, his eyes were hotly indignant as he answered his father.

"Can you see me coming to you with any confidence? Honestly now, can you? You would have made me feel that I was a fool. You may be a demon at law with an uncanny nose for scenting out the truth in a case, but you go blooey when it comes to knowing your own son."

"Phil!" Mrs. Carr protested faintly.

He pressed her hand against his cheek. "It's all right, Mother. He's had it coming to him for some time."

He smiled at his father; Phineas Carr's fingers clinched on his coat lapel. "Now that is off my chest I will proceed with the saga of the kidnapping of the fair Milly, if you can call it kidnapping when the victim is rarin' to go. When Hale said at the close of court yesterday that he would present one more witness in the morning, Terrence and I were sure he meant Milly Pike. I had seen him scowl at her when she came into the court-room. Hitty Betts had reported that the girl had been talking to Mr. Leigh. That didn't look good to us. We didn't know to what she was prepared to swear, but we determined to put her where she couldn't swear to anything—unless at me."

"Do you know the penalty for tampering with a witness?"

Philip shrugged. "Don't roar, Judge. Of course I do. You understand, don't you, Mother? I wanted to help Pamela, the girl I am going to marry."

Pamela's senses whirled like a merry-go-round gone mad, steadied. Her eyes flashed to Scott Mallory. Had he exclaimed before he turned to stare down into the fire, or had she imagined it? With a joyous croon, Mrs. Carr flung her arm about her.

"My dear! My dear! Is it true? I am the happiest woman in the world. Now I have someone to whom to leave my pearls!"

Pamela's tongue clove to the roof of her mouth, her throat dried, her eyes were drawn to Phineas Carr as by a magnet. His seemed to bore into her soul before he looked at his son. He understood, thank heaven! He knew that Phil was taking her love for granted.

"This is joyous news, Philip—but, don't misunderstand me, my boy, when I ask you to finish the saga of the fair Milly, before we—we—offer our sincere congratulations—if—they are in order."

His voice was affectionately friendly. His wife regarded him with wistful radiance, his son, incredulously.

"I can't believe it is you, sir, speaking as one

gentleman to another. There isn't much more to
it. Terry and I had sniffed smoke where there was
no fire. When I pinned the girl down to confession
she admitted brassily:

"'I've got a crush on Terry Leigh. All the girls
in the village got their Academy boy-friend. They
bet me I couldn't get him. I bet I could. Only excuse I had to go up to the Leigh place was to get
eggs. I talked to his father when I couldn't see
him.' Her tone was nasty as she added, 'I'm off
him for life. He set the rooster on me. Anyway,
there's someone else I like much better.' So there
you are! I'm a flat tire. I spent my day kidnapping
a witness who wasn't a witness after all. If you had
needed more proof that I was not cut out for the
legal profession, Father, you've got it in the way I
dug for evidence where there wasn't any. Now,
we'll talk about Pam and me — and the stage
settings."

Scott Mallory abruptly flung his cigarette into the
smoldering wood-coals. His face was white, his
smile twisted.

"Then this is where a mere outlander makes his
exit. I'm off to New York tonight for a few weeks,
Mr. Carr. Upon my return we will settle up the
details of this *cause celebre*."

"Just a moment, Mallory. I've been unjust so
many times to Philip that I'm afraid he'll misunderstand me now." Phineas Carr steadied his voice.
"Happy as I would be if it were true, Miss Pamela

has not yet corroborated Philip's statement. For a recently engaged girl she seems singularly disturbed."

Pamela was only dimly conscious of Mrs. Carr's shocked, "Phin!" She looked at Scott Mallory. His expression was cold as the Arctic pole and about as remote. A lot he cared if she were engaged to Philip Carr. Hadn't Phil said that he had been preferring Hilda? She could change the pattern of her life by accepting Philip — his mother's pearls — but, she didn't want a man, any man, in her life. Fifty thousand dollars of her own! She had forgotten that, forgotten that there need be no more cooking or catering or serving for her. She smiled at Philip Carr as she shook her head.

"I am sorry. I —"

"Hi, Pam!"

Terrence hailed her from the threshold. "I told Mr. Carr at the court-house I'd come for you at five. Phil, I nearly laughed my head off when I found you'd lit out with a witness what wasn't a witness. We were some little detectives, been over-feeding on mystery stories, what? I hear the second Mrs. Leigh's counsel walked out on her. Been hanging round the post-office to get the dope on what people were saying. They are strong for you, Pam."

Pamela linked her arm in his. She blinked furiously to keep back tears as she looked up at him, he was such a dear.

"Terry — Terry!" She swallowed a sob of

sheer excitement. "You may practise your curve! You may fire every egg through the barn window! Father has deposited fifty thousand dollars with Mr. Carr for you."

Her brother flung a protecting arm about her shoulders, his eyes were terrified, his face colorless

"Pull yourself together, Pam! I knew this strain would get you if you didn't have a change of scene. Father's crack-up, Cecile's get-away, creditors hounding, patrons fussing. Cooking! Cooking! Cooking! Keeping the old frog kicking! Round and round. It's the treadmill that gets the farmers' wives. Cheer up, Pam, everything's going to be all right. Mr. Scott, you tell her!"

Scott Mallory put his hand on the boy's shoulder, his eyes were unashamedly full of tears, his voice husky.

"Steady, Terrence. Your sister is stating facts. Evidence at the trial brought out the fact that your father has been hoarding a fortune in rare stamps. Today his agent, Brown, bought enough of them to enable him to repay you and Pamela the money your mother left you."

Terrence went limp. "Do you mean it! Do you mean that Father will go on his own again?"

No thought of what the money would mean to him, merely an overwhelming sense of freedom from his father's incessant fault-finding. Pamela herself knew that sense as of a spirit uncaged.

"Milly Pike, who be you, to tell me whether I

can come into this house or not? Get out of my way, an' stay there."

With the last word Mehitable Betts appeared on the threshold. Her pansy bonnet was awry, a gray shawl dragged from one shoulder, she gripped a straw suitcase. Mrs. Carr nodded dismissal to the angry-eyed, pink-frocked maid, who hovered behind her. Phineas Carr pushed forward a chair.

"Come in, Miss Betts. We must have been waiting tea for you."

The gaunt woman straightened like a martinet. Sniffed.

"I won't take tea. I came to give notice to Pamela."

Again! Pamela sighed, remembered that it didn't matter. Every reservation had been cancelled. The "Closed" sign would remain out until one-time patrons forgot the Silver Moon. She was sorry in a way, making good had been thrillingly interesting. Quite from force of habit, not because she thought it of importance, she inquired:

"What is the matter now, Hitty?"

"Matter!" Miss Betts dropped her suitcase with a thud, the better to hitch her spectacles into place. "Matter! Your father's second wife's up at the house with him!"

"What!" Pamela and Terrence united in the exclamation.

Miss Betts' lips puckered satisfaction. "Land's sake, I thought you'd be surprised. They're up

there on the porch. That smart parrot knows something irregular's going on. When he isn't tooting
like an auto horn, he's shivering and ruffling his
feathers and croaking 'Goo'bye! Goo'bye!'"

"Are — are they talking together — like
friends?"

"Well, I wouldn't call her conversation friendly,
Pamela, I'd call it mushy. He didn't look's though
he was considering poisoning her, either. She's
trying to get him again, I guess. I heard her say,
'Motoring in England would set you on your feet,
Harold. Let's go.' You ought to see that dog of
yours, Terry. Lying on the grass, head on his paws,
dejected like, as though he couldn't bear life another
minute."

Terrence chuckled. "It sounds domestic enough,
Hitty. What sent you flying off the handle?"

The glare of outraged Miss Betts should have
withered him.

"Domestic! Your Pa comes to me and he says,
lordlike,

"'Mrs. Leigh will be here for supper, Hitty.
Serve it on the porch.' I looked at him an' I says,
'I *was* working for Pamela. I'm *leaving* this
minute.' He just raised his brows in that way he
has and walked out. As I was reaching for my hat
I heard him say,

"'Pamela'll be here soon and she'll get supper
for us, Cecile.'"

For one terrifying instant Pamela thought her

mind would snap from fury. Every ship in the room seemed to be flying along under bellying sails. She struggled to piece her voice together, it came raggedly.

"I get supper for them! With a cheque for fifty thousand dollars in my pocket! I won't go back to Grandmother Leigh's house while Cecile is there. She can cook. I'm through! Terrence, go to the Inn and stay until you hear from me. I'm going away by myself to — New York — I'll stay with Madge Jarvis! No, Phil, don't touch me! I haven't gone crazy, though I may sound so. Your father understands. Ask him. Don't be afraid of him. Tell him at once what a hit your settings have made. He will be so proud of you. I don't love you. I'm sorry. I don't love anyone except — except Terry." She stopped at the door.

"Thank you all for what you have done for me. I — I've just got to get away!"

Her heart was pounding, her breath came as if she had been running as she jumped into the sedan. She threw it into gear and sent it roaring along the drive.

Chapter XXIII

————

THE road stretched ahead, silken smooth, between spreading fields already slumbering in the rosy afterglow. On the crest of a miniature hill Pamela stopped the car. Over the tops of a clump of scrub oaks she could see the dunes, humped like *papier mâché* shapes against a darkening sky, with foaming shallows at their bases. Houses, which looked for all the world like gigantic marshmallows scattered in a genie's flight, dotted the foreground. A lovely village, a village to return to, not one in which to spend one's youth.

She drove on. A rim of burnished copper hung on the far horizon for an instant before it dropped out of sight. With its passing, familiar objects and sounds took on an unexpected strangeness. She passed the court-house. How gray and stolid! What stories it could tell of the meting of justice, perhaps the defeat of justice. Lengthening shadows, unearthly flickers where gold-washed leaves stirred restlessly under a caressing breeze. Murmur of little night-prowlers awakening in wood and field. Carpets of moss. Maze of willows. Paths through lush meadows worn by plodding feet. Darting birds. Munching cows gazing with ruminative eyes. Old horses going coltish in their hind legs. A church bell summoning the faithful. Happy-go-lucky cedar fences neither knowing nor caring whither they straggled, unmotivated as she was now.

The road proved not so straight as she remembered. Was it because she was alone? Now that the tumult and the shouting within her had died down she would better check-up emotionally, her life seemed all loose ends. Where was she going? To New York, she had said. A frenzied determination to escape had shaken her when Hitty had reported Cecile's presence at the Silver Moon with her husband. Had it been caused by jealousy? No. She still loved her father but she would rather not see him again until the memory of these last months had dimmed.

A quick thinker, Cecile. Doubtless she had figured that as she had been discredited in the trial her best move was to be reinstated as Harold Leigh's wife — now that she knew that he had money. They were waiting for Pamela to return to get supper for them, were they? If they waited for that they would starve! Oh, but they wouldn't starve. Cecile could cook. And then — and then her husband could turn a postage stamp or two into a magic carpet to transport her to England. Steady! Why boil-up over something which had passed?

What had the Carrs thought of her outburst?

With the question came a picture of the room she had left. Against a background of ships of every conceivable type and material, she visualized Mrs. Carr's wistful face; Philip tugging at his small mustache, his expression crestfallen; Phineas Carr with fingers clutching his flower-bedecked lapel, watching his son with sympathetically understanding eyes; Terrence crimson with indignation; Mehitable Betts, her grim mouth clamped with satisfaction at the reaction to her announcement; Scott —

At the imminent risk of ditching the car Pamela closed her lids tight. Even that didn't shut out his eyes, they burned into her soul. Where had she taken the turning which had smashed their friendship? When Hilda Crane's sister had dotted her life-line with an offer for the cottage? The plot-complex again!

She forced her attention to her surroundings, glanced at the speedometer. She had driven fifty miles! She would stop for the night at the first attractive inn. She could make New York tomorrow. She had twenty dollars, some change in her purse and a cheque for fifty thousand. She must spend the cash carefully. Fifty thousand! Unbelievable! No more catering at the Silver Moon. In retrospect, even that didn't seem so hard; hadn't the Chowder House brought Scott into her life? She had liked her patrons, most of them. Nothing now between her and her chosen work. Life, liberty and the pursuit of plot-germs! At present her mind was as empty of ideas for stories and articles as a squeezed orange was of juice; but once she touched her typewriter they would come trooping along, she knew from experience. She was approaching a village. She looked at the gas-gauge. She would better stop and have the tank filled.

A pleasant street. Gardens bordered and starred with spring flowers colorless in the twilight, filched of their fragrance by a moist breeze which scattered it prodigally. Nice old houses, their ancient glories mellowed by time and the absence of fresh paint. A little white church with presumably a dove-gray parsonage beside it. Its familiarity had a dreamlike quality. A garage!

A man in greasy overalls hurried from the dark interior before she stopped the sedan. He touched a lock of rough hair, sunbursts of fine lines crinkled about his eyes as he smiled.

"How much, Miss?"

"All the tank will hold."

He disappeared behind the car. As she waited, she watched a brilliant star prick through an indigo sky, impale itself on the church spire where it hung like a bit of glittering tinsel on the top of a Christmas tree. Lovely night! Freakishly unreal, though; were it not for the odor of gasoline she would think she was living a dream, nothing unreal about the smell.

The garage keeper's concerned face appeared at the car window.

"Say, Miss, yer tank's leaking something terrible."

Existence shed its dreamlike quality to bump into facts.

"How can it leak?"

The man's smile revealed teeth startlingly white in contrast to their begrimed setting.

"I don't know how it can, Miss, but it does."

"How quickly can you repair it?"

He scratched his head contemplatively. "Run her into the shop. I'll take a look."

Pamela regarded him thoughtfully. If she were a judge of human nature — she flattered herself that she was — the man was honest and respectable. He hadn't discovered the leak merely to give himself work. She drove into the garage.

From the top of a packing-box she watched him as, flat on his back, he poked around under the car with his flashlight. It was evident from his absorption that he was an engine addict.

Her glance traveled round the dusky shop. One shelved wall was entirely given over to what might be generically termed "parts." There were bunches of waste by the oily dozen; a gas-tank on wheels; grease and tire-rim machines; a battery-charger in the act of transfusion; new tires, a squad of them in a corner; boxes of tubes; a wrecked flivver, a complete and perfect thing of its kind. On a bench near the window reposed a pile of thick sandwiches and a steaming cup. Pamela's eyes came back to the prostrate figure on the floor. Tank conditions must be serious to keep the mechanic there all this time. Lucky he had discovered the leak; else she might have been hung up between towns without food for man or beast, figuratively speaking.

The thought set hunger gnawing. She had been unable to so much as taste the luncheon Hitty had provided. With the thought came the remembrance of Terrence's laughter. What wonder he had "laughed his head off" when he visualized Philip Carr speeding away with a witness who wasn't a witness? Later, Eddie Pike's melodramatic accusation had entirely submerged the tea-party. She had been driving at supper time. She was hollow to her toes. She was entitled to be low in her mind; hunger set Terrence and his father prowling for someone to bite, it reduced her spirit to its lowest denominator.

She slid from the box, circled a puddle of gasoline, jumped a water-hazard. She gently nudged the mechanic's boot, shouted to make herself heard above his pounding and tapping.

"How long will it take?"

The man wriggled out, sat up. He wiped his hot face with a hand which left a sardonic streak from eye to nose. Not so good. After all, he didn't look so dependable as she had thought.

"Can't tell yet, Miss. You'd better sit down an' take it easy."

"But, I am starving. Any place near where I can get something to eat?"

From the hoplessness of his expression she deduced that eating wasn't being done this month in the village. Or—eyes narrowed, she regarded him speculatively—was he trying to keep her here?

He scratched an ear, jiggled the tools in his hand. He was stalling. What would she better do? Insist upon driving out, leaky tank or no leaky tank?

"Let me think— Car just stopped outside. Excuse me, Miss; can't afford to lose a sale."

He hurried away wiping oily hands on oilier waste. Pamela heroically turned her back on the sandwiches. Even if she did suspect the man of double-crossing her, it would be like stabbing him in the back to snitch any part of his supper. She looked at the clock. Getting late. She was strong for adventure but this one lacked a sense of timeliness.

Was the tank really leaking? She doubled like a jackknife in an attempt to look under the car. Her hat fell off. She caught it before it reached the floor. Gas would be dripping if the leak were as serious as the man had intimated. She couldn't see a drop, there was no puddle visible. He had tricked her—

"To get the proper perspective you should be flat on your back."

"Scott!"

Pamela straightened. The suddenly right-side-up shop whirled. She backed against the bumper of her car, clenched her hands behind her.

"I'm not going back! I am not going back!"

Mallory's face, which had been a ghostly blur,

took on form and color, dark color. He caught her shoulder.

"Come away from that dirty car! You will spoil your clothes." He drew her forward. "I am not here to drag you back. The mechanic says it will take time to find the leak. If you want to go on tonight you'd better come with me."

"When did he tell you that?"

"When he was filling up for me. Said he had a job inside which might take a couple of hours."

"Oh, he did! What communicative souls men are. Babbling brooks have nothing on them. I suspect he is trying to put something across."

"Mike Shaughnessy wouldn't do that!"

"Mike? You know him then?"

"I—I usually stop here on my way back and forth. Remember I told you I went to the parsonage across the street once with a wedding party? Mike and I got rather fratty then so I buy gas here on my way up and down."

Pamela listened with her ears, not with her mind. She remembered his story on the way home from Boston about the eloping couple. She had been half asleep which fact accounted for the dreamlike quality of the church and dove-gray house when she had passed it a while ago.

"Pam!" Mallory's voice, the grip of his hands on hers shocked her back to the present. "What has come between us? You know that I love you, don't you? You know that yarn of Phil Carr's about

Hilda Crane and me was straight fiction, don't you?"

She kept her eyes on his hands. She hadn't known that a gassy, oily garage could seem so like heaven. She lingered outside the gates.

"Why should I know?" She steadied her traitorous voice. "I am not a mind-reader. You came to the village often, but not to the Silver Moon."

His grip tightened. His voice was husky from repression.

"The day I went to warn Carnation Carr to keep his hands off my client, he showed me the risk if I tried your case, said that I would be vulnerable because—because I loved you. He's a prince! He advised that I keep away from you until after the trial. I had told him about meeting Cecile in New York and of her evident suspicion. My calls upon Hilda were a smoke-screen—I couldn't hurt her heart, she hasn't any—an excuse for being in the village to consult with him."

He tilted her chin. "Look at me, Pam. You believe me, don't you?"

Her eyes met his. "Yes, I—" He pressed his lips hard on hers. Her hands clung tight about his neck, he loosened his arms only to crush her close again.

"Say, Mr. Mallory—"

Scott held Pamela as in a vise when she would have slipped away.

"I will be out in a minute, Shaughnessy. Put—

put in a quart of oil — and — and see if the tires need air."

"I get you!"

The mechanic's words were curiously choked. Was he laughing as he bolted from the shop? Pamela looked accusingly at the man who still held her as if he never would let her go.

"Scott!"

"I know what you are going to say. Guilty! Terrence phoned Mike to keep you here until I came. We knew that my roadster would cover the ground in half the time it would take the sedan."

"Suppose I hadn't stopped?"

"Your brother knew the amount of gas in the tank, figured from your hasty departure that you wouldn't stop until you had to."

She tilted her head back against his shoulder.

"Scott, are you sure I am not dreaming?" Her laugh was shaky as she laid her hand on the face swooping to hers. "You needn't kiss me again to make me realize that you — and — I are not a dream. I meant about Father. Is it possible that a collection of stamps can mean so much money?"

"Several years ago one sold for a million and a half. Count Ferrary's netted three million."

"Not dollars!"

"Dollars. Your father's must be tremendously valuable. When you first told me that he was interested in stamps, I wondered. His insistence that his new wife should not be told of his hobby was suspicious. I began to investigate. I knew that you would not listen to me if I told you that I loved you, while you felt you must make a home for him. Right, wasn't I?"

She nodded. "I suspected before that you were a mind-reader."

"I didn't dare trust myself with you — much — it tore me to pieces to be with you and not tell you that I loved you — have you in my arms. Nothing for me to do but find a fortune for him. I found it. He was furiously angry, but, he got over it. Brown was shaking with eagerness when he paid over those two cheques. I doubt if what he bought made much of a dent in one of the most famous collections in the world."

"How did you persuade him to pay Terrence and me?"

"I didn't have to do much persuading. As he improved in health his conscience began to prick. I just encouraged him to make good. I was bound to protect your interests. You were my first Leigh client, you retained me to fire S. Linsky before I talked with your father about his bills."

"Father is right. You are an unflinching person."

He drew her hands to his lips.

"I mean to be now, then never again with you. Marry me tonight, will you — Gorgeous?"

"Scott! Are you mad?"

"Come back! I can argue more eloquently when I have you in my arms. By your own admission you don't care for a wedding splurge. You say that you won't return to the Silver Moon while your stepmother is there — from Hitty's account it looks as if she intended to stay for a while, till she gets that allowance — at least. I must be in New York tomorrow night for a conference with clients from the Argentine, will be there two weeks. After that — well, I have an option on a penthouse for the winter. You may have it all silver walls and egg-shell lacquer if you like."

"That is a shameless bribe." In spite of the turmoil within her, Pamela smiled at him. He kissed her.

"Don't do that again. I — I can't think."

"Why think?"

His shaken whisper drew her heart to her throat. She struggled for composure, mocked gaily:

"One can't get married without a license, can one?"

He tapped his breast pocket. "What do you think I was doing while Terrence sneaked in the back door of the Silver Moon — with the almost ex-married close together in a secluded corner of the porch — and packed your suitcase and picked up your top-coat? I was at the house of the town clerk getting a special license."

"Did Terry know that — that —"

"We were to be married? He did. When I told him, he grinned that one-sided smile of his and said, like the soldier he is:

"'Tell Pam that it will be a relief to me to have her away from that cook-stove at the Silver Moon. Tell her to think of me in the stilly night practising my curve with the prize Plymouth Rock eggs.'"

Pamela brushed her eyes against a blue serge breast to clear them of tears. Was that Scott's heart pounding?

Mallory gently smoothed back her hair. "Carnation Carr helped me get that special license."

"Scott, I had a premonition the night I met Mr. Carr in his Ship Room, that he would change the pattern of my life."

"Your departure from that same room this afternoon was a smash. Philip started after you. His father caught his arm. Said with a tenderness of which I did not believe that juggernaut of an advocate capable:

"'That is Mallory's job, Phil.'"

"How did he know?"

"Know! He knew in our first interview. Everyone knew I was mad about you."

"I didn't."

"Your mistake." He laid his cheek on her hair. "Coming with me?"

"To New York?"

"To the parsonage across the street first. Your senior counsel attended to that bit of business for me too. Great things, telephones."

She regarded him with mock gravity. "Do you

know, Scott, it is being borne in upon me how terribly afraid Carnation Carr was that I would marry his only child."

"Don't get him wrong. He would have adored you for a daughter, but — you won't like this — he said that the first time you mentioned my name, he knew you loved me. His assurance was all that kept me going, these last interminable weeks."

His eyes darkened. Pamela was beginning to know that look.

"Coming?"

"Yes."

He raised her hand to his lips. Slipped a ring on her finger, a blazing planet of a diamond set in a twinkling constellation of lesser stars. "I came prepared to make you wear this the moment the trial was over. It will have to serve for a wedding ring too. Like it?"

She looked at him in answer.

Perhaps in time, the haze, behind which lurked the past fifteen minutes, might lift and she would remember clearly the sequence of events, Pamela thought as she followed the stepping-stones from the parsonage door to the shining roadster. She had only a confused sense of a kindly white-haired clergyman with a book; of a placid woman with a mammoth cameo pin at her lace collar; of an amber-haired school-girl; Scott's eyes glowing through the fog; the pressure of his hand, the uneven richness of his voice answering,

"I do."

Mallory pulled her coat from the car. "Better put this on." He drew it about her shoulders with disturbing care. He observed casually as he started the roadster:

"Mike Shaughnessy will take the sedan back to Terrence."

"Was there really a leak in the gas-tank, Scott?"

A note in his laugh set her pulses rioting. "He seems like an honest man."

Moonlight softly blurred the world. Silver dews shimmered on the meadows. The roadster skirted a produce-laden wagon; the lumbering farm horses pricked dejected ears, shuffled hairy fetlocks and relapsed into a plod.

"We'll have a fine day for the trip tomorrow."

Fair tomorrow! Terrifying and disillusioning much of the year behind her; but fair tomorrow and all the tomorrows so long as she and Scott were together, Pamela told herself passionately.

Down the road the lights of a long building twinkled invitingly. Mallory drove more slowly as he asked:

"Hungry?"

"Starving. I had just realized when you crashed into the garage, that I had eaten nothing since breakfast."

"We will stop somewhere for supper at once." He threw a newly possessive arm about her shoulders. "Suppose we stay at that inn ahead tonight? It is a good one."

Pamela kept her eyes on her locked fingers. "You mean — stop here and — and go on to New York tomorrow?"

"Yes. Don't you intend ever again to look at the man you have married — Mrs. Mallory?"

Pamela's lashes swept up. The unguarded, passionate light in Scott Mallory's eyes softened.

"Sweet child!" he whispered tenderly and kissed her gently on the lips.

At the hospitably open door of the inn he caught her hand, drew her into the shadow.

"Happy, dear?"

The hint of remorseful anxiety in his low voice, the husky break in the last word, gave wings to her heart. After all, it was Scott, who, since the day he had stepped into the green and white kitchen had been unfailingly tender; Scott, who loved her, with whom she was crossing this strange threshold. Her radiant eyes confirmed the lilt in her voice as she answered:

"Happy? Top of the world!"